OLD PRIEST AND NEW PRESBYTER

*Episcopacy and Presbyterianism
since the Reformation with especial relation to the
Churches of England and Scotland*

BEING
THE GUNNING LECTURES DELIVERED IN THE
UNIVERSITY OF EDINBURGH 1953–54
AND
THE EDWARD CADBURY LECTURES IN THE
UNIVERSITY OF BIRMINGHAM
1954–55

CONIVGI ET ADIVTRICI
DEVOTISSIMAE

OLD PRIEST AND NEW PRESBYTER

BY

NORMAN SYKES, F.B.A.

*Dixie Professor of Ecclesiastical History and
Fellow of Emmanuel College, Cambridge*

CAMBRIDGE
AT THE UNIVERSITY PRESS
1957

PUBLISHED BY
THE SYNDICS OF THE CAMBRIDGE UNIVERSITY PRESS
Bentley House, 200 Euston Road, London, N.W. 1
American Branch: 32 East 57th Street, New York 22, N.Y.

First Edition 1956
Reprinted 1957

Made and printed in Great Britain by
William Clowes and Sons, Limited, London and Beccles

CONTENTS

PREFACE

THIS study sprang from the invitation of the Council of the University of Edinburgh, on the recommendation of the Senatus Academicus, to deliver the Gunning Lectures during the academic session 1953–4. I am grateful to the University for the honour thus done me; and particularly to the Very Reverend Principal John Baillie and to his colleagues of the Faculty of Divinity for their kindness and hospitality which made my visit to New College so pleasant and enjoyable.

The six lectures thus delivered were expanded and given as the Edward Cadbury Lectures in the University of Birmingham in the academic session 1954–5; and I should desire to express my thanks to the Council of that University for the honour of its invitation; and especially to the Reverend Professor G. W. H. Lampe for his kindness and entertainment, which contributed so much to the enjoyment of my visits to Birmingham.

In view of the provenance of the invitation, it seemed proper that I should choose a subject of interest to the church of Scotland no less than to the church of England. I cannot hope to make an original contribution to knowledge on such a well-worn theme; but I believe that I have offered some new items of information, and I have endeavoured to interpret the subject in its historical context during the successive centuries of post-Reformation ecclesiastical history.

I ought to add perhaps that the manuscript of the lectures was sent to press before the first meeting of the Joint Committee of the Convocations of Canterbury and York on the Church of South India (on which I had the privilege of serving); and that the whole was therefore finished without knowledge of the recommendations which that committee was to reach, and which have been accepted by the said Convocations whilst the proofs were in my hands.

I owe much to the privilege of conversations with Dr Gordon Donaldson, Reader in Scottish History in the University of Edinburgh, on the theme of the English and Scottish Reformations. And I am particularly indebted to my colleague and friend the Reverend Barry D. Till, Fellow and Chaplain of Jesus College, Cambridge, for his kindness in compiling the index and reading the proofs, and I should like to express my most grateful thanks to him for his pains and patience.

NORMAN SYKES

Emmanuel College, Cambridge
July 1955

Thanks to the discovery of Du Pin's *Commonitorium* and other documents relating to Archbishop Wake's correspondence both with Gallican divines of the Sorbonne and with foreign Protestants, since the delivery of these lectures, it has been possible to give a fuller and more authentic account of these matters than was hitherto possible. Nevertheless the lectures are left unchanged, since the full account of these episodes may be found in my *William Wake, Archbishop of Canterbury 1657–1737* (2 volumes, Cambridge University Press, 1957), to which reference may be made.

N.S.

May 1957

I

THE GODLY PRINCE AND THE GODLY
BISHOP

'WE talked', recorded Boswell of a conversation with
Dr Johnson, 'of the Roman Catholick religion, and how
little difference there was in essential matters between
ours and it.' . . . 'True Sir,' commented the doctor, 'all
denominations of Christians have really little difference
in point of doctrine, though they may differ widely in
external forms. There is a prodigious difference between
the external form of one of your Presbyterian churches
in Scotland and a church in Italy; yet the doctrine
taught is essentially the same.' The observation is paral-
leled by another remark of Johnson anent 'the discor-
dant tenets of Christians': 'For my part, Sir, I think all
Christians, whether Papists or Protestants, agree in the
essential articles, and that their differences are trivial,
and rather political than religious.'[1] Even when due
allowance has been made for the important distinction,
characteristic of Johnson's age, between fundamental
and non-essential articles of faith, the optimism of his
diagnosis may seem singularly fallacious in view of the
intractable divergencies not only between the church of
Rome and all other Christian churches, but also between
the several churches of the Reformation. For where a
sufficient and substantial agreement in doctrine seems to
exist, problems of church polity and order have presented
formidable barriers to union. Old Priest and New Presbyter, not to mention Giant Pope, have found it difficult

1 Boswell, *Life of Johnson* (ed. G. B. Hill, rev. L. F. Powell), II, 150; I, 405.

to dwell together in unity; and no church as yet has discovered the recipe of that magic elixir which maketh men to be of one mind in a house. Contemporary conditions, however, alike in the mission field and nearer home in the totalitarian states, conspire to press upon the Christian churches the necessity of a re-examination of the causes and ground of their differences; and it is in the hope that even a cursory re-examination of a limited part of the field of ecclesiastical relations may serve some useful end, that I have ventured in this series of lectures to consider particularly the Anglican position as regards episcopacy, presbyterianism, and papacy, with especial reference to the relations of the two national churches of this island, those of England and Scotland. In approaching this theme it is necessary to begin by an examination of the Anglican Elizabethan settlement, and therein especially of the theory of 'the godly prince' which was a fundamental principle of its constitution.

'By the goodness of almighty God and his servant Elizabeth we are.' The gracious and grateful recognition by Richard Hooker of the services rendered to the church of England by Queen Elizabeth I throughout her long and vital reign represents a practical rather than theoretical apologia for the royal supremacy. But if this phrase from the dedication of Book V *Of the Laws of Ecclesiastical Polity* had regard primarily to the historical circumstances of his age, the rest of his work, with the concordant testimony of a great cloud of contemporary Anglicans, leave no room for doubt of the theological importance of the doctrine of 'the godly prince' in their rationale of the church, its ministry, and its relation to the state. At this distance of time and amid such different conditions of ecclesiastical and political development, the Reformation apotheosis of 'the godly prince' strikes

2

an unfamiliar, if not actually uncongenial, note on our ears; and there is a strong resultant tendency to discount the prominence and centrality of this theme in the theology no less than the ecclesiology of the sixteenth century. Yet there can be no doubt that the rediscovery in the historical books of the Old Testament of 'the godly prince', and the argument therefrom *a fortiori* to the authority of the christian sovereign, was one of the most important and significant themes of the Reformers, alike Lutheran, Calvinist, and Anglican. It is with a historical consideration and survey of the position and power of the christian prince, therefore, that any exposition of the Anglican theory of the church and episcopacy in the sixteenth century must take its beginning.

John Whitgift in his controversy with Thomas Cartwright distinguished between the 'establishment' of the christian church under a persecuting magistrate and under a godly ruler. In the apostolic age

there was then no church 'established' in any civil government; because the magistrates did then persecute and not defend the church. The church in the apostles' time was 'established' in doctrine most perfectly; in discipline, government, and ceremonies, as was convenient for that time, and as the church may be in time of persecution; but the time was not yet come whereof the prophet said, 'Kings shall be thy nursing-fathers and princes shall be thy nursing-mothers'; therefore it was not 'established' in any civil government, neither did it so publicly and openly shew itself. . . .

If you speak of the church, as it is a communion and society of the faithful and elect only, and of the government thereof, as it is only spiritual; then is it most certain that the church is as thoroughly established, as perfectly governed, as gloriously decked and beautified, in time of persecution, as it is or can be under the civil magistrate. But, if you speak of the external society of the church, which comprehendeth both good and evil, and of the outward government of it, then neither it is

3

nor can it be in such a perfect state, nor so thoroughly established, or outwardly adorned, in the time of the cross, as it is and may be under a christian prince.[1]

His conclusion therefrom was that 'the church may be established without the magistrate, touching true faith and the spiritual government of it by Christ in the heart and conscience of man, but not touching the visible society and the external government'. The precedent so plainly set forth in the Old Testament could not be contradicted in the New; nor was there anything in the royal supremacy repugnant to the headship of Christ over his church.

If you mean the universal church [he replied again to Cartwright], only Christ is the Head, neither hath he any vicegerent to supply that universal care over the whole church. But, if you speak of particular churches, as the church of England, the church of Denmark, then, as the prince is the chief governor and head of the commonwealth under God, so is he of the church likewise. For it is certain that the christian magistrate under Christ hath as great authority as the magistrate had under the law. But then the civil magistrates had chief authority, both in matters of the commonwealth and of the church also . . .; therefore the magistrate ought to have the same now in like manner.[2]

It was unthinkable moreover that a christian prince should have no greater authority in the church than the profane and persecuting Emperor Nero; for 'christian princes have, and must have, the chief care and government of the church next under God'; and 'one of the most singular benefits that God bestoweth on his church in this world is, that he giveth unto it christian kings and princes; from whose office and authority whosoever doth detract and withdraw anything, injurieth the ordinance

1 Whitgift, *Works*, vol. I, pp. 390–1 (Parker Society).
2 *Ibid*. vol. III, p. 198.

4

of God, and sheweth himself unthankful for so great a benefit'.[1] In a christian state, therefore, the authority of the magistrate, that is the royal supremacy, was certainly of the *bene esse*, if not without exception of the *esse* of the church, according to Whitgift's teaching.

Whitgift indeed was contending against an adversary who wished to replace the Elizabethan settlement by a regime fashioned after the pattern of the best reformed churches stemming from Geneva. But John Jewel had made a similar defence of the royal supremacy against the advocate of papal authority, Thomas Harding. In his *Apologie or Answere in defence of the Churche of Englande*, he affirmed that

we truly grant no further liberty to our magistrates than we know hath both been given them by the word of God, and also confirmed by the examples of the very best-governed commonwealths. For, besides that a christian prince hath charge of both tables committed to him by God, to the end he may understand that not temporal matters only, but also religious and ecclesiastical causes, pertain to his office; besides also that God by his prophets often and earnestly commandeth the king to cut down the groves, to break down the images and altars of idols, and to write out the book of the law for himself; and besides that the prophet Esaias saith 'A king ought to be a patron and nurse of the church'; I say, besides all these things, we see by histories and by examples of the best times that good princes ever took the administration of ecclesiastical matters to pertain to their duty.[2]

To Queen Elizabeth I herself indeed Jewel applied the words of the prophet that 'she is unto us as a comfortable water in a dry place, as a refuge for the tempest, and as the shadow of a great rock in a weary land'; and he continued in hardly less eulogistic vein:

[1] *Ibid.* vol. iii, pp. 218 and 166.
[2] Jewel, *Works*, vol. iii, pp. 97–8 (Parker Society).

5

The greatest blessing which God giveth to any people is a godly prince to rule over them. The greatest misery that can fall upon a people is to have a godly prince taken from them. For by a godly prince he doth so rule the people as if God himself were with them in visible appearance.[1]

From such premisses it was a very moderate conclusion that 'it is lawful for a godly prince to command bishops and priests; to make laws and orders for the church; to redress the abuses of the sacraments; to allege the scriptures; to threaten and punish bishops and priests, if they offend'.[2]

The importance attaching to such affirmations was not that the royal supremacy was a convenient *ruse de guerre* to employ against the pretensions of the papacy as a point of political theory and statecraft (though, as the imperialists of the middle ages in their controversy with the papalists had discovered, it was certainly that); but that the Reformers appealed to the testimony of scripture. In the word of God they found no papacy; but they found in the Old Testament the type and pattern of the godly prince 'over all persons and in all causes within his dominions supreme'; and from this they deduced the authority of the christian sovereign. In point of fact the 'godly prince' captured the imagination of the sixteenth-century Reformers as the 'shaliach' has done that of some contemporary exegetes.

For princes are nursing fathers of the church . . . [observed Jewel again]; neither for any greater cause hath God willed governments to exist, than that there might be always some to maintain and preserve religion and piety. Princes therefore nowadays do most grievously offend, who are called indeed Christians, but who sit at ease, follow their pleasures, and patiently suffer impious rites and contempt of God, leaving all unto the bishops, to those very men to whom they know that all religion is a

1 Jewel, *Works*, vol. IV, p. 1153. 2 *Ibid.* vol. I, p. 287.

laughing stock; as if the care of the church and of God's people belonged not to them, or as if they were pastors but of sheep and oxen, as it were, and had care of their bodies, and not also of their souls. They remember not that they are God's servants, chosen of purpose to serve him.[1]

Such exhortation might be laudable when addressed to rulers who were hindering the inauguration of reform; but did it imply that a godly prince who embraced the Reformation might sit loose to episcopacy? Upon occasion Whitgift used expressions patient of such an interpretation. Two of his fixed principles of argument were: first, that 'the diversity of time and state of the church requireth diversity of government in the same'; from which he deduced that 'God hath given the chief government of his church to the christian magistrate, who hath to consider what is most convenient'; and secondly, that 'it is plain that any one certain form or kind of external government perpetually to be observed is nowhere in the scripture prescribed to the church'; from which it followed likewise that 'the charge thereof is left to the christian magistrate, so that nothing be done contrary to the word of God'.[2] Taken in their literal sense these statements might seem to leave a very considerable latitude to the civil power, since the only check to its judgment of 'what is most convenient' was the proviso that 'nothing be done contrary to the word of God'. Indeed Whitgift could say further that

the archbishop doth exercise his jurisdiction under the prince and by the prince's authority; for, the prince having the supreme government of the realm, in all causes and over all persons, as she doth exercise the one by the lord chancellor, so doth she the other by the archbishops.[3]

1 *Ibid.* vol. IV, pp. 1125–6.
2 Whitgift, *Works*, vol. III, pp. 176 and 215.
3 *Ibid.* vol. II, p. 246.

And in corresponding terms Jewel, in exhorting the faithful 'to pray to God that he will stir up and set forth men to instruct his people', added the rider:

Yet that nothing embarreth the authority of princes. For, as God calleth him inwardly in the heart whom he will have to be a minister of his word, so must he be authorised of his prince by outward and civil calling.[1]

The definition of the church in the Anglican formularies was therefore of paramount importance in this connection. Article 19 of the Thirty-nine Articles of Religion, 'Of the Church', affirmed that 'The visible Church of Christ is a congregation of faithful men, in which the pure Word of God is preached, and the Sacraments duly administered according to Christ's ordinance in all those things that of necessity are requisite to the same.' The correspondence between this article and Article VII of the Confession of Augsburg has been often noted: 'The Church is a congregation of saints, in which the Gospel is purely taught and the Sacraments rightly administered.' Moreover, in Book IV of his *Institutes of the Christian Religion*, Calvin declared that 'wherever we find the word of God purely preached and heard, and the sacraments administered according to the institution of Christ, there, it is not to be doubted, is a church of God'.[2] To the definition in the Thirty-nine Articles it is serviceable to add that contained in the second part of the Homily for Whitsunday:

[1] Jewel, *Works*, vol. II, p. 1022, Sermon IV.

[2] Article 19: 'Ecclesia Christi visibilis est coetus fidelium, in quo verbum Dei purum praedicatur, et sacramenta, quoad ea que necessario exigantur, iuxta Christi institutum recte administrantur.'

Article VII of the Confession of Augsburg: 'Est autem Ecclesia congregatio Sanctorum, in qua Evangelium recte docetur, et recte administrantur Sacramenta.'

Calvin, *Institutio Christianae Religionis* (1559), Lib. IIII, Cap. i. 9: 'Ubi enim cumque Dei verbum sincere praedicari atque audiri, ubi sacramenta ex Christi instituto administrari videmus, illic aliquam esse Dei Ecclesiam nullo modo ambigendum est.'

The true church is an universal congregation or fellowship of God's faithful and elect people, built upon the foundation of the apostles and prophets, Jesus Christ himself being the head corner-stone. And it hath always three notes or marks, whereby it is known; pure and sound doctrine; the sacraments ministered according to Christ's holy institution; and the right use of ecclesiastical discipline. This description of the church is agreeable both to the scripture of God and also to the doctrine of the ancient fathers, so that none may justly find fault therewith.[1]

Similarly the *Declaration of Certain Articles of Religion*, put forth by the archbishops and bishops in 1559, acknowledged 'that church to be the spouse of Christ, wherein the word of God is truly taught, the sacraments orderly ministered according to Christ's institution, and the authority of the keys duly used'.[2] To Whitgift, however, 'the essential notes of the church be these only; the true preaching of the word of God and the right administration of the sacraments'.[3]

In Jewel's *Apologie* against the Romanist attacks, he affirmed

that there is one church of God, and that the same is not shut up (as in times past among the Jews) into some one corner or kingdom, but that it is catholic and universal, and dispersed throughout the whole world; ... and that this church is the kingdom, the body, and the spouse of Christ; and that Christ alone is the prince of this Kingdom; that Christ alone is the head of this body; and that Christ alone is the bridegroom of this spouse.[4]

This, however, said nothing of the notes or marks of the church; and Jewel's chief point against his adversaries was that the scriptures are the basis and foundation of the church: 'It behoveth us rather to search the

---

1 *The Homilies* (Oxford, 1859), p. 462.
2 E. Cardwell, *Documentary Annals of the Reformed Church of England*, vol. I, p. 264.
3 Whitgift, *Works*, vol. I, p. 185.
4 Jewel, *Works*, vol. III, p. 59.

9

scriptures, as Christ hath advised us, and thereby to assure ourselves of the church of God: for by this trial only, and by none other, it may be known'; and again, 'by these ancient learned fathers, it is plain that the church of God is known by God's word only, and none otherwise'.[1] But when it was asked precisely what the scriptures declare to be the true marks of the church, Jewel afforded little clear guidance. Of the two characteristics, truth and unity, he gave the precedence to truth:

Of a truth unity and concord doth best become religion; yet is not unity the sure and certain mark whereby to know the church of God [Indeed] ... The catholic church of God standeth not in multitude of persons, but in weight of truth. Otherwise Christ himself and his apostles had not been catholic; for his flock was very little; and the catholic or universal consent of the world stood against it.[2]

This was a useful *argumentum ad hominem* in defence of the Church of England against Rome; but Jewel carried the practical question little forward when he affirmed that

the church of God is in God the Father, and in the Lord Jesus Christ; it is the company of the faithful, whom God hath gathered together in Christ by his word and by the Holy Ghost, to honour him, as he himself hath appointed; this church heareth the voice of the Shepherd.[3]

It is, however, significant that neither Article 19 nor Whitgift nor Jewel said anything of a particular form of ministry being essential to the church. Article 23, 'Of Ministering in the Congregation', indeed, required a minister to be 'lawfully called and sent', and defined 'those we ought to judge lawfully called and sent' as having been 'chosen and called to this work by men who have public authority given unto them in the Congregation, to call and send Ministers into the Lord's vine-

---

1 Jewel, *Works*, vol. III, pp. 152–3.   2 *Ibid.* pp. 620 and 268.
3 *Ibid.* vol. II, p. 819.

yard'. Similarly Article 36, 'Of Consecration of Bishops and Ministers', contented itself with affirming the Ordinal to

contain all things necessary to such Consecration and Ordering; neither hath it anything that of itself is superstitious and ungodly. And therefore whosoever are consecrated or ordered according to the Rites of that Book ... we decree all such to be rightly, orderly, and lawfully consecrated and ordered.

Likewise Hooker, whose part in the controversy belonged to a later stage than Jewel and Whitgift, declared that the unity of the visible church

consisteth in that uniformity which all several persons thereunto belonging have, by reason of that one Lord whose servants they all profess themselves, that one Faith which they all acknowledge, that one Baptism wherewith they are all initiated. The visible church of Jesus Christ is therefore one, in outward profession of those things, which supernaturally appertain to the very essence of Christianity, and are necessarily required in every particular Christian man.[1]

Of 'the notes of external profession' by which those who appertained to the visible body of the church were recognisable, Hooker did not doubt 'that one of the very chiefest is Ecclesiastical Polity'.[2]

The particular form of polity established by the godly prince in the church of England was set forth in the Preface to the Ordinal, in these terms:

It is evident unto all men diligently reading holy Scripture and ancient Authors, that from the Apostles' time there hath been these Orders of Ministers in Christ's Church: Bishops, Priests, and Deacons. Which Offices were evermore had in such reverend estimation, that no man, by his own private authority might presume to execute any of them, except he were first called, tried, examined, and known to have such qualities as

[1] Hooker, *Ecclesiastical Polity*, III, i, 3-4.
[2] *Ibid.* i, 14.

were requisite for the same; and also by public Prayer, with Imposition of hands, approved and admitted thereunto. And therefore, to the intent these Orders should be continued and reverently used and esteemed in the Church of England, it is requisite that no man (not being at this present Bishop, Priest, or Deacon) shall execute any of them, except he be called, tried, examined, and admitted thereunto, according to the Form hereafter following.[1]

Thus from the outset of its reformation the church of England continued the episcopal succession, and required its ministers to have received episcopal ordination or consecration. Indeed, next to their advocacy of the 'godly prince', the Anglican reformers were at pains to restore the godly bishop, in contradistinction to the

---

[1] As interpretative of this statement, attention is sometimes directed to the rubrics in the Ordinal, requiring the preaching of a sermon. It is instructive to examine the evidence in this regard.

(i) In the first version of the Ordinal, 1550, the rubric at the Ordering of Deacons stated that 'there shall be an exhortation, declaring the duty and office of such as come to be admitted *Ministers*, how necessary such orders are in the church of Christ, and also, how the people ought to esteem them in their vocation'.

At the Ordering of Priests the rubric simply reads: 'When the exhortation is ended, then shall be sung for the Introit to the Communion, this Psalm.'

At the Consecrating of an Archbishop or Bishop, there was *no* provision for a sermon or exhortation.

(ii) In the revision of 1552 no change was made, nor in 1559.

(iii) In 1662 the following changes were made.

At the Form and Manner of Making of Deacons the rubric read: 'there shall be a Sermon or Exhortation, declaring the duty and office of such as come to be admitted *Deacons*; how necessary that Order is in the Church of Christ; and also how the people ought to esteem them in their office'.

At the Ordering of Priests, the rubric concerning the sermon was the same, with the substitution of 'come to be admitted Priests', for 'Deacons'.

At the Consecrating of an Archbishop or Bishop, the rubric after the Gospel was changed from its earlier form: 'After the gospel and *Credo* ended': to 'After the Gospel, and the Nicene Creed, *and the Sermon* are ended.' Thus the sermon at the consecration of a bishop first makes its appearance in 1662.

It would seem therefore that the evidence of the rubrics is too slight and precarious to carry weight. For if emphasis be laid upon the rubric at the Ordering of Deacons and Priests, requiring an exhortation 'how necessary such orders are in the church of Christ', it may be a matter of delicacy to account for the lack of such provision at the consecrating of a bishop, where, even after 1662, the subject of the sermon is not mentioned.

corrupt prelacy of the later middle ages, against which they had revolted.[1]

And as for the bishop of Rome [observed Jewel], except he do his duty as he ought to do, except he minister the sacraments, except he instruct the people, except he warn them and teach them, we say that he ought not of right once to be called a bishop, or so much as an elder. For a bishop, as saith St Augustine, is a name of labour and not of honour.

Or again, as he wrote to his friend Josiah Simler, 'we require our bishops to be pastors, labourers, and watch-men'.[2] 'The Institution of a Christian Man' of 1537 had laid stress upon these aspects of the episcopal office:

For surely the office of preaching is the chief and most principal office, whereunto priests or bishops be called by the authority of the gospel; and they be also called bishops or archbishops, that is to say, superattendants or overseers, to watch and to look diligently upon their flock, and to cause that Christ's doctrine and his religion may be truly and sincerely conserved, taught, and set forth among Christian people, according to the mere and pure truth of scripture; and that all erroneous and corrupt doctrine and the teachers thereof, may be rejected accordingly.[3]

The same emphasis was to be found in the Form of Consecrating of an Archbishop or Bishop in the Ordinal. In the interrogatories addressed by the archbishop to the bishop-elect, stress was laid upon the obligation faithfully to exercise himself in the holy scriptures, both as the standard of doctrine and the rule of life; and after the imposition of hands, the Bible was delivered to the bishop with the exhortation to 'give heed unto reading, exhortation, and doctrine. Think upon these things contained in this book. Be diligent in them. . . . Take heed

[1] See Paul Broutin, S.J., *L'Évêque dans la Tradition Pastorale du XVIème Siècle* (1953), for the influence of this concept in the Counter-Reformation.
[2] Jewel, *Works*, vol. III, p. 308; *Zurich Letters*, i, 50–1.
[3] C. Lloyd, *Formularies of Faith* (Oxford, 1825), pp. 109–10.

unto thyself, and unto teaching, and be diligent in doing them.' Similarly the section of the *Reformatio Legum Ecclesiasticarum* which dealt with the office and dignity of bishops in the church, bade them to feed and govern both clergy and people with sound doctrine, grave authority, and prudent counsel, not lording over their flocks but showing themselves true servants of the servants of God: and remembering that authority and jurisdiction in the church had been given to them for the winning of many to Christ, confirming those who were already of Christ's flock and restoring the lapsed.[1]

It was precisely in order to emphasise the pastoral and evangelistic functions of the godly bishop that some of the reformers preferred the title of 'superintendent'. For the bishops had exercised so much dominion and rigour, and been such Papalins [observed Strype], that the very name of *bishop* grew odious among the people, and the word *superintendent* began to be affected, and came in the room; and the rather, perhaps, being a word used in the Protestant churches of Germany. This the Papists made sport with. But see what favourable construction one who was a bishop himself, put upon this practice and the reason he assigned hereof.

Strype proceeded thereupon to quote John Poynet, bishop of Winchester:

Who knoweth not that the name *bishop* hath been so abused, that when it was spoken the people understood nothing else but a great lord, that went in a white rochet with a wide shaven

---

[1] *Reformatio Legum Ecclesiasticarum: De Episcoporum gradu ac dignitate in Ecclesia,* cap. 10: 'Episcopi, quoniam inter caeteros Ecclesiae ministros locum principem tenent, ideo sana doctrina, gravi authoritate, atque provido consilio, debent inferiores ordines cleri, universumque populum Dei regere et pascere, non sane ut dominentur eorum fidei, sed ut seipsos vere servos servorum Dei exhibeant, sciantque authoritatem et jurisdictionem ecclesiasticam non alia de causa sibi praecipue creditam esse, nisi ut suo ministerio et assiduitate homines quam plurimi Christo jungantur, quique jam Christi sunt, in eo crescant et exaedificentur, atque si nonnulli deficiant, ad pastorem Christum dominum reducantur, et per salutarem poenitentiam instaurentur.' (Ed. E. Cardwell, pp. 103–4.)

crown, and that carried an oil box with him, wherewith he used once in seven years, riding about, to *confirm* children &c. Now to bring the people from this abuse, what better means can be devised than to teach the people their error by another word out of Scripture of the same significance: which thing, by the term *Superintendent* would in time have been well brought to pass; ... and the word *superintendent* being a very Latin word, made English by us, should in time have taught the people, by the very etymology and proper signification, what thing was meant when they heard that name, which by this term *bishop* could not so well be done, by reason that bishops in time of popery, were *overseers* in name but not in deed. I deny not ... that the name *bishop* may be well taken; but because the evilness of the abuse hath marred the goodness of the word, it cannot be denied but that it was not amiss to join for a time another word with it in his place, whereby to restore that abused word to his right signification. And the word *Superintendent* is such a name, that the papists themselves ... cannot find fault withal.[1]

The authority of Jewel could also be urged in favour of the use of *superintendent* as emphasising the concept of 'the godly bishop'. For, he argued against Harding,

whereas it hath pleased you, as well here as elsewhere, to sport yourself with superintendents and superintendentships, and to refresh your wits with so vain a fantasy of your own; if ye had been so deeply travailed in the doctors, new or old, as ye bear us in hand, ye might easily have known that a superintendent is an ancient name and significth none other but a bishop. St Augustine saith: Vocabulum episcopatus inde ductum est, quod ille, qui praeficitur, eis, quibus praeficitur, superintendit. ... Ergo ἐπισκοπεῖν ... Latine dicere possumus superintendere. Again he saith: Quod Graece dicitur Episcopus, hoc Latine superintentor interpretatur. Chrysostom saith: Episcopus, ex eo dictus quod omnes inspiciat. St Hierome saith: ἐπισκοποῦντες, id est, superintendentes. Anselmus saith: Episcopus ... [Latine] superintendens dicitur. Beda likewise

---

[1] J. Strype, *Ecclesiastical Memorials*, II, ii, 141 (*anno* 1553).

saith: Episcopus . . . Latine superintendens dicitur. Petrus de Palude saith: Episcopus dicitur Superintendens; et Petrus fuit Superintendens toti mundo. . . . Your own Thomas of Aquine saith: Episcopi dicuntur ex eo, quod superintendunt. Therefore, M. Harding, if modesty move you not, yet at least for your gravity's sake, leave playing with these vain and childish follies. The bishops of England have this day not only the same name, but also the same room, and authority, and jurisdiction that other bishops have ever had before.[1]

In view of this stout insistence on the episcopal succession in the church of England, it is the more important to observe that Jewel interpreted this succession as one of doctrine, not of sees. In his *Defence of the Apology* he animadverted severely on the popes' claim to succession from Peter:

They are gone from faith to infidelity, from Christ to anti-Christ. And yet, all other things failing, they must hold only by succession; and, only because they sit in Moses' chair, they must claim the possession of the whole. This is the right and virtue of their succession.[2]

Similarly in reply to Harding's challenge as to his own succession to the former bishops of Sarum, Jewel affirmed:

To be short, we succeed the bishops that have been before our days. We are elected, consecrate, confirmed, and admitted as they were. If they were deceived in anything, we succeed them in place, but not in error. They were our predecessors, but not the rulers and standards of our faith. Or rather, to set apart all comparison of persons, the doctrine of Christ this day, M. Harding, succeedeth your doctrine, as the day succeedeth the night; as the light succeedeth darkness; and as the truth succeedeth error.[3]

---

[1] Jewel, *Works*, vol. IV, p. 906. It is interesting further to observe that when the University of Oxford conferred the honorary degree of D.D. on Adam Samuel Hartmann of the Moravian Brethren in 1680, he was described as 'Ecclesiarum Unitatis Fratrum Bohemarum . . . Superintendens seu Episcopus.'

[2] *Ibid.* vol. III, p. 325.   [3] *Ibid.* p. 339.

And, to summarise the matter, he observed succinctly to his adversary, 'Succession, you say, is the chief way for any christian man to avoid antichrist. I grant you, if you mean the succession of doctrine.'[1] Or again, 'God's grace is promised to a good mind, and to one that feareth God, not unto sees and successions.'[2] Indeed, for Jewel the touchstone of episcopacy was its soundness of doctrine and its discharge of the work of an evangelist, not its succession of place. He challenged Harding to prove the papal succession by showing that the contemporary pope followed the example of Peter:

that is, that he runneth up and down into every country to preach the gospel, not only openly abroad, but also privately from house to house; that he is diligent, and applieth that business in season and out of season, in due time and out of due time; that he doth the part of an evangelist, that he fulfilleth the work and ministry of Christ; that he is the watchman of the house of Israel, receiveth answers and words at God's mouth, and, even as he receiveth them, so delivereth them over to the people; ... that he doth not feed his own self, but his flock; that he doth not entangle himself with the worldly cares of this life; that he doth not use a sovereignty over the Lord's people; that he seeketh not to have other men minister to him, but himself rather to minister unto others; that he taketh all bishops as his fellows and equals; that he is subject to princes, as to persons sent from God. ... Unless therefore the popes do the like nowadays, as Peter did the things aforesaid, there is no cause at all why they should glory so of Peter's name and of his succession.[3]

It is noteworthy, furthermore, that notwithstanding the pressure of polemic from the presbyterians, neither Whitgift nor Hooker abandoned their position that no form of polity is exclusively prescribed in scripture. This characteristic of their apologetic indeed was observed with surprise and regret by Keble:

[1] *Ibid.* p. 348.   [2] *Ibid.* p. 103.   [3] *Ibid.* p. 104.

Now, since the episcopal succession had been so carefully retained in the Church of England, and so much anxiety evinced
to render both her liturgy and ordination services strictly conformable to the rules and doctrines of antiquity, it might have
been expected that the defenders of the English hierarchy
against the first Puritans should take the highest grounds, and
challenge for the bishops the same unreserved submission, on
the same plea of exclusive apostolical prerogative, which their
adversaries feared not to insist on for their elders and deacons.
It is notorious, however, that such was not in general the line
preferred by Jewel, Whitgift, Bishop Cooper, and others, to
whom the management of that controversy was entrusted
during the early part of Elizabeth's reign. They do not expressly disavow, but they carefully shun, that unreserved appeal
to antiquity, in which one would have thought they must have
discerned the very strength of their cause to lie. It is enough,
with them, to shew that the government by archbishops and
bishops is ancient and allowable; they never venture to urge
its *exclusive* claim, or to connect the succession with the validity
of the holy Sacraments.[1]

In his argument against Cartwright, Whitgift expressly
stated in his Preface to *The Defence of the Answer to the
Admonition* that the external government of the church

hath both a substance and a matter about which it is occupied,
and also a form to attain the same, consisting in certain offices
and functions, and in the names and titles of them. The substance and matter of government must indeed be taken out of
the word of God, and consisteth in these points, that the word
be truly taught, the sacraments rightly administered, virtue
furthered, vice repressed, and the church kept in quietness and
order. The offices in the church, whereby this government is
wrought, be not namely and particularly expressed in the
scriptures, but in some points left to the discretion and liberty
of the church, to be disposed according to the state of times,
places, and persons.[2]

In the body of his *Defence*, he expanded this by arguing
that, although

1 *Works of Hooker* (ed. John Keble), vol. i, p. lix.
2 Whitgift, *Works*, vol. i, p. 6.

in a church collected together in one place and at liberty, government is necessary . . . that any one kind of government is so necessary that without it the church cannot be saved, or that it may not be altered into some other kind thought to be more expedient, I utterly deny; . . . because I find no one certain and perfect kind of government prescribed or commanded in the scriptures to the church of Christ; which no doubt should have been done, if it had been a matter necessary unto the salvation of the church.[1]

As a practical illustration of this position, he stated explicitly that

I condemn no churches that have appointed any order for the electing of their pastors which they think to be agreeable to their state, and most profitable for them; for therefore I say that no certain manner or form of electing ministers is prescribed in the scripture, because every church may do therein as it shall seem to be most expedient for the same. That may be profitable for the churches of Geneva and France, which would be most hurtful to this church of England.[2]

In reply to Cartwright's principle that 'those things only are to be placed in the church which God himself in his word commandeth', Whitgift did not hesitate to say:

it is untrue in matters of 'ceremonies, rites, orders, discipline, and kind of government'; which being external matters and alterable, are to be altered and changed, appointed and abrogated, according to time, place, and person; 'so that nothing be done against the word of God'.[3]

Indeed, he held it

no derogation at all from the apostolical church to have the orders of it in divers points altered; for, though such were most convenient then for that state, time, and persons, yet are they not so now in respect of this state, time, and persons; so that the form of the apostolical churches was then perfite and absolute, though now it admit (in the respect of divers circumstances) alteration.[4]

[1] *Ibid.* p. 184.   [2] *Ibid.* p. 369.
[3] *Ibid.* p. 284.   [4] *Ibid.* p. 414.

In explanation of this position, he observed that

it is well known that the manner and form of government used in the apostles' time and expressed in the scriptures, neither is now, nor can or ought to be observed, either touching the persons or the functions; for we have neither apostles, prophets, workers of miracles, gifts of healing, diversity of tongues, widows, or such like; all which pertained to the government of the church in the apostles' time, and were parts of it. . . . And, seeing that the church is not bound to this form, so plainly expressed in . . . scripture, I see not how you can bind it to the self-same form of government used in the apostles' time.

Accordingly he insisted emphatically 'that there is no one certain kind of government in the church which must of necessity be perpetually observed'; and stigmatised the contrary assertion of his adversary as one which 'cannot stand with the truth and with learning'.[1] So axiomatic did this position become that Bishop Cooper in his *Admonition* averred that 'surely, as grave, learned men as most that have written in this time . . . do make proof of this proposition, that one form of church government is not necessary in all times and places of the Church'.[2]

Almost identical with this standpoint was the exposition given by Hooker of the necessity and nature of polity in the church. Of the necessity of some form of ordered regimen for 'all societies Christian' he had, of course, no doubt. 'Even so, the necessity of polity and regiment in all Churches may be held without holding any one certain form to be necessary in them all.'[3] He, like Whitgift, rejected the easy way of retort to the presbyterian claim of divine right by asserting a parallel authority for episcopacy:

If therefore we did seek to maintain that which most advantageth our own cause, the very best way for us and the strongest

[1] Whitgift, *Works*, vol. III, p. 214; vol. I, p. 187.
[2] T. Cooper, *Admonition to the People of England* (1847 edition), p. 66.
[3] Hooker, *Ecclesiastical Polity*, III, ii, 1.

against them were to hold even as they do, that in Scripture there must needs be found some particular form of church polity which God hath instituted, and which for that very cause belongeth to all churches, to all times. But with any such partial eye to respect ourselves, and by cunning to make those things seem the truest which are the fittest to serve our purpose, is a thing which we neither like nor mean to follow.[1]

Instead, he based his reply on the same distinction as that made by Whitgift, between 'matters of faith and in general matters necessary unto salvation' on the one hand, and things 'of a different nature', namely, 'ceremonies, order, and the kind of church government' on the other hand; and he affirmed that whilst the former were things *necessary*, the latter, in which he expressly included 'matters of government', were 'in the number of things *accessory*'.[2] The difference between Hooker and his opponents lay not in the question whether ecclesiastical polity was from God (for, argued Hooker, 'nor is it possible that any form of polity, much less of polity ecclesiastical, should be good unless God himself be author of it'); but whether 'no form of church polity is . . . to be lawful, or to be of God, unless God be so the author of it that it be also set down in Scripture'. Therefore he challenged his critics to say 'whether their meaning be that it must be there set down in whole or in part. For if wholly, let them shew what one form of polity ever was so.'[3]

In constructing his own apologia for episcopacy, accordingly, he did not demand an exclusive authority from scripture. He was persuaded 'that God's clergy are a state, which hath been and will be, as long as there is a church upon earth, necessary by the plain word of God himself'; and from this he deduced that

[1] *Ibid.* x, 8.   [2] *Ibid.* iii, 4.   [3] *Ibid.* ii, 1.

forasmuch as where the clergy are any great multitude, order doth necessarily require that by degrees they be distinguished; we hold there have ever been and ever ought to be in such case at leastwise two sorts of ecclesiastical persons, the one subordinate unto the other; as to the Apostles in the beginning, and to the Bishops always since, we find plainly both in Scripture and in all ecclesiastical records, other ministers of the word and sacraments have been.[1]

The chief difficulty in assessing Hooker's doctrine of episcopacy arises from the disputed authenticity of Books VII and VIII of his great work. If they are accepted as even substantially from his own hand, his testimony to a change of opinion since writing the earlier books is of evident importance:

Now although we should leave the general received persuasion held from the first beginning, that the Apostles themselves left bishops invested with power above other pastors; although, I say, we should give over this opinion, and embrace that other conjecture which so many have thought good to follow, and which myself did sometimes judge a great deal more probable than now I do, merely that after the Apostles were deceased, churches did agree amongst themselves for the preservation of peace and order, to make one presbyter in each city chief over the rest, and to translate into him that power by force and virtue whereof the Apostles, while they were alive, did preserve and uphold order in the Church . . .: this order taken by the church itself (for so let us suppose that the Apostles did neither by word nor deed appoint it) were notwithstanding more warrantable than that it should give place and be abrogated, because the ministry of the Gospel and the functions thereof ought to be from heaven.[2]

Into the detailed argument concerning Books VII and VIII, still continuing, it is not germane to our present purpose to enter; but without pronouncing upon the critical issues involved, it may be useful to enquire what doctrine of episcopacy emerges from their contents.

[1] Hooker, *Ecclesiastical Polity*, III. xi, 20. [2] *Ibid.* VII, xi, 8.

A thousand five hundred years and upward the Church of Christ hath now continued under the sacred regiment of bishops. Neither for so long hath Christianity been ever planted in any kingdom throughout the world but with this kind of government alone; which to have been ordained of God, I am for mine own part even as resolutely persuaded, as that any other kind of government in the world whatsoever is of God.[1]

From this historical evidence,

this we boldly therefore set down as a most infallible truth, 'That the Church of Christ is at this day lawfully, and so hath been sithence the first beginning, governed by bishops, having permanent superiority and ruling power over other ministers of the word and sacraments.'[2]

Indeed a later passage appears to carry the emphasis still higher :

Wherefore let us not fear to be herein bold and peremptory, that if anything in the church's government, surely the first institution of bishops was from heaven, was even of God, the Holy Ghost was the author of it.[3]

Of the difference at least in emphasis, if not further, between the earlier and later books *Of the Laws of Ecclesiastical Polity* in respect of episcopacy, there can be little doubt. But even in these later books, the author is content to ascribe to episcopacy apostolic, not dominical, authority. To Hooker moreover all good forms of polity, civil as well as ecclesiastical, are established by God. It would seem therefore that to him episcopacy, by reason of its historic tradition from the apostolic age to his own times, had demonstrated its divine authority. But this was very different from the claim that it is the exclusive form of ministry prescribed by the scriptures.

Similarly Whitgift made his appeal to historical tradition in favour of episcopacy:

[1] *Ibid.* vii, i, 4.   [2] *Ibid.* iii, 1.   [3] *Ibid.* v, 10.

23

There is no man of learning and modesty, which will without manifest proof condemn any order, especially touching the government of the church, that was used and allowed during the time of the primitive church, which was the next five-hundred years after Christ. . . . Neither was there any function or office brought into the church during all that time, allowed by any general council or credible writer, which was not most meet for that time, and allowable by the word of God.[1]

Again, he urged against Cartwright that

this authority, which the bishops and archbishops now exercise, came first from the apostolical church, then from the example of the primitive church for the space of five hundred years after the apostles' time; thirdly from the councils of Nice, Antioch, and Constantinople, and all the best and purest councils that ever were; and, last of all, from the authority of the prince and by the consent of this whole church and realm of England.[2]

At a later time, after his elevation to the primacy, in controversy with Beza, he likewise affirmed that

we make no doubt but that the episcopal degree, which we bear, is an institution apostolical and divine; and so always hath been held by a continued course of times from the Apostles to this very age of ours.[3]

Equally noteworthy is the fact that Richard Bancroft, the faithful henchman of Whitgift, averred in respect of 'the state of the question betwixt the Church of England and the Precisians touching the government thereof', that

the difference betwixt us is, that they say those names only (as Pastors, Doctors, Elders, and Deacons with their titles, Dispensatores Ministeriorum [sic] Christi etc.), their functions, and duties . . . are to be remitted and still retained, which they have squared us out in their platform; whereas the Church of England doth hold and defend, that so the substance be observed, the Word of God truly preached, the Sacraments

---

[1] Whitgift, *Works*, vol. II, p. 182.   [2] *Ibid.* p. 407.
[3] Strype, *Whitgift*, vol. II, p. 170.

rightly administered, virtue furthered, vice suppressed, and that the Church be quietly and orderly governed, the names, titles, duties and offices, whereby these things are attained, be not namely and particularly expressed in the Scriptures; but are in some parts left to the discretion and liberty of the Church, to be disposed according to the estate of times, places, and persons.[1]

Similarly in his famous sermon at Paul's Cross on 9 February 1588 he maintained the same position as Whitgift and Hooker. He reproached the presbyterians with the novelty of their system of church government, arguing that it was

a very strange matter, if it were true, that Christ should erect a form of government for the ruling of his Church to continue from his departure out of the world until his coming again; and that the same should never be once thought of or put into practice for the space of fifteen hundred years.

In like manner he rebuked them for forsaking the communion of a lawful and reformed church, affirming that

it hath ever been reckoned a most certain ground and principle in religion; that the church which maintaineth without error the Faith of Christ, which holdeth the true doctrine of the Gospel in matters necessary to salvation, and preacheth the same; which retaineth the lawful use of those Sacraments only which Christ hath appointed; and which appointeth vice to be punished, and virtue to be maintained; notwithstanding in some other respects and in some other points it may have many blemishes, nay divers and sundry errors, is yet to be acknowledged for the mother of the faithful, the house of God, the ark of Noah, the pillar of truth, and the spouse of Christ.

With regard to the form of church polity, he ranged himself firmly behind Jewel, observing that

for the better understanding whereof, you must know that the church of God ever since the apostles' times, hath distributed

---

[1] *Tracts ascribed to Richard Bancroft* (ed. Albert Peel), p. 95 (Cambridge, 1953). For 'dispensatores *ministeriorum* Christi', read 'dispensatores *mysteriorum*' as in I Cor. iv. 1.

the ecclesiastical ministry principally into these three parts, Bishops, Priests, and Deacons; according as it is contained in the *Apology* of the Church of England.[1]

Thus, with Bancroft, as with Whitgift and Hooker, episcopacy was defended as being of apostolical, not of dominical, provenance; and the appeal to history and tradition constituted the ground of its justification, not the allegation of any exclusive prescription of scripture.

But if episcopacy is to be retained, what are the specific functions which the bishop alone must perform in the church? In Book VII *Of the Laws of Ecclesiastical Polity* his office is thus succinctly defined:

A Bishop is a minister of God, unto whom with permanent continuance there is given not only power of administering the word and sacraments, which power other Presbyters have; but also a further power to ordain ecclesiastical persons, and a power of chiefty in government over presbyters as well as laymen, a power to be by way of jurisdiction a Pastor even to Pastors themselves.[2]

Whitgift concurred that 'it is the general consent of all the learned fathers, that it pertaineth to the office of a bishop to order and elect ministers of the word'[3]; and this was indeed the unvarying rule of the ordinal for persons ordained in England for ministry in the church of England. But, in conformity with a widespread tendency of his age, he laid chief emphasis upon Jerome's statement, 'What does a bishop do that a presbyter does not except ordain', as evidence of the identity of presbyter and bishop in respect of order. Thus, 'The Institution of a Christian Man', after affirming of the *potestas clavium* that

---

[1] Bancroft, *Sermon preached at Paul's Cross*, pp. 10, 11–12, 82.
[2] Hooker, *Ecclesiastical Polity*, VII, ii, 3.
[3] Whitgift, *Works*, vol. I, p. 437.

this office, power, and authority was committed and given by Christ and his apostles unto certain persons only, that is to say, unto priests and bishops whom they did elect, call, and admit thereunto by their prayer and imposition of hands, [had continued that] in the New Testament there is no mention made of any degrees or distinctions in orders, but only of deacons or ministers, and of priests or bishops.[1]

Whitgift accordingly held that

it is not to be denied but that there is an equality of all ministers of God's word *quoad ministerium*: 'touching the ministry'; for they have all like power to preach the word, to minister the sacraments: that is to say, the word preached, or the sacraments ministered, is as effectual in one (in respect of the ministry) as it is in another. But *quoad ordinem et politiam*: 'touching order and government', there always hath been and must be degrees and superiority among them.[2]

In so reasoning he was following in the wake of Jewel, who not only cited this passage of Jerome, but repeatedly quoted also his saying, 'Noverint episcopi se magis consuetudine, quam dispositionis dominicae veritate, presbyteris esse majores' ('Let bishops understand that they be greater than the priests by order and custom [of the church] and not by the truth of God's ordinance').[3] And again, he asked what Harding meant by saying that 'they which denied the distinction of a bishop and a priest were condemned of heresy':

Thinketh he that priests and bishops hold only by tradition? Or is it so horrible an heresy as he maketh it, to say that by the scriptures of God a bishop and a priest are all one? Or knoweth he how far and unto whom he reacheth the name of an heretic?

Verily Chrysostom saith: Inter episcopum et presbyterum interest ferme nihil; Between a bishop and a priest in a manner there is no difference.

---

1 C. Lloyd, *Formularies of Faith*, pp. 104–5.
2 Whitgift, *Works*, vol. II, p. 265.   3 Jewel, *Works*, vol. I, pp. 340, 379.

St Hierome saith, somewhat in rougher sort: Audio quendam in tantam erupisse vecordiam, ut diaconos presbyteris, id est, episcopis anteferret: ... cum apostolus perspicue doceat, eosdem esse presbyteros quos episcopos: I hear say there is one become so peevish that he setteth deacons before priests, that is to say, before bishops; whereas the apostle plainly teacheth us that priests and bishops be all one.

St Augustine saith: Quid est ... episcopus nisi primus presbyter, hoc est, summus sacerdos? What is a bishop but the first priest, that is to say, the highest priest? So saith St Ambrose: Episcopi et presbyteri una ordinatio est; uterque enim sacerdos est. Sed episcopus primus est: There is but one consecration of priest and bishop; for both of them are priests. But the bishop is the first.

All these, and other more holy fathers, together with St Paul the apostle, for thus saying, by M. Harding's advice, must be holden for heretics.[1]

For Jewel, Whitgift, and Hooker therefore the royal supremacy was the keystone of the arch of ecclesiastical polity, since it 'may be proved by most certain warrants of Holy Scripture', and episcopacy had proved itself of divine authority by its continuance from the apostolic age until their own times; whilst in the Church of England both the godly prince and the godly bishop had co-operated to reform abuses and restore sound doctrine. The conclusion of Keble was both just and apt:

Lest it should be imagined that we are here conceding more than we really mean to concede regarding the views of the writers in question, two propositions are subjoined, as comprising the substance of the argument by which they resisted the demands of the Puritans.

1. The whole Church, being naturally the subject in which all ecclesiastical power resides, may have had originally the right of determining how it would be governed.
2. Inasmuch as the Church did determine from very early times to be governed by bishops, it cannot be right to swerve

1 Jewel, *Works*, vol. III, p. 439.

from that government, in any country where the same may be maintained, consistently with soundness of doctrine, and the rights of the chief magistrate, being Christian.[1]

The reservations in this summary are as important as the affirmations of principle; and, no less than the positive positions, represented an integral element in the Anglican tradition as set forth by Jewel, Whitgift, and Hooker. It was the peculiar felicity of the church and realm of England in their eyes to have realised all these conditions in its ecclesiastical reformation. But what of church polity in less happy lands, where prince and episcopate had joined hands to oppose the restoration of sound doctrine and the effecting of reform? And what attitude should the church of England adopt towards its Protestant brethren faced by the harsh necessity of choosing between soundness of doctrine and perfectness of polity? And what in turn would be the attitude of those presbyterian Protestants towards the maintenance in England of episcopacy, which to them represented with the monarchy the oppression of the church, whereas to Hooker it seemed no other or less than 'the temperature of excess in all estates, the glue and soder of the public weal, the ligament which tieth and connecteth the limbs of this body politic each to other'?[2]

[1] *The Works of Hooker* (ed. John Keble), I, lxii–lxiii.
[2] Hooker, *Ecclesiastical Polity*, VII, xviii, 12.

II

A PARITY OF MINISTERS ASSERTED

'THE gospel and the church', wrote Whitgift in his *Defence of the Answer to the Admonition,*

was in queen Mary's time here in England; but it was persecuted, not 'established', not maintained, not allowed of, nor professed by the public magistrate and the laws of the land; and therefore of necessity a great difference between the government of it then and the government of it now; the outward show of it then and the outward show of it now; the placing of ministers then and the placing of them now.[1]

By this timely and homely reminder to his fellow-churchmen of the contrast between the position of their church under Mary Tudor and under her successor Elizabeth I, the author not only recalled the providential mercy which had delivered them from the present situation of many of their Protestant brethren in less happy lands; but laid down also the maxim that under conditions of oppression and persecution churches might be driven perforce and justifiably to acquiesce in the lack of something of the perfection of polity, and yet maintain the essentials of a true and reformed church. If the alternative lay between soundness of doctrine and the retention of episcopacy; if princes and bishops, instead of promoting, were actively opposing the necessary reform of the church, then other forms of church order might be adopted, until it pleased God to turn again the captivity of Sion. 'I say', he observed in another place of the *Defence,* 'there may be seniors in the time of persecution,

[1] Whitgift, *Works,* vol. I, p. 391.

when there is no christian magistrate, not that there ought of necessity to be.'[1]

Circumstances alter cases; and unusual conditions demanded abnormal remedies. Such, for example, Hooker judged to have been the case of Calvin at Geneva:

This device I see not how the wisest at that time living could have bettered, if we duly consider what the present estate of Geneva did then require. For their bishop and his clergy being (as it is said) departed from them by moonlight, or howsoever, being departed, to choose in his room any other bishop, had been a thing altogether impossible. And for their ministers to seek that themselves alone might have coercive power over the whole church, would perhaps have been hardly construed at that time. But when so frank an offer was made, that for every one minister there should be two of the people to sit and give voice in the ecclesiastical consistory, what inconvenience could they easily find which themselves might not be able always to remedy?[2]

Cartwright indeed had argued that if elders had been profitable in the apostolic age, they should be much more serviceable to the church in time of peace and under a christian prince; but Whitgift replied that

this is a poor and feeble reason: The church found seniors in the time of persecution: *ergo*, there ought rather to be seniors under a christian prince than in the time of persecution. Or this, the church is now better able to find seniors; *ergo*, it ought now rather to be governed by seniors. . . . But we ask not what the church was able to do then or what it is able to do now; but whether the same government ought to be now that was then; and whether a christian magistrate have no more authority in the government of the church now, than the heathenish and persecuting magistrate had then. . . . God hath much better provided for his church by placing in it civil and christian magistrates, whose authority is so ample and large, than by

[1] *Ibid.* vol. III, p. 166.
[2] Hooker, *Ecclesiastical Polity*, Preface, ii, 4.

placing seniors; wherefore, where christian magistrates be, the government of seniors is superfluous.[1]

But if arguments drawn from the church in time of persecution did not apply to its condition when protected by a godly prince, they were valid and could furnish precedents for contemporary Protestants suffering oppression. As Whitgift had already hinted, it was not necessary to look to Geneva in the times of Calvin for examples; they could be found at home during the reign of Mary Tudor. For under her short rule, congregations of true Protestants had met in secret (as the Puritans, under her successor, were to remember and imitate) for the worship of God and the maintenance of a corporate church life.

Although the church seemed at first to be entirely overthrown and the godly were dispersed in every quarter, yet a congregation of some importance collected itself at London, chose its ministers by common consent, appointed deacons, and in the midst of enemies more sharp-sighted than Argus and more cruel than Nero, the church of God was again restored entire, and, in a word, complete in all its parts. And though it was often dispersed by the attacks of its enemies, and a very great number of its members perished at the stake, it nevertheless grew and increased every day.[2]

A parallel account of this congregation was given by members of the Plumbers' Hall church before the Ecclesiastical Commissioners on 20 June 1567, when John Smith averred that

we bethought us what were best to do; and we remembered that there was a congregation of us in this city in queen Mary's days; and a congregation at Geneva, which used a book and order of preaching, ministering of the sacraments and discipline, most agreeable to the word of God, which book is

---

[1] Whitgift, *Works*, vol. III, p. 180.
[2] *Zurich Letters*, 2nd series, no. lxii, p. 160.

allowed by that godly and well-learned man, Master Calvin and the preachers there; which book and order we now hold.[1]

Thus an English church under the cross met in London during Mary Tudor's days, appointed its ministers and deacons without reference to bishops or sovereign, and illustrated Whitgift's principle that in such circumstances the lack of episcopacy was no barrier to a corporate worship and discipline. But not only was this precedent fashioned at home in England; still more revealing was the history of the companies of exiles who sought refuge in continental cities during the reign of Mary, and there found themselves emancipated alike from the liturgy and polity of the church in England. In the congregation at Frankfort, after the controversy between Knoxians and Coxians had been determined in the expulsion of Knox by the civil magistrates, Richard Cox on 28 March 1555

assembled all such as had been Priests and Ministers in England to his lodging; and there declared ... that he thought it requisite that they should consult together, whom they thought most meet to be a Bishop, or Superintendent, or Pastor; with the rest of the Officers, as Seniors, Ministers, and Deacons.[2]

There is much of importance as well as interest in Thomas Fuller's account of the proceedings which ensued:

After the departure, or rather the driving away, of Mr Knox, Dr Cox and his adherents clearly carried all, and proceeded to the election of Officers in their Congregation. But first a fit title for him that was to take charge of their souls, then a proper person for that title.

1. *Bishop* (though first in nomination) was declined as improper, because here he had no inspection over any Diocese, but only a cure of a congregation, on which very account Mr Scory (though formerly bishop of Chichester) when

---

[1] Grindal, *Remains*, p. 203.
[2] *Troubles at Frankfort* (ed. E. Arber), pp. 72, 77.

preacher to the Congregation at Emden, took upon himself the title of Superintendent.

2. *Superintendent* was here also waived, as the same in effect, only a bad Latin word instead of a good Greek.

3. *Minister* also was misliked for the principal Preacher (though admitted to signify his assistants), perchance as a term of too much compliance with the opposite party.

4. *Pastor* was at last pitched upon, as freest from exception, most expressive of the office, and least obnoxious to offence.

Then was Mr Whitehead chosen their Pastor; yet so as two Ministers, four Elders, and two Deacons were joined to assist him.[1]

Here was evidence of congregations of English exiles rejecting the name of bishop and preferring those of pastor or superintendent, and setting up also the discipline of the reformed church by the appointment of elders and deacons. Moreover it is noteworthy that these companies included four persons who had been bishops in Great Britain: John Scory, formerly bishop of Chichester, at Emden; John Bale of Ossory, at Frankfort and Basle; John Poynet of Rochester and Winchester, at Strasburg; and Miles Coverdale of Exeter, at Frankfort, Aarau, and Geneva; none of whom sought to have the pre-eminence over his brethren in the novel circumstances of their exile. Thus Anglican divines had set the pattern and precedent for Whitgift's later avowal that 'there may be seniors in time of persecution when there is no christian magistrate'.

Their period of exile indeed was too short for expedient to harden into principle; and for their somewhat lukewarm attempt at keeping 'the face of an English church' to decline into capitulation before the pattern of the best reformed churches amongst which their lot was cast. But even this short interval had been long

[1] Thomas Fuller, *Church History* (ed. Brewer), vol. IV, pp. 218–9 (Bk. VIII. 6) (Oxford, 1845, 6 vols.).

enough to bring English churchmen face to face with the problem of preserving the church in the teeth of royal and episcopal oppression; and to evoke their sympathies for their brethren whose oppression was continued. For themselves, once more the godly prince was to prove the linchpin of the body politic; for with the accession of Elizabeth I and the dispossession of the surviving bishops of her predecessor's reign, the church of England returned to the path of reformation with an episcopate recruited predominantly from the personnel of the returned exiles. If it was natural for them to maintain a close correspondence with their former hosts and to seek their counsel concerning the perfecting of the Elizabethan settlement, it was not so certain what attitude their continental brethren might adopt towards episcopacy, which in their experience was associated with the Holy Roman emperors, or the Valois kings of France, or their kinswomen in Scotland, Mary of Guise and Mary Stewart. Might not the difference of their fortunes drive a wedge between the restored Anglican exiles and their former protectors, in whose cities they had eaten the bread of banishment and at whose hands they had received lessons in organising the liturgy and polity of a church under the cross? Would the Anglican episcopacy prove a divisive rather than an eirenic element in their relations with foreign Protestants?

It is generally agreed that the first reformers, both Lutheran and Calvinist, had no objection to episcopacy in principle. As Professor G. D. Henderson has succinctly stated, 'none of the earlier reformation standards rejects episcopacy', and during the first phase of the movement 'there is no trace of reforming hostility to the office of a bishop'. The Augsburg Confession used very guarded and moderate language concerning the episcopate,

35

emphasising the difference between the proper ecclesiastical authority of bishops and the temporal powers extrinsically added thereto. Article VII of Part II of the Confession, *De Potestate Ecclesiastica*, observed that

there have been great controversies touching the power of bishops; in which many have incommodiously mingled together the Ecclesiastical power and the power of the sword. . . . These faults did godly and learned men long since reprehend in the Church and for that cause our teachers were compelled, for the comfort of men's consciences, to show the difference between the ecclesiastical power and the power of the sword. . . .

Now their judgment is this; that the power of the keys, or the power of the Bishops, by the rule of the Gospel, is a power or commandment from God of preaching the Gospel, of remitting or retaining sins, and of administering the Sacraments. . . . This power is put in execution only by teaching or preaching the Word and administering the Sacraments, either to many or to single individuals, according to their calling. . . .

Therefore, when the question touches the jurisdiction of Bishops, dominion must be distinguished from ecclesiastical jurisdiction. Again, by the Gospel, or as they term it, by divine right, bishops—that is, those who have the administration of the Word and Sacraments committed to them—have no other jurisdiction at all but to remit sin, also to judge in regard to doctrine and to reject doctrine inconsistent with the Gospel, and to exclude from the communion of the Church, without human force but by the Word, those whose wickedness is notorious. And herein of necessity the Churches ought by divine command to render obedience unto them, according to the saying. He that heareth you, heareth me. But when they teach or decree anything contrary to the Gospel, then have the churches a commandment of God, which forbiddeth obedience to them. . . .

Besides these things, there is a controversy whether Bishops or Pastors have power to institute ceremonies in the church, and to establish laws concerning meats, holy days, grades and orders of ministers. . . . Concerning which we teach that Bishops have no power to ordain anything contrary to the Gospel.

The conclusion of the argument was that

bishops might easily retain lawful obedience, if they did not urge men to observe traditions which they cannot keep with a good conscience. For they command celibacy, and will receive none unless they promise not to teach the pure doctrine of the Gospel. The churches ... ask only that the bishops should remit unjust burdens, which are novel and contrary to the custom of the catholic church. . . . For Peter forbids bishops to be lords and be imperious over the churches. Now our purpose is not to have authority taken from the bishops; but this one thing only is requested, that they would suffer the Gospel purely to be taught, and that they would relax a few observances, which cannot be received without sin.[1]

This standpoint was reaffirmed in the Schmalkaldic Articles, which also allowed episcopacy as rightly exercised:

If the bishops were real bishops who served the church and the gospel, we could for the sake of peace and unity in the church, permit them to ordain and confirm our ministers, but not as though it were a matter of necessity. . . .

Now, as they are not real bishops, nor wish to be, but secularised lords and princes, ... persecuting and condemning those who are properly called to the ministry, the church has no need to remain without ministers because the bishops refuse to co-operate.

Therefore, according to the example of the early church and early fathers, we ourselves have to ordain suitable persons to this ministry.

The same Articles also affirmed that

the Gospel has given to those who are placed at the head of the churches, the command to preach the Gospel, to give absolution, and to administer the sacraments. Further, they have the power of jurisdiction, that is the power to excommunicate those whose crimes are notorious, and to readmit penitent sinners. All are agreed ... in admitting that by divine authority these powers belong in common to those who preside over the churches, whether they be called pastors or bishops.[2]

[1] B. J. Kidd, *Documents of the Continental Reformation*, pp. 283-8.
[2] Schmalkaldic Articles, III, X.

37

On the other hand, Luther, like Jewel, interpreted apostolic succession as a succession of doctrine, not of office ('Evangelium soll die successio sein'); and he recognised only one essential ministry of the church, that of preaching the Word and administering the sacraments. This ministry he held to be the gift of God to the church, that by its exercise faith might be created in the people. 'In order that we may obtain this faith', ran Article V of the 1531 version of the Augsburg Confession, 'the ministry of teaching the gospel and ministering the sacraments has been instituted'; and Article XIV affirmed 'concerning ecclesiastical order, we teach that no one ought to teach publicly in the church nor to administer the sacraments, unless he has been duly called'.[1] This calling and commission could be given by simple ministers, since Luther held that 'we who preach the gospel have the power of ordaining' ('Nos qui praedicamus Evangelium, habemus potestatem ordinandi'). Maintaining also that in the New Testament 'bishop' and 'presbyter' were synonyms, Luther himself exercised the right to ordain in practice. Granted favourable political and ecclesiastical conditions, indeed, the Lutheran Church in Germany might have followed the model of the Church of Sweden or that of England. But episcopal ordination would not have been regarded as essential nor the preservation of episcopal succession as vital. When this hope proved vain, Luther still recognised the need for overseers or superintendents of the ministry; and instituted such officers to exercise the power of jurisdiction traditionally associated with the episcopal office. Local conditions were responsible in

[1] *Sylloge Confessionum*, pp. 124, 127, Article V: 'Ut hanc fidem consequamur, institutum est ministerium docendi Evangelii et porrigendi sacramenta.' Article XIV: 'De ordine ecclesiastico docent, quod nemo debet in ecclesia publice docere aut sacramenta administrare, nisi rite vocatus.'

large measure for the particular forms and names of ecclesiastical polity in the several Lutheran churches. Outside Sweden and Finland, however, the power of ordination was not restricted to the bishop; and the office of superintendent or 'bishop' was based not upon a difference of order but upon a distinction of function.

Calvin, as has already been observed, held that 'wherever we find the word of God purely preached and heard, and the sacraments administered according to the institution of Christ, there, it is not to be doubted, is a church of God'. Furthermore, where these essential conditions were fulfilled, there was no ground for separating from the communion of the church:

When we affirm the pure ministry of the word, and pure order in the celebration of the sacraments, to be a sufficient pledge and earnest, that we may safely embrace the society in which both these are found, as a true church; we carry the observation to this point, that such a society should never be rejected as long as it continues in those things, although in other respects it may be chargeable with many faults. It is possible, moreover, that some fault may insinuate itself into the preaching of the doctrine, or the administration of the sacraments, which ought not to alienate us from its communion.[1]

To such a degree did Calvin press these principles as to write that

so highly does the Lord esteem the communion of his church, that he considers everyone as a traitor and apostate from religion, who perversely withdraws himself from any Christian society which preserves the true ministry of the word and sacraments.[2]

His own exposition of the nature of the ministry is well known; that he regarded apostles, prophets, and evangelists as extraordinary officers of the apostolic church, 'not instituted to be of perpetual continuance'; that

---

1 Calvin, *Institutes*, bk. IV, cap. I, sect. ix, xii (trans. J. Allen, 2 vols., 1844).
2 *Ibid.* sect. x.

pastors and teachers on the other hand 'sustain an ordinary office in the church', being assisted by elders and deacons; that 'the province of pastors is the same as that of the apostles, except that they preside over particular churches respectively committed to each of them'; and that 'in calling those who preside over churches by the appellations of "bishops", "elders", and "pastors", without any distinction, I have followed the usage of the scripture, which applies all these terms to express the same meaning'.[1] Moreover, 'no one shall assume a public office in the church without a call'; the choice of ministers should be made with the consent of the people, but other pastors should preside over the election; and ordination should be by imposition of hands of the pastors. The distinction between presbyter and bishop Calvin affirmed to have arisen in order 'to guard against dissension, the general consequence of equality', amongst the presbyters of a city; and 'this arrangement was introduced by human agreement, on account of the necessity of the time'. But the episcopacy thus established was constitutional, not monarchical; 'every assembly . . . for the sole purpose of preserving order and peace, was under the direction of one bishop, who, while he had the precedence of all others in dignity, was himself subject to the assembly of the brethren'.[2] Nor did this superiority exempt the bishop from the obligation personally to dispense the word and sacraments; and Calvin's criticism of the contemporary episcopate was based upon the neglect by bishops of the primary duty of their office, and upon the recognised abuses and scandals associated both with their appointment and the discharge of their responsibility.

[1] Calvin, *Institutes*, bk. IV, cap. III, sect. iv, v, viii.
[2] *Ibid.* sect. x, xv, xvi; cap. IV, sect. ii.

There remained, however, the question of ecclesiastical discipline, which Calvin associated with the government of the church:

'Governors', I apprehend to have been persons of advanced years, selected from the people, to unite with the bishops in giving admonitions and exercising discipline. . . . From the beginning every church has had its senate or council, composed of pious, grave, and holy men, who were invested with that jurisdiction in the correction of vices, of which we shall soon treat. Now that this was not the regulation of a single age, experience itself demonstrates. This office of government is necessary, therefore, in every age.[1]

This exercise of discipline was connected with the power of the keys; whereby the authority of binding and loosing

is dispensed to us by the ministers and pastors of the church, either in the preaching of the gospel, or in the administration of the sacraments; and this is the principal exercise of the power of the keys, which the Lord has conferred on the society of the faithful.[2]

This discipline consisted first of private admonitions; and secondly of public admonition

before the tribunal of the church, that is the assembly of the elders, and there to be more severely admonished by public authority, that if he reverence the church, he may submit and obey; but if this do not overcome him, and he still persevere in his iniquity, our Lord then commands him, as a despiser of the church, to be excluded from the society of the faithful.[3]

It was universally agreed that provision must be made for 'the punishment of wickedness and vice and the maintenance of true religion and virtue'; but differences existed as to the best means of achieving this end. Whitgift, as has been remarked, held that 'where christian magistrates be, the government of seniors is superfluous';

[1] *Ibid.* bk. IV, cap. III, sect. VIII.   [2] *Ibid.* cap. I sect. xxii.
[3] *Ibid.* cap. XII, sect. ii.

and he could call to his support the redoubtable authority of Erastus, who likewise affirmed that 'wherever the
magistrate is godly and christian, there is no need of any
other authority, under any other name or title, to rule
and punish; as if the godly magistrate differed in nothing
from the heathen'.[1]

There existed, therefore, considerable grounds for
mutual co-operation and alliance between the churches
of the Reformation. On the one side such typical
Anglicans as Whitgift and Hooker, whilst defending
tenaciously the retention of episcopacy on the basis of
history and tradition, denied that any one form of
government was prescribed in scripture in such wise as
to allow of no departure from it. On the other side,
Calvin himself held that 'one church should not despise
another on account of a variety of external discipline':[2]
and there was a general agreement that the essential
notes of a true church were the preaching of the Word
purely and the administration of the sacraments according to Christ's ordinance. Moreover there was a good
deal in common on the controverted terrain of church
polity and order between the offices of bishop and superintendent; for Lutheranism retained some episcopal
functions in its superintendents, and some Anglicans
were prepared to regard the choice of title as indifferent
provided that the pastoral nature of the office was safeguarded and realised. From the amalgam of these
varieties of Protestantism there might have emerged the
ecclesiastical equivalent of that mixed polity so beloved
of Aristotle, which could have embraced episcopal,
presbyteral, and lay elements in a balanced whole. For

1 Erastus, *Explicatio Gravissimae Quaestionis*, Thesis LXXIV: 'Ubicunque igitur
magistratus est pius et christianus, ibi alio nullo est opus, qui alio nomine ac
titulo vel gubernet vel puniat, quasi nihil a profano magistratu pius differet.'
2 Calvin, *Institutes*, bk. IV, cap. X, sect. xxxii.

even in matter of nomenclature there was considerable agreement. If Calvin denounced the Roman bishops because 'by their ordination they create not presbyters to rule and feed the people, but priests to offer sacrifice', Whitgift on his side explained away the offensive word 'priest' in his observation that:

I am not greatly delighted with the name, nor so desirous to maintain it; but yet a truth is to be defended. I read in the old fathers that these two names *sacerdos* and *presbyter* be confounded. I see also that the learned and the best of our English writers, such I mean as write in these our days, translate this word *presbyter* so; and the very word itself, as it is used in our English tongue, soundeth the word *presbyter*. As heretofore use hath made it to be taken for a sacrificer, so will use now alter that signification, and make it to be taken for a minister of the gospel. But it is mere vanity to contend for the name, when we agree of the thing.

Hooker indeed would have 'priest' fall into desuetude:

I rather term the one sort of clergy *Presbyters* than *Priests*, because in a matter of so small moment, I would not offend their ears to whom the name of Priesthood is odious, though without cause.... Seeing then that sacrifice is no part of the church ministry, how should the name of Priesthood be thereunto rightly applied?... Wherefore to pass by the name, let them use what dialect they will, whether we call it a Priesthood, a Presbytership, or a Ministry, it skilleth not. Although in truth the word *Presbyter* doth seem more fit, and in propriety of speech more agreeable than *Priest* with the drift of the whole gospel of Jesus Christ.

Likewise Jewel, declaring that 'there is no reason' to account Holy Orders a sacrament, bade his opponent 'here note, this ministry of the church was not ordained to offer sacrifice for forgiveness of sins'.[1] Thus far,

---

[1] Calvin, *Institutes*, bk. iv, cap. v, sect. iv. Whitgift, *Works*, vol. iii, p. 351. Hooker, *Ecclesiastical Polity*, v, lxxviii, 2, 3. Jewel, *Works*, vol. ii, pp. 1229, 1331.

therefore, in Maitland's phrase, 'there was agreeable harmony in dogma and little controversy over polity'.[1]

During the first decade and a half of the reign of Elizabeth I, indeed, the possibilities of such close and harmonious co-operation between the churches of England and Scotland were bright. In the first place many of the leaders were well known to each other, and had shared common experiences. John Knox, John Spottiswoode, and William Harlow had all served in England; whilst John Willcock and Christopher Goodman were Englishmen who had served in Scotland. Moreover the *Book of Discipline* of 1560 required, as 'a thing most expedient for this time', the appointment of twelve or ten superintendents, to whom territorial dioceses were assigned, and 'to whom charge and commandment shall be given to plant and erect churches, to set order, and appoint ministers'. In harmony with English precept also, it further required that these superintendents

must not be suffered to live as your idle bishops have done heretofore; neither must they remain where they gladly would; but they must be preachers themselves, and such as make no long residence in any one place, till their churches be planted and provided of ministers or at the least of readers.

They were, indeed, to be constitutional rulers, 'subjected to the censure and correction of the ministers and elders, not only of the chief town, but also of the whole province' over which they were appointed 'overseers'.[2] Similarly the 'Form and Order of the Election of the Superintendent, which may serve in election of all other Ministers' of 1561 required the preaching of a sermon on 'the necessity of Ministers and Superintendents' and the qualities of these officers. The superintendent, there-

---

[1] *Cambridge Modern History*, vol. II, p. 590.
[2] W. C. Dickinson, *John Knox's History of the Reformation in Scotland*, vol. II, p. 291.

fore, 'was such a bishop as can exist in a Church which knows neither the necessity of episcopal ordination, nor the inviolable parity of ministers; and the existence of the office left the door open for the introduction of an episcopate into the Scottish reformed church'.[1] John Knox, furthermore, had no doubt that the civil magistrate should inaugurate the work of reformation:

Now let us consider [he wrote in his *Petition* of 1558], whether the reformation of religion falling into decay and punishment of false teachers do appertain to the civil magistrates and nobility of any realm. I am not ignorant that Satan of old time for maintenance of his darkness, hath obtained of this blind world two chief points; former, he hath persuaded princes, rulers, and magistrates that the feeding of Christ's flock pertaineth nothing to their charge, but that it is rejected upon the bishops and state ecclesiastical; and secondly, that the reformation of religion, be it never so corrupt, and the punishment of such as be sworn soldiers in their kingdom, are exempted from all civil power and are reserved to themselves and to their own cognition. But that no offender can justly be exempted from punishment and that the ordering and reformation of religion with the instruction of subjects, doth especially pertain to the civil magistrate, shall God's perfect ordinance, his plain Word, and the facts and examples of these that of God are highly praised, most evidently declare.[2]

Here evidently were the makings of both the godly prince and the godly bishop! But political and ecclesiastical conditions in Scotland did not permit of their realisation as they had done in England. For though the Edinburgh parliament had initiated the process of reform, neither Mary of Guise nor Mary Stewart were evident prototypes of the godly prince; and the popish bishops held on to their offices notwithstanding. Actually only five of the ten superintendents provided for in the

---

[1] G. Donaldson, 'The Scottish Episcopate at the Reformation', *English Historical Review*, vol. LX (1945), pp. 349–64.

[2] John Knox, *Works* (ed. D. Laing), vol. IV, pp. 485–6.

Book of Discipline were appointed; but conforming bishops, such as Alexander Gordon of Galloway, Adam Bothwell of Orkney, and Robert Stewart of Caithness, were commissioned to act as superintendents and to plant kirks in their dioceses. And one of the new superintendents, the Laird of Dun, John Erskine, later explicitly identified 'bishop' with 'superintendent', and argued for the scriptural authority of the office.

The administration of the power is committed by the kirk to bishops or superintendents. Wherefore to the bishops or superintendents pertaineth the examination and admission to offices and benefices of spiritual cure, whatsoever benefice it be, as well bishoprics, abbacies, and priories as the inferior benefices. That this pertaineth by the Scripture of God to bishops or superintendents is manifest. . . . Thus we have plainly expressed by Scriptures that to the office of a bishop pertaineth the examination and admission to spiritual cure and office, and also to oversee them who are admitted, that they walk uprightly and exercise their office faithfully and purely. To take away this power from the bishop or superintendent is to take away the office of a bishop that no bishop be in the kirk; which were to alter and abolish the order which God hath appointed in his Kirk.[1]

During the first two decades of its reformation, indeed, the Church of Scotland enjoyed a mixed polity, combining elements representative of episcopal and presbyteral authority in the church and of the power of the godly magistrate in the state. Kirk sessions were already in existence; but the Classis did not take root till later. With the runaway flight of Mary and the regencies of Moray and Morton, the way was opened for a further approximation to the Anglican pattern of polity by the introduction in 1572 at the Convention of Leith of a Protestant episcopacy. For it was there decreed 'that the

1 D. Calderwood, *History of the Church of Scotland*, vol. III, pp. 157–8.

names and titles of archbishops and bishops are not to be altered, or innovat; nor yet the bounds of the dioceses confounded; but to stand and continue in time coming as they did before the reformation of religion'; that every metropolitan or cathedral seat should have a 'chapter of learned ministers'; and that bishops should 'exercise no further jurisdiction in spiritual functions than the superintendents have and presently exercise', and 'that all archbishops and bishops be subject to the Kirk and General Assembly thereof *in spiritualibus* as they are to the king *in temporalibus*'. Moreover, in 'the order of admission of bishops and others entering to spiritual promotions', it was desired that 'so far as may be, the order of the Kirk of England be followed'. Accordingly, promotion to the episcopate was to be by means of a *congé d'élire* accompanied by a Letter Missive from the regent to the cathedral chapter (though the chapter, unlike their English confrères, enjoyed the right to crave a new nomination, if they found the first nominee 'not qualified in whole or part of the qualities required in a bishop'); and then by Royal Letters Patent under the Great Seal for the consecration of the bishop-elect; who was to take an oath to the king as 'the only lawful and supreme Governor of this realm as well in things temporal as in the conservation and purgation of religion'. With the ratification of these provisions by the Assembly at Perth in August of the same year, the new order started on its way. It may be noted in passing that the Perth Assembly omitted the name of 'bishop' from its list of 'certain names, as archbishop, dean, archdeacon, chancellor, chapter', which it deemed 'slanderous and offensive to the ears of many', and which it received only as an interim measure and desired to be 'changed to others less offensive'. Thus at the institution of John

Douglas to the archbishopric of St Andrews, the rite was conducted according to the order for the admission of superintendents, with the significant substitution of the imposition of hands upon the recipient instead of the mere 'taking by the hand'. The Superintendent of Fife, Winram, preached the sermon; and Bishop Stewart of Caithness, the Superintendent of Lothian John Spottis-woode, and the Minister of Leith David Lindsay laid hands upon Douglas; who henceforth styled himself 'Archbishop of St Andrews and Superintendent of Fyfe'. If in certain quarters the new prelates were contume-liously described as Tulchan bishops, it could not be foreseen whether they might not yet develop according to the pattern prevailing in England.

Ironically enough, it was from England at this very juncture that the movement originated which was to come near to overthrowing episcopacy in the Church of England and was to plant the presbyterian order firmly in the Church of Scotland. It might without injustice be called 'the Cambridge Movement'; for its leader, Thomas Cartwright, was Lady Margaret's Professor of Divinity, most of its adherents were from that university, and it was at first an academic movement which spread later from the colleges to the parishes. With the publi-cation in 1572 of the *Admonitions to Parliament,* both the tempo and temper of ecclesiastical discussion were changed. To their authors, 'we in England are so far off from having a church rightly reformed according to the prescript of God's Word, that as yet we are not come to the outward face of the same'. Instead, therefore, of minor accommodations of the existing church polity, the new reformers demanded the complete supersession of diocesan episcopacy and of the Book of Common Prayer. In this 'reform of the reformation' seignories were indispensable, and the new watchword of 'parity of ministers' was introduced:

Now, then, if you will restore the church to his ancient officers, this you must do. Instead of an Archbishop or Lord Bishop, you must make equality of ministers. Instead of Chancellors, Archbishops, Officials, Commissaries, Proctors, Doctors, Summoners, Churchwardens, and such like: you have to plant in every congregation a lawful and godly seignory. The Deaconship must not be confounded with the Ministry. . . . And to these three jointly, that is the Ministers, Seniors, and Deacons, is the whole regiment of the Church to be committed.

In like manner the Book of Common Prayer was aspersed as but 'an unperfect book, culled and picked out of that popish dunghill, the Mass Book, full of all abominations'; and the conclusion of the matter was clear and far-reaching: 'But in a few words to say what we mean. Either we must have a right ministry of God and a right government of his church, according to the scriptures set up (both which we lack), or else there can be no right religion.'[1] Thanks to the maxim of the advocates of this new order of 'tarrying for the magistrate', the realisation of their programme by constitutional means was impossible in England. For neither the godly magistrate in the person of the queen, nor the godly bishops as represented by her episcopate, could stomach such demands; and Elizabeth also had means at her disposal, by virtue of the royal prerogative, of preventing her faithful commons from repeating their successful strategy of 1559, when they had overthrown the royal policy for the first parliament of the reign and had forced the enactment of an Act of Uniformity, with the Prayer Book of 1552 substantially attached thereto.

In Scotland the fortunes of war went otherwise. For

[1] W. H. Frere and C. E. Douglas, *Puritan Manifestos*, pp. 9, 16, 21, 6.

in 1574 there returned the protagonist of the corresponding Scottish presbyterian movement, Andrew Melville, forcefully, if variously, described as 'The Hildebrand of Presbytery', ἐπισκοπομάστιξ, *episcoporum exactor*, and 'the flinger-out of bishops'; who, after six years of study in France and five years' further teaching and study at Geneva, was fully cognisant of the opinions and views of Calvin's successor, Theodore Beza. Now therefore was the axe to be laid to the root of the tree of Morton's Protestant prelacy. For whereas Knox had been always conscious of the close relationship of the Reformation in Scotland with that in England, Melville looked for authority and alliance to the reformed churches abroad. Accordingly the General Assembly and parliament agreed in 1580 that

forasmuch as the office of a bishop, as it is now used and commonly taken within this realm, hath no sure warrant, authority, or good ground out of the Book and Scriptures of God, but is brought in by the folly and corruption of men's inventions, to the great overthrow of the Kirk of God; the whole Assembly of the Kirk in one voice, after liberty given to all men to reason in the matter, none opposing himself in defending the said pretended office, finds and declares the same pretended office, used and termed as is above said, unlawful in itself, as having neither fundament, ground nor warrant in the Word of God.

In 1581 also the Assembly adopted the *Second Book of Discipline*, of which the two chief reforms were the dropping of the office of superintendent (largely because it had been the Trojan horse by which episcopacy had been reintroduced) and the institution of the new court of the presbytery. 'One generation cometh and another goeth'; and both in England and Scotland, as Grindal remarked to Bullinger, 'they are young men who disseminate these opinions'. A new company of leaders, 'doctors' rather than 'pastors', was coming to the fore, determined to press rigid and exclusive claims for presbyterianism as the only form of polity prescribed and commanded in scripture. If in 1566 'the Superintendents, Ministers and Commissioners of Kirks within the realm of Scotland' could write to 'their brethren the Bishops and Pastors of England'—albeit in behalf of those Puritan ministers refusing to wear the surplice—now the 'brethren' of Melville were Cartwright, Travers, and the authors of the *Admonitions*, who in their turn asked plaintively, 'Is discipline meet for Scotland and is it unprofitable for this realm?'

Nor was the correspondence confined to this island. A novel feature of the presbyterian aggression was its revelation that abroad, in Geneva and in Zurich also, an old generation had passed and another succeeded. Now the Anglican bishops, still faithful correspondents of their foreign mentors, displayed a new self-confidence and a more positive assertion of the rights of episcopacy. Bishop Cox demanded of Rodolph Gualter:

Has not the management and conservation of ecclesiastical rites from the very origin of a well-constituted church been at all times under the especial control of bishops? Have not the despisers and violators of such rites been rebuked and brought to order by the bishops? [1]

Similarly, Bishop Horne assured Bullinger that it was 'some men of inferior rank and standing, deficient indeed both in sagacity and sense, and entirely ignorant and unknown', who were the leaders of the movement; and who 'call together conventicles, elect their own bishops', and separate from the church. [2] Nor was it out of keeping with this novel spirit that Cox should roundly designate

[1] *Zurich Letters*, 1st series, no. xciv, p. 236.
[2] *Ibid.* no. xcviii, p. 248.

the rebels as copying the examples of 'the Donatists of old and the Anabaptists now', and compare them again to 'the Anabaptists, Donatists, papists and all the good-for-nothing tribe of the sectaries'.[1]

More important, however, were the replies of the continental divines; for they revealed an equally significant gulf between Geneva and Zurich. From Zurich indeed the Anglican prelates received consoling words. Gualter censured those who 'require the names of archbishops, bishops, and other officials to be entirely abolished', in terms of measured severity:

I wish they would act with greater modesty, and that in altering the constitution of state or church they would not assume to themselves greater piety than they possess. . . . It appears to me better to bear with patience the imperfections of the kingdoms of this world, so long as purity of doctrine and liberty of conscience remain inviolate, than by disputing about the external government of the church to bring the whole into danger. And I wonder that they entertain such an aversion to the name of bishop, which they cannot but know was in use in the time of the apostles, and always too retained in the churches in after times; we know too that archbishops existed of old, whom they called by another name *patriarchs*. And if in later times they have occasioned so much offence by reason of their tyranny and ambition . . . I do not yet see what is to hinder that, on the removal of the abuses, those persons may be bishops and called such, who, placed over a certain number of churches, have the management of such things as pertain to the purity of religion and doctrine.

Even in regard to popular election of ministers as against appointment by bishops, he urged the 'great need of prudence and moderation, lest while we are urging an extreme right, many persons may have occasion of complaining that we have done them injustice'. St Paul had commanded all things to be done decently and in order;

[1] *Zurich Letters*, 1st series, no. cix, pp. 284 *seq.*

and, added Gualter, 'I do not see how this can be the case without a certain distinction of ecclesiastical office.' In the entire city and canton of Zurich, only one church had the right of electing its ministers.

Among us at least (to bring forward this by way of example), who, by the singular mercy of God have now for fifty years enjoyed the free preaching of the gospel, the election of ministers in many of the parishes rests with the Bishop of Constance and the popish abbots, who from the donation of former sovereigns, possess the tithes and largest revenues in the canton of Zurich. And should we seek to deprive them of their right and possession, which has now been established by long prescription, what disturbances should we occasion, what danger should we bring upon our churches! It seems to us also more advisable that they should enjoy their right together with the tithes, and allow us peace and freedom of religion, and suffer themselves to be so far controlled by our most noble senate, as not to appoint any incumbent to the churches, who has not been brought up in our church and approved by a lawful examination.[1]

In corresponding vein Bullinger also wrote to Bishop Sandys:

But these parties are endeavouring to erect a church, which they will never raise to the height they wish; nor if they should erect it, will they be able to maintain it. I have seen the heads of their fabric, as delineated by you, with respect to which I have long since declared my sentiments. The first proposition, that the civil magistrate has no authority in ecclesiastical matters; and also the second, that the church admits of no other government than that of presbyters, or the presbytery; these two, I say, they hold in common with the papists, who also displace the magistrate from the government of the church, and substitute themselves alone in his place. Whose opinion I have confuted in my refutation of the pope's bull, and in defence of the queen of England and her noble realm, which I sent you two years since. I wish that there were no lust of dominion in

_____
[1] *Ibid.* 2nd series, no. xciv, pp. 225 *seq.*

the originators of this presbytery! Nay, I think the greatest caution is necessary that the supreme power be not placed in this presbytery, much more that it be not an exclusive government.[1]

On these issues the heirs of Zwingli at Zurich differed sharply and completely from Calvin's successor at Geneva. Beza indeed supported the English rebels:

For, since an outward call (after due examination as to doctrine and moral character) not by any single individual, but at least by a congregation of the brethren, is as it were the basis and foundation of an ecclesiastical ministry, what can be more abominable, what more extravagant, than that assumed power of the bishops, by which they admit at their pleasure parties not so called, but who enter the ministry of their own accord; and immediately, without assigning them any cure, approve them as qualified either to serve, as they call it, or to teach; at length, on the vacancy of any preferment . . . they appoint this or that individual to whatever churches they please? If we enquire into church discipline, what can it be in a country, where, just the same as under the papacy, they have in the place of a lawfully appointed presbytery, their deans, chancellors, and archdeacons?

In this 'state of the Anglican churches, which, as it appears to me, is very wretched and altogether beyond endurance', the Puritan ministers who had asked whether they could 'with a good conscience remain in the ministry under these conditions' received a reply which, all things considered, was in the negative; though Beza was prepared to allow a middle course, that 'after a respectful protest to the bishop' they might 'continue in the ministry until the matter is decided in parliament'.[2]

Nor was Beza's counsel based simply on a reciprocation of what he believed to be Elizabeth's inveterate

[1] *Zurich Letters*, 2nd series, no. xcviii, pp. 240 *seq.*   [2] *Ibid.* no. liii, pp. 127 *seq.*

dislike of the church of Geneva. His own opinions on episcopacy were immoderate both in form and content. For he divided bishops into three sorts: of God, of Man, and of the Devil. The first were synonymous, both in the New Testament and in the reformed churches, with pastors; and were 'called bishops in regard of the sheep committed unto them'. The second kind were

brought into the church by the alone wisdom of Man, besides the express word of God; [and embraced] a certain power given to one certain Pastor above his other fellows, yet limited with certain orders or rules provided against tyranny. They which bear this office of bishop, are called bishop in regard of their fellow-elders, or the whole clergy, as watchmen set over the clergy.

As for the third genus, 'The Bishop of the Devil', its origin and history were thus unsympathetically delineated:

Even as that kind of bishop ordained of God, degenerated little by little into an human ordinance ... so this of the devil is sprouted forth of the corruption of the bishop brought in by man. Of this most intolerable corruption there are foul, most manifest, and undoubted marks. Some of this kind of bishops have wholly singled themselves from the elderships, so that they have nothing to do with them. Some have wholly abolished them. And that they have challenged unto themselves, and I know not to what officials, the whole guidance of the church, and chiefly the authority to elect, to depose, and to excommunicate, so as they not only are above others, but as it were, alone do exercise lordship over God's heritage.

This diabolical bishop was altogether contrary to the Word of God, where 'the authority of all Christ's Ministers in the church seems to be equal'.[1]

Thus the lines of division were made plain. Geneva in the person of Beza and Scotland in that of Melville stood

[1] *The Judgment of a most reverend and learned Man from beyond the seas concerning a Threefold Order of Bishops* (Theodore Beza), 1580.

over against Zurich as represented by Gualter and Bullinger and against the church of England. If the fame of Geneva under Calvin had far exceeded that of the Zurich of Zwingli, the latter was now to have its revenge by its support of the Anglican settlement.[1] And as a gracious and flattering return, Bullinger's *Decades* of sermons were prescribed for reading and study by the clergy of the church of England by authority of Whitgift himself as archbishop of Canterbury.

Not until James VI had escaped from the 'Ruthven raiders' in 1583 did the cause of episcopacy revive in Scotland, when the administration of Arran and the royal policy veered round again to prelacy. Patrick Adamson, archbishop of St Andrews since 1576 and the king's adviser in ecclesiastical matters, when accused before the General Assembly 'that he fathered on the Scriptures the superiority of pastors above pastors', and also of 'taking on him authority in his person contrary to the Word of God', retorted proudly that 'ye have mothered on the Scriptures equality of pastors, which is Anabaptistry', and further offered 'to prove that the office of a bishop, as it is in my person, in all points is according to God's Word, and agreed upon by his majesty's conference, and I entered thereunto by a lawful calling'.[2] The fact of Adamson's mission to England to confer with Archbishop Whitgift identified the episcopalian party in Scotland both with the church of England and with the suspected inclinations of James VI.[3] After the fall of Arran, therefore, in 1585 the General Assembly, followed by parliament, restored the full

---

[1] For the influence of Zurich on England see Helmut Kressner, 'Schweizer Ursprünge des anglikanischen Staatskirchentums' (*Schriften des Vereins für Reformations-geschichte*, Nr. 170, Jahrgang 59).

[2] D. Calderwood, *History of the Church of Scotland*, vol. IV, pp. 499–500.

[3] G. Donaldson, 'The Attitude of Whitgift and Bancroft to the Scottish Church', *Transactions of the Royal Historical Society*, 4th series, vol. XXIV.

presbyterian programme of church polity, with its graded hierarchy of courts, kirk sessions, presbyteries, synods, and General Assembly. But despite this resolute action, it was evident that the prospects of episcopacy were bound up with the personal fortunes of the Scottish king; and it was from this standpoint that the most offensive passage of Bancroft's famous sermon at Paul's Cross in defence of episcopacy lay in his assertion that James VI had not changed his views on matters ecclesiastical, and, notwithstanding the restoration of presbyterianism in Scotland, was but tarrying the Lord's leisure until he should come to the throne of England and circumstances should thereby favour his policy again.[1] Indeed, Bancroft's open attacks on the church of Scotland in his 'Dangerous Positions and Proceedings' and 'A Survey of the Pretended Holy Discipline' greatly exacerbated Scottish feeling. Yet the future lay with James and with Bancroft. For in 1597 Bancroft became bishop of London; in 1603 James VI became also James I of England; and in the following year the new king raised his bishop of London to the archbishopric of Canterbury in succession to Whitgift. Not in Zurich and Geneva only, nor alone in the academies and parishes of England and Scotland were new men rising; in the highest places of state and church one generation was coming as another passed. What might not be anticipated by the church of Scotland from a sovereign who was shortly to startle the Hampton Court Conference with his maxim of 'No bishop, no king', and from a primate whom Andrew Melville had designated as 'the capital enemy of all the Reformed churches of Europe'?

[1] W. O. Chadwick, 'Richard Bancroft's Submission', *Journal of Ecclesiastical History*, vol. III (1952), pp. 58–73.

III

AN IMPARITY OF MINISTERS DEFENDED

'WHAT think we of the reformed churches?' asked Jeremy Taylor in his treatise *Of the Sacred Order and Offices of Episcopacy*.

For my part I know not what to think; the question hath been so often asked, with so much violence and prejudice, and we are so bound by public interest to approve all that they do, that we have disabled ourselves to justify our own. For we were glad at first of abettors against the errors of the Roman church; we found these men zealous in it; we thanked God for it, as we had cause; and we were willing to make them recompense by endeavouring to justify their ordinations, not thinking what would follow upon ourselves; but now it is come to that issue that our own episcopacy is thought not necessary, because we did not condemn the ordinations of their presbytery.[1]

It was natural that the presbyterian aggression, inaugurated in England by Cartwright and by the authors of the *Admonitions to Parliament*, and supported from abroad by the thunders of Beza at Geneva, should have produced a sense of irritation and indignation on the part of Anglican divines; who, whilst defending their own tradition of episcopacy, had carefully and pointedly refrained from claiming for it an exclusive scriptural prescription, but had allowed presbyterian ordinations and polity where circumstances necessitated them. Equally to be expected was the more emphatic note which crept not only into the correspondence of English bishops with their continental mentors, but also into the apologetic works which multiplied during the last generation of the

[1] Jeremy Taylor, *Works* (ed. R. Heber), vol. v, p. 118.

reign of Elizabeth I in championship of episcopacy as retained, yet reformed, in the church of England. The presence of this increased emphasis is not difficult to detect or to defend. Perhaps its most outstanding, if not its most important, expression may be seen in the writings of Thomas Rogers on the Thirty-nine Articles. Rogers was a chaplain of Richard Bancroft, both as bishop of London and archbishop of Canterbury; and in the first version of his work, entitled *The English Creed, consenting with the True, Ancient, Catholic, and Apostolic Church*, in 1585, he observed, in commenting on Article 23, 'Of Ministering in the Congregation', in his fifth Proposition:

They are lawful Ministers which be ordained by men lawfully appointed to the calling and sending forth of Ministers; [for] so in the primitive church by the Apostles were Pastors and Elders ordained; who, by the same authority, ordained other Pastors and Teachers; whence it is that the church as it hath been, so it shall till the end of the world be provided for. . . . They are tied every man to his charge, which they must faithfully attend upon, except urgent occasion do enforce the contrary. The calling of these men is termed a general calling, and it is the ordinary, and in these days the lawful, calling allowed by the Word of God. So testify with us the true Churches elsewhere in the world.

On Article 36, 'Of Consecration of Bishops and Ministers', he contented himself with the comment: 'This Article simply is none Article of the Catholic Church; and so much thereof as is universally received, hath already both by the Holy Scripture been confirmed, and allowed by our neighbour Churches in the 23 Article.'[1]

In the revised version, however, published in 1607, under the title of *The Catholic Doctrine of the Church of England, an Exposition of the Thirty-Nine Articles*, whilst the

[1] Rogers, *op. cit.* (1585), pp. 26, 76.

commentary on Proposition 5 of Article 23 was the same, in that on Article 36 he argued two Propositions: first, 'It is agreeable to the word of God and practice of the primitive church, that there should be archbishops, bishops, and such like differences and inequalities of ecclesiastical ministers'; and secondly, that whosoever were consecrated or ordered according to the Anglican Ordinal, were rightly, orderly, and lawfully consecrated and ordered. In the proof of the former of these propositions, he observed that

albeit the terms and titles of archbishops we find not, yet the superiority which they enjoy, and the authority which the bishops and the archbishops do exercise, in ordering and consecrating of bishops and ecclesiastical ministers, is grounded upon the Word of God; [and he affirmed further that] from the apostles' days hitherto there never wanted a succession of bishops, neither in the east nor western churches, albeit there have been from time to time both marprelates and mock-prelates to supplant their states, and ill-prelates abusing their functions and places, to the discredit of their calling and profession. So provident hath the Almighty been for the augmentation of his glory and people, by this kind and calling of men.

Amongst the 'adversaries unto this truth', Rogers numbered the Anabaptists and 'the Disciplinarians or Puritans among ourselves', who contended that 'an equality must be made of ministers'.[1] Evidently the two versions of the work testified to a distinct stiffening of the author's attitude towards episcopacy.

Indeed the ground of controversy was shifting. For in face of the presbyterian claim that its form of polity alone was prescribed in holy scripture, it was not sufficient to appeal to the royal supremacy and to rest episcopacy upon the will of the godly prince. It must be shown to be

[1] Rogers, *op. cit.* (1607), Parker Society (ed. J. J. S. Perowne, 1854), pp. 329–31.

at least not repugnant, and if possible agreeable, to the Word of God; and whilst maintaining its close relationship to the royal supremacy, to have an equal authority with its rival from the Bible itself. Accordingly Dr John Bridges, dean of Salisbury, in his formidable *Defence of the Government established in the Church of England for Ecclesiastical Matters* of 1587 (running to 1,400 closely printed quarto pages), traced the imparity of ministers to apostolic times, and deduced therefrom that episcopacy was of apostolic origin.

For, although no such ordinance appropriating the name Bishop, be expressed in the manifest Word of God; yet the ordinance of the matter is plainly expressed: as we have shewed out of Timothy, Calvin's and Beza's plain confession of the same; And the name also applied to Timothy in the subscription of the 2nd Epistle, if that may go for Scripture. But let the application of the name be not so much the express ordinance of God, as of godly men, and those in the apostles' times; and now, the apostles alive, being not unwilling thereunto, was this ordinance of man good or ill? [1]

And again, of the apostolic provenance of episcopacy, he wrote:

And that this was the practice of the primitive church, from the apostles' age universally both for times and places, the fathers' own testimonies conferred with the ancient ecclesiastical histories do sufficiently record. [2]

Even more emphatic was the testimony of Hadrian Saravia, a Dutchman of Spanish extraction, who, after ministering in the Channel Islands and next discharging the office of divinity professor at Leyden, settled in England and received preferment in the church of England. In his *De Diversis Gradibus Ministrorum Evangelii*, published in 1590, he held bishops to be necessary to the

---

[1] J. Bridges, *op. cit.* p. 280.   [2] *Ibid.* p. 292.

church, and episcopal government to be the best and of divine authority.[1] He distinguished three functions of the church's ministry: the preaching of the Word, the administration of the sacraments, and the authority of government in the church, of which the first two were common to bishops and presbyters, but the last reserved to bishops only. Moreover this last branch of ministerial office included both the ordination of ministers and the administration of discipline; and therewith an imparity between presbyter and bishop, which was of dominical as well as of apostolical appointment.[2] Likewise, just as the preaching of the Word and administration of the sacraments were essential to the church for all ages, so it was with ecclesiastical polity in that form which had been instituted by our Lord himself, handed down by the apostles, and confirmed by the fathers.[3] Episcopacy, therefore, was an example of that unvarying tradition of the church which Saravia held to be immutable; since he believed that the apostles had established nothing in the church which they had not received from the Lord; and the sum of his argument was succinctly stated in the heading to his 21st chapter: 'Episcopi sunt divina institutione et apostolica traditione instituti.'[4] There could be no doubt of the unequivocal standpoint

---

[1] H. Saravia, *Diversi Tractatus Theologici* (London, 1611): 'Quod me attinet, Episcopos Ecclesiae necessarios arbitror, et eam disciplinam et gubernationem Ecclesiae esse optimam et divinam, quam pii Episcopi, cum veri nominis presbyteris, ex praescripto verbi Dei et veterum conciliorum administrant' (Preface: 'Candido Lectori', p. 2).

[2] Saravia, *op. cit.*: 'In hac tertia parte non parva inter eos invenitur inaequalitas, propter diversos authoritatis gradus, quos primo Dominus statim ab initio et postea Apostoli constituerunt' (cap. I, p. 2).

[3] 'Sic etiam regiminis forma, quae ab ipso Domino fuit instituta, et ab Apostolis tradita, ac usu Patrum confirmata, permanere debet' (cap. XIV, p. 16).

[4] 'Quod inde ab Apostolorum temporibus et Patribus per universum terrarum orbem factum ab omnibus Ecclesiis legimus usque ad nostra tempora, canonem Apostolorum immutabilem esse judico' (cap. XX, p. 22). 'Apostolos nihil constituisse in Ecclesia, quod a Domino non acceperint, certum est' (cap. XXI, p. 24).

of Saravia on episcopacy, the loss of which in the reformed churches of the continent he deeply deplored.[1]

In similar vein Matthew Sutcliffe's *A Treatise of Ecclesiastical Discipline*, published in 1591, held that 'the office of bishops and ministers hath authority and confirmation from God, the office of doctors, barely teaching, is a devise of man'; and argued that this form of polity was derived from Christ:

That order which Jesus Christ prescribed, the Apostles diligently observed and maintained. For they did not only keep an Apostolical dignity themselves and shewed their authority in their actions, but on the Ministers which they appointed, they set notable marks of difference.[2]

Moreover, he emphasised the necessity of succession in government as well as in doctrine: 'now if that doctrine and government be always necessary to the world's end, then, as there is a succession of doctrine, so there must always be a succession of government'.[3] But the most thorough and emphatic treatise on this subject was Thomas Bilson's *The Perpetual Government of Christ's Church*, published in 1593, in which the coping-stone was set upon the Elizabethan apologetic for episcopacy. Bilson distinguished in the apostles 'four things needful for the first founding and erecting of the church, though not so for the preserving and maintaining thereof; and four other points that must be perpetual in the church of Christ'. These permanent functions were 'the dispensing the word, administering the sacraments, imposing of hands, and guiding the keys to shut or open the kingdom of heaven'; of which the two first 'must be general to all pastors and presbyters of Christ's church';

---

[1] 'Tantum veterem ordinem conservandae disciplinae in Ecclesia Christi necessarium, et a Patribus summo studio observatum, sublatum esse deploro; et ne prorsus nostri saeculi calamitate tollatur, vehementer timeo' (Prologus, p. 2).
[2] M. Sutcliffe, *op. cit.* pp. 101, 43.   [3] *Ibid.* pp. 51–2.

and the last two, 'singularity in succeeding and superiority in ordaining, have been observed from the apostles' times, as the peculiar and substantial marks of episcopal power and calling'.[1] The episcopal form of polity, thus traditional in the church, was not a matter of choice, but of divine appointment: 'we must not frame what kind of regiment we list for the ministers of Christ's church, but rather observe and mark what manner of external government the Lord hath best liked and allowed in his church, even from the beginning'.[2] Moreover the authority of the keys was originally vested in the apostles and by them transmitted to the church, not *vice versa*; and the officers succeeding to this authority after the apostles were the bishops:

And this singularity of one pastor in each place descended from the apostles and their scholars in all the famous churches of the world by a perpetual chair of succession, and doth to this day continue. . . . Of this there is so perfect record in all the stories and fathers of the church, that I much muse with what face men that have any taste of learning can deny the vocation of bishops came from the apostles. For if their succession be apostolic, their function cannot choose but be likewise apostolic; and that they succeeded the apostles and evangelists in their churches and chairs, may inevitably be proved, if any Christian persons or churches deserve to be credited.[3]

Thus episcopacy was of apostolic origin and was in fact the perpetual form of government to be observed in the church:

Now that in the churches planted by the apostles and their coadjutors, one hath been severed from the rest of the presbyters and placed above the rest in the honour of the episcopal chair, before there were any general councils to decree that manner of government, and so continued even from the

---

[1] Bilson, *op. cit.* (1842 edition), pp. 11–13.
[2] *Ibid.* p. 35.   [3] *Ibid.* pp. 319–20.

apostles' persons and hands to this present age; the perpetual succession of bishops in those principal churches where the apostles and their helpers preached and governed, and likewise in all other churches of the world following their steps, will strongly and fully confirm. If the apostles placed bishops with their own hands; if departing or dying they left bishops to succeed them; if their disciples and scholars embraced and used that course to set bishops over presbyters for saving the church from schisms and left it to their aftercomers; I trust there are few men ... but ... will acknowledge the first distinction and institution of bishops from and above presbyters was, if not commanded and imposed by the apostles' precepts on the church, yet at least ordained and delivered unto the faithful by their example, as the best way to maintain the peace and unity of the church; and consequently the unity of the church (which Austin speaketh of) that the bishop's office should be greater than the presbyter's and the decree of the whole world (which Jerome mentioneth) were derived from the apostles and confirmed by them, and may not be reversed and repealed after 1,500 years, unless we challenge to be wiser and better able to order and govern the church of Christ than the apostles were.[1]

Thus the presbyterian claim for divine appointment was met by a counter-assertion for episcopacy; though its association with the royal supremacy was still emphasised. Bridges, for example, could describe the godly prince as 'the means to salvation', and affirm that 'the christian king is God's vicar'.[2] And Bilson could echo the sentiments of Whitgift in urging that

those churches under persecution had none that could justly challenge to rule the rest; ours hath a lawful monarch professing the faith, to whom by God's law the government of all crimes and causes ecclesiastical doth rightly belong; and therefore the private and popular regiment of afflicted churches must cease, since God hath blessed this realm with a public, peaceable, and princely government. . . . What need we suffrages of

---

1 *Ibid.* pp. 332-3.
2 Bridges, *op. cit.* pp. 1367, 1185 (marginal headings).

lay elders to reform disorders and abuses in pastors, when we have open and known laws to work the same effect with more force and better speed? In popular states and persecuted churches some pretence may be made for that kind of discipline; in christian kingdoms I see neither need nor use of lay elders.[1]

But if Bridges, Bancroft, and Bilson were firm in their incipient doctrine of 'no bishop, no king', in the new apologetic episcopacy was finding its own authority and support by appeal to that very Word of God from which Cartwright had quarried his programme of presbyterianism.

The work thus begun under Elizabeth was continued in the Stuart century, when the Anglican defence of episcopacy became even more emphatic and confident. John Keble discerned a 'marked distinction' between 'the school of Hooker and that of Laud, Hammond, and Leslie in the two next generations'; though maintaining that the great Elizabethan himself had 'laid down principles, which, strictly followed up, would make this claim [for episcopacy] exclusive'.[2] The foundations of the seventeenth-century Anglican apologetic indeed were the same substantially as in the previous epoch; but firmer deductions were drawn from the historical evidence and greater weight placed upon the authority of bishops *divino jure*. Thus Bishop Joseph Hall could 'plead the divine right of episcopacy', in the sense that 'that government whose foundation is laid by Christ, and whose fabric is raised by the apostles, is of divine institution'; and that 'episcopacy is an eminent order of sacred function, appointed by the Holy Ghost in the evangelical church for the governing and overseeing

[1] Bilson, *op. cit.* pp. 213–14. Cf. Bancroft, *A Survey of the Pretended Holy Discipline*, p. 63: 'They take from Christian princes and ascribe to their pretended regiment, the supreme and immediate authority under Christ in causes ecclesiastical.'

[2] J. Keble, Preface to Hooker's *Works*, vol. i, p. lxxvii

thereof; and for that purpose, besides the administration of the word and sacraments, endued with power of imposition of hands and perpetuity of jurisdiction'. Indeed, he considered that 'to depart from the judgment and practice of the universal church of Christ ever since the apostles' times, and to betake ourselves to a new invention, cannot but be, besides the danger, vehemently scandalous'.[1] These were strong words from one of the Anglican representatives at the Synod of Dort; and stronger might perhaps be expected naturally from other quarters. Archbishop Laud, to whom Hall submitted his *Episcopacy by Divine Right* before its publication, held firmly that 'bishops might be regulated and limited by human laws in those things which are but incidents to their calling; but their calling, as far as it is *divino jure*, by divine right, cannot be taken away' and that 'this is the doctrine of the church of England'.[2] Richard Field, in his comprehensive treatise *Of the Church*, was peculiar in denying that the episcopate was a separate order, and in espousing without qualification the opinion of Jerome that the presbyterate and episcopate are one order; notwithstanding, he maintained that 'bishops alone have the power of ordination, and no man may regularly do it without them'.[3] Similarly Bishop Lancelot Andrewes did not hesitate to affirm, in controversy with Cardinal Perron, not only his own view but that 'our Church doth hold, there is a distinction between Bishop and Priest and that *divino jure*', tracing this difference of the two orders to their respective succession from the apostles and the seventy, appointed by Christ himself; yet at the same time he held that these matters of polity *ad agenda*

---

[1] J. Hall, *Works*, vol. x, pp. 158, 183, 180.
[2] W. Laud, *Works*, vol. IV, pp. 310–11.
[3] R. Field, *Of the Church*, bk. v, p. 704.

Ecclesiae spectant, not to the *credenda.*[1] Again, the *Convocation Book concerning the Government of God's Catholic Church and the Kingdoms of the whole World,* of Bishop John Overall, maintained that Christ

did by the direction of the Holy Ghost and ministry of his Apostles, ordain in the New Testament, that there should be in every national church, some ministers of an inferior degree . . . and over them bishops of a superior degree, . . . and lastly above them all, archbishops and in some especial places patriarchs.[2]

Even higher ground was taken by Bishop Jeremy Taylor, who in his *Episcopacy Asserted* wrote that

although we had not proved the immediate divine institution of episcopal power over presbyters and the whole flock, yet episcopacy is not less than an apostolical ordinance and delivered to us by the same authority that the observation of the Lord's day is. . . . And therefore it is but reasonable it should be ranked among the *credenda* of Christianity, which the Church hath entertained upon the confidence of that which we call 'the faith of a Christian', whose Master is truth itself.[3]

It would be easy to accumulate further evidences of the assertion of episcopacy *divino jure* from the works of Francis Mason, Henry Hammond, Bishop Robert Sanderson, Archbishop James Bramhall, and Herbert Thorndike; but to pile Pelion upon Ossa is needless where the tradition of a positive Anglican apologetic is so strong. Indeed a quotation from Sanderson may well be accepted as summarising the argument. After making the well-known observation that the claim for *divinum jus* may either imply a positive divine precept, or simply an apostolical institution, he continued:

Now that the government of the churches of Christ by bishops is of Divine Right in that first and stricter sense is an opinion at

[1] L. Andrewes, *Minor Works,* p. 29; *Opuscula,* p. 187.
[2] J. Overall, *Convocation Book,* p. 156 (1690 edition).
[3] J. Taylor, *Works,* vol. v, pp. 68–9.

least of great probability, and such as may more easily and upon better grounds be defended than confuted. . . . Yet because it is needless to contend for more, where less will serve the turn, I find that our divines that have travailed most in this argument . . . do rather choose to stand to the tenure of episcopacy *ex Apostolica designatione* than to hold a contest upon the title of *Jus Divinum*, no necessity requiring the same to be done. . . . Sufficient it is for the justification of the Church of England in the constitution and government thereof, that it is (as it certainly is) of Divine Right in the latter and larger signification; that is to say, of Apostolical institution and approbation; exercised by the Apostles themselves and by other persons in their times, appointed and enabled thereunto by them, according to the will of our Lord Jesus Christ, and by virtue of the commission they had received from him.[1]

In part, it may be observed, this new emphasis upon episcopacy was the result of the dual attack upon the church of England by Romanist and presbyterian opponents and of its own afflictions during the Interregnum when the little city of Zoar seemed to have fallen beyond restoration; but it was due also in part to contemporary patristic studies, especially in relation to the First Epistle of Clement, the Epistles of Ignatius, and the works of Cyprian.

Nevertheless, it is of equal importance to observe that the Anglican asserters of episcopacy generally stopped short of unchurching the foreign reformed churches and of denying the validity of their ministry and sacraments. Episcopacy was the rule and was essential where it could be had; but in cases of necessity it might be dispensed with, and such necessity was judged to be the sad fortune of these churches. Hooker allowed that the whole church might even change the episcopal form of polity:

The whole body of the church hath power to alter, with general

[1] R. Sanderson, *Episcopacy not prejudicial to Regal Power*, 1647 (1683 edition), sect. II, v, pp. 14–15.

consent and upon necessary occasions, even the positive laws of the apostles, if there be no command to the contrary and it manifestly appears to her that change of times have clearly taken away the very reasons of God's first institution. . . . Bishops, albeit they may avouch with conformity of truth that their authority hath thus descended even from the very apostles themselves, yet the absolute and everlasting continuance of it they cannot say that any commandment of the Lord doth enjoin; and therefore must acknowledge that the church hath power by universal consent upon urgent cause to take it away, if thereunto she be constrained through the proud, tyrannical, and unreformable dealings of her bishops, whose regiment she hath thus long delighted in.[1]

This was a very hypothetical case; but the circumstances of some local and national churches were practical and actual; and Hooker likewise recognised the possibility that they might violate tradition in the matter of ordination:

Whereas hereupon some do infer that no ordination can stand but only such as is made by bishops . . . to this we answer that there may be sometimes very just and sufficient reason to allow ordination made without a bishop. The whole church visible being the true original subject of all power, it hath not ordinarily allowed any other than bishops alone to ordain; howbeit as the ordinary course is ordinarily in all things to be observed, so it may be in some cases not unnecessary that we decline from the ordinary ways.[2]

Of the conditions justifying the admission of men to the ministry 'extraordinarily yet allowably', he gave two examples: the first where God raised up special agents whose mission he authenticated 'by manifest signs and tokens from heaven'; and the second 'extraordinary kind of vocation', where

the exigence of necessity doth constrain to leave the usual ways of the church, which otherwise we would willingly keep;

---

[1] Hooker, *Ecclesiastical Polity*, vii, v, 8.   [2] *Ibid.* xiv, 11.

where the church must needs have some ordained, and neither hath nor can have possibly a bishop to ordain; in case of such necessity the ordinary institution of God hath given often-times, and may give, place. And therefore we are not simply without exception to urge a lineal descent of power from the apostles by continued succession of bishops in every effectual ordination. These cases of inevitable necessity excepted, none may ordain but only bishops.[1]

Almost exactly parallel was the argument of George Downham, chaplain to James I and afterwards bishop of Derry, in his sermon preached at the consecration of the bishop of Bath and Wells in 1608 and maintained in his *Defence of the Sermon*; of which Dr Mason observed that 'both sermon and *Defence* are referred to with great respect by all subsequent writers of that and the following age'.[2] Downham laid down that

what function or government is of apostolical institution, that is to be acknowledged a divine ordinance in respect of the first institution, as having God the author thereof; the episcopal function or government by bishops is of apostolical institution, therefore the episcopal function is a divine ordinance.

But whilst holding that the ancient church ascribed the ordinary right of ordination to bishops only, it did not

so appropriate it unto them, as that extraordinarily and in case of necessity, it might not be lawful for presbyters to ordain; and much less teaching, (as the papists imagine) absolutely a nullity in the ordination which is not performed by a bishop. For suppose a church either altogether destitute of a bishop, or pestered with such as the popish prelates are, heretical and idolatrous, by whom no orthodoxall ministers might hope to be ordained; we need not doubt but that the ancient fathers would, in such a case of necessity, have allowed ordination without a bishop, though not as regular according to the rules of ordinary church government, yet as effectual and as justi-fiable in the want of a bishop.

[1] *Ibid.* xiv, 11.
[2] A. J. Mason, *The Church of England and Episcopacy*, p. 65.

He rebutted the retort that if episcopacy was a divine ordinance, there could be no church without it:

For whereas it hath been proved that the government of the churches by bishops is an apostolical and divine ordinance, may not we also infer, that all churches are so necessarily and perpetually tied unto it, as that no other form of government is warrantable in the church of God? and that not only this government is lawful, but that it only is lawful? ... For although we be well assured that the form of government by bishops is the best, as having not only the warrant of Scripture for the first institution, but also the perpetual practice of the church from the apostles' time to our age for the continuance; notwithstanding we doubt not, but where this may not be had, others may be admitted; neither do we deny but that silver is good, though gold be better.[1]

In similar vein Whitgift in his controversial exchanges with Beza, whilst affirming the apostolic origin and authority of episcopacy and defending its retention in the church of England, emphasised that in so doing he was 'nowhere opposing the discipline of any other church or in the least reflecting thereon'; but rather wished 'that every particular church would mind its own business and not prescribe the laws of rites and the manner of government to others'.[2] Following his example Bridges averred that

the difference of these things is not directly material to salvation, neither ought to break the bond of peace and christian concord. But they may think and wish well to us, and we in the name of the Lord think well and wish good luck to them. Yea, to wish that they had no better state then we have, on condition that they had no worse, and might always have as good, I think all our neighbour reformed churches would be soon entreated to say *Amen*.[3]

So in defending the Anglican system, 'we prescribe not to all places, nor prejudicate any other churches that are

[1] G. Downham, *A Sermon defending the honourable function of Bishops* (1608), pp. 42, 56, 94.   [2] Strype, *Whitgift*, vol. II, pp. 165, 172.   [3] Bridges, *op. cit.* 87.

not in, nor of, the state of the churches in England and Ireland'.[1] Again, Bishop Cooper (who suffered such harsh ridicule from the pen of Martin Marprelate) affirmed of the foreign churches that

all these churches . . . I doubt not but have been directed by the Spirit of God to retain this liberty, that in external government and other outward orders, they might choose such as they thought in wisdom and godliness to be the most convenient for the state of their country and disposition of the people.[2]

Even Saravia admitted the force of practical necessity, though protesting that the exception must not overthrow the rule.[3]

Richard Field likewise, in examining the contention of the Romanists that 'the reformed churches are not the true churches of God', particularly because presbyterian ordinations 'are clearly void, and so by consequence, many of the pretended reformed churches, as namely those of France and others, have no ministry at all', set himself to consider 'whether the power of ordination be so essentially annexed to the order of bishops, that none but bishops may in any case ordain'. In reply he alleged two cases of exception and necessity, namely 'wherein all bishops were extinguished by death or fallen into heresy'; and concluded: 'Who then dare condemn all those worthy ministers of God, that were ordained by presbyters in sundry churches of the world, at such times as bishops in those parts where they lived, opposed themselves against the truth of God and persecuted such as professed it?'[4] Even more striking were the admissions

---

[1] *Ibid.* p. 1196. [2] T. Cooper, *Admonition to the People of England*, p. 67.

[3] Saravia, *op. cit.* p. 2: 'Quando mecum cogito temporum iniquitatem et quorundam locorum statum in quibus Deo placuit per pios et doctos viros recolligere ex captivitate Babylonica dispersas oves, non video quomodo veri potuerint restitui episcopi. . . . Tamen quod extra ordinem factum est necessitate quadam, paucis quibusdam in locis et uno tantum saeculo, universo orbi legem non praescribit.' [4] Field, *op. cit.* bk. III, pp. 154–71.

of Andrewes in respect of the ministry of the foreign reformed churches in his correspondence with Peter Du Moulin:

Nevertheless if our form be of divine right, it doth not follow from thence that there is no salvation without it, or that a church cannot consist without it. He is blind who does not see churches consisting without it; he is hard-hearted who denieth them salvation. We are none of these hard-hearted persons we put a great difference between these things. There may be something absent in the exterior regiment, which is of divine right, and yet salvation to be had. . . . To prefer a better, is not to condemn a thing. Nor is it to condemn your church if we recall it to another form, namely our own, which the better agrees with all antiquity.

Again, in a subsequent letter Andrewes wrote:

You ask whether your churches have sinned in the matter of divine authority. I did not say that. I said only that your churches lacked something which is of divine authority; but the fault is not yours but that of the evil of the times. For your France did not have kings so favourable to the reformation of the church as did our England; but some time, when God grants better days, that which is now lacking, can be supplied by his grace. Meantime, however, the name of 'bishop', which occurs so often in the Scriptures, ought not to have been abolished. For what advantage is there to abolish the name whilst retaining the thing? And you have retained the thing without the name.[1]

[1] Andrewes, *Opuscula*, pp. 191, 211: 'Nec tamen si nostra forma divini juris sit, inde sequitur, vel quod sine ea salus non sit, vel quod stare non possit Ecclesia. Caecus sit, qui non videat stantes sine ea Ecclesias; Ferreus sit, qui salutem eis neget. Nos non sumus illi ferrei; latum inter ista discrimen ponimus. Potest abesse aliquid quod divini juris sit, (in exteriore quidem regimine) ut tamen substet salus. . . . Non est hoc damnare rem, melius illi aliquid anteponere. Non est hoc damnare vestram Ecclesiam, ad formam aliam, quae toti antiquitati magis placuit, (id est) ad nostram revocare. . . . Quaeris tum peccentne in jus divinum Ecclesiae vestrae? Non dixi. Id tantum dixi, abesse ab Ecclesiis vestris aliquid, quod de divino jure sit; culpa autem vestra non abesse, sed injuria temporum. Non enim tam propitios habuisse Reges Galliam vestram, in Ecclesia reformanda, quam habuit Britannia nostra; interim ubi dabit meliora Deus, et hoc quoque, quod jam abest, per Dei gratiam suppletum iri. At interea Episcopi nomen, quam tam saepe in Sacris est, abolendum non fuisse. Quanquam, quid attinet abolere nomen, retinere rem? Nam et vos rem retinetis, sine titulo.'

Where so staunch a believer in episcopacy as Andrewes had led the way, none need blush to follow. Accordingly Hall's conclusion that episcopacy 'for the main substance is now utterly indispensable, and must so continue to the world's end', was qualified by the explanation:

indispensable by any voluntary act; what inevitable necessity may do in such a case, we now dispute not; necessity hath dispensed with some, immediately divine laws. Where then that may be justly pleaded, we shall not be wanting both in our pity and in our prayers.

Therefore he could write of the foreign reformed churches that

we love and honour those sister churches as the dear spouse of Christ. We bless God for them; and we do heartily wish unto them that happiness in the partnership of our administration which I doubt not but they do no less heartily wish unto themselves. . . . First, our position is only affirmative, implying the justifiableness and holiness of an episcopal calling, without further implication. Next, when we speak of divine right, we mean not an express law of God requiring it upon the absolute necessity of the being of a church, what hindrances soever may interpose, but a divine institution, warranting it where it is and requiring it where it may be had. Every church therefore, which is capable of this form of government, both may and ought to affect it, as that which is with so much authority derived from the apostles to the whole body of the church upon earth; but those particular churches to whom this power and faculty is denied, lose nothing of the true essence of a church, though they miss something of their glory and perfection, whereof they are barred by the necessity of their condition.

Indeed he held that these churches

were forced to discard the office, as well as the men; but yet the office because of the men; as popish, not as bishops; and to put themselves for the present into such a form of government, at a venture, as under which they might be sure without violent interruption to sow the seeds of the . . . Gospel.[1]

1 Hall, *Works*, vol. x, pp. 245, 282, 152-3.

The same point was stated even more forcefully by George Downham, who affirmed that the foreign Protestants 'were forced with the loss of the episcopal government to redeem the most precious jewel of the Gospel, which is to be redeemed (if need be) with the loss of all outward things'.[1]

The distinction made by Hall between the essence and the perfection of a church was underlined and emphasised by Bramhall. In replying to the accusation that 'a considerable party of episcopal divines in England do unchurch all or most of the Protestant churches, and maintain the Roman church to be a true church, and them to be no true churches', he denied the charge:

I cannot assent to his minor proposition that either all or any considerable part of the episcopal divines in England do unchurch either all or the most part of the Protestant churches. No man is hurt but by himself. They unchurch none at all, but leave them to stand or fall to their own Master. They do not unchurch the Swedish, Danish, Bohemian churches, and many other churches in Polonia, Hungaria, and those parts of the world, which have an ordinary uninterrupted succession of pastors, some by the names of Bishops, others under the name of Seniors unto this day. . . . They unchurch not the Lutheran churches of Germany, who both assert episcopacy in their Confessions, and have actual Superintendents in their practice, and would have Bishops name and thing if it were in their power.

His opponent's mistake arose

from not distinguishing between the true nature and essence of a church, which we do readily grant them, and the integrity or perfection of a church, which we cannot grant them without swerving from the judgment of the catholic church.[2]

Bramhall further distinguished 'episcopacy itself' from 'popish episcopacy, that is, the abuse not the thing';

[1] G. Downham, *A Sermon defending the Honourable Function of Bishops*, p. 96.
[2] Bramhall, *Works*, vol. III, pp. 517–18.

from 'an absolute necessity by divine right of such and such an episcopacy, endowed with such or such degrees of power or pre-eminence'; and from 'such an episcopacy as is held to differ from presbyterate in the very power of order'. Moreover he argued for episcopacy as *via tutissima*, 'the safest way'; for

seeing there is required to the essence of a church, first a pastor, secondly a flock, thirdly a subordination of this flock to this pastor, where we are not sure that there is a right ordination, what assurance have we that there is a church? I write this not to prejudge our neighbour churches. I dare not limit the extraordinary operation of God's Spirit, where ordinary means are wanting, without the default of the persons. He gave his people manna for food whilst they were in the wilderness. Necessity is a strong plea. Many Protestant churches lived under kings and bishops of another communion; others had particular reasons why they could not continue or introduce bishops; but it is not so with us. . . . It is charity to think well of our neighbours, and good divinity to look well to ourselves. But the chief reason is, because I do not make this way to be simply necessary, but only shew what is safest, where so many Christians are of another mind. I know that there is great difference between a valid and a regular ordination; and what some choice divines do write of case of necessity; and for my part am apt to believe that God looks upon his people in mercy with all their prejudices; and that there is a great latitude left to particular churches in the constitution of their ecclesiastical regiment, according to the exigence of time and place and persons, so as order and His own institution be observed.[1]

In particular, he applied this principle to the Lutheran churches, arguing that they had the thing whilst abandoning the traditional name:

The practice of all the Protestant churches in the dominions of the king of Sweden and Denmark, and the most of them in

[1] *Ibid.* pp. 473–5.

High Germany, do plainly prove it; ... all these have their bishops or superintendents, which is all one.

In support of his contention, he appealed to the often-quoted opinion of Hierome Zanchius, that

in the churches of the Protestants, Bishops and Archbishops are not really wanting, whom (changing the good Greek names into bad Latin names) they call Superintendents and General Superintendents; where neither the good Greek names nor bad Latin names take place, yet there also there use to be some principal persons, in whose hands almost all the authority doth rest.[1]

It is not without interest to observe that Laud also accepted the Lutheran churches as possessing the *res* if not the *nomen* of episcopacy:

For in Sweden they retain both the thing and the name; and the governors of their churches are, and are called, bishops. And among other Lutherans the thing is retained, though not the name. For instead of bishops they are called superintendents, and instead of archbishops, general superintendents. And yet even here too these names differ more in sound than in sense. For bishop is the same in Greek that superintendent is in Latin. Nor is this change very well liked by the learned. Howsoever, Luther, since he would change the name, yet did very wisely that he would leave the thing, and make choice of such a name as was not altogether unknown to the ancient church.[2]

The plea of inevitable necessity, however, did not commend itself to Jeremy Taylor, who held that whilst 'necessity may excuse a personal delinquency', he had never heard 'that necessity did build a church'. For 'if God means to build a church in any place, he will do it by means proportionable to that end; that is, by putting

[1] Bramhall, *Works*, vol. III, p. 480.

[2] Laud, *Works*, vol. III, p. 386. Cf. G. Downham, *A Defence of a Sermon*: 'To speak only of the reformed churches in Europe, is it not evident that the far greater part of them is governed by bishops and which is all one with bishops, by Superintendents' (p. 148).

them into a possibility of doing and acquiring those things which himself hath required of necessity to the constitution of a church'. If the plea of necessity be true, then in such case 'there is no church there to be either built or continued, but the candlestick is presently removed'. To him it was rather a question 'what we think of the primitive church than what we think of the reformed churches'. Yet even Taylor was not prepared to allow his logic to outrun charity. Although doubting the plea of necessity both on theological and historical grounds, he likewise shrank from unchurching non-episcopal churches:

But shall we then condemn those few of the reformed churches whose ordinations have always been without bishops? No, indeed; that must not be; they stand or fall to their own master. And though I cannot justify their ordinations, yet what degree their necessity is of, what their desire of episcopal ordinations may do for their personal excuse, and how far a good life and a catholic belief may lead a man in the way to heaven, although the forms of external communion be not observed, I cannot determine. For aught I know their condition is the same with that of the church of Pergamus: 'I know thy works, and where thou dwellest, even where Satan's seat is; and thou holdest fast my faith, and hast not denied my name.' *Nihilo minus habeo adversus te pauca*, some few things I have against thee; and yet, of them, the want of canonical ordinations is a defect which I trust themselves desire to be remedied; but if it cannot be done, their sin is indeed the less, but their misery the greater. ... But this I would not have declared so freely, had not the necessity of our own churches required it, and that the first pretence of the legality and validity of their ordinations been buoyed up to the height of an absolute necessity; for else why shall it be called tyranny in us to call on them to conform to us and to the practice of the catholic church, and yet in them be called a good and holy zeal to exact our conformity to them?[1]

[1] Taylor, *Works*, vol. v, pp. 119-21.

Equally firm as a defender of episcopacy was Thorndike, who desired to restore the constitutional exercise
of episcopacy by the association of presbyters with
bishops therein; yet was prepared to make allowances
for the foreign reformed churches:

Be it pardonable for our neighbours and brethren of the
reformed Churches abroad, to have overseen the succession of
the Apostles, because they could not discern it, as they found
it blended with such abundance of accessories, especially in the
persons of men that hated to be reformed.

With these churches he desired the maintenance of
fraternal relations, without compromising the claims of
episcopacy:

The honour and esteem which the learned of the reformed
churches abroad have professed of the state of our churches,
and our charity in excusing the necessities of theirs and acknowledging the efficacy of the ministry which they use, will be
sufficient through God's goodness, to actuate the correspondence we desire to preserve with them, without those innovations which they never required at our hands to such
purpose.[1]

In the specific matter of presbyterian ordinations,
Thorndike admitted that his conviction of the necessity
of episcopacy seemed to 'make void the ordinations of
the reformed churches of France, and others reformed
according to Calvin, and so make them no churches'.
In reply, he averred

that it was necessary for the French, as well as for ourselves, to
reform themselves. That it was necessary for all to reform themselves unto the form of the primitive catholic church, I say, we
do not agree; I say that, till we do agree, there remains no hope
of unity, because no rule for reformation in the church.

In the meantime, circumstances alter cases: 'all that can
be questioned is, how it may appear, that it was not of

[1] Thorndike, *Works*, vol. I, pt. I, pp. 92–4.

choice but of necessity, that they embraced that way of settling and propagating their reformation which they embraced'. He wished indeed that the Reformed had followed the Lutherans in setting up 'such a form of episcopacy as they could of themselves'. But though they had not, 'very many learned and religious persons of those churches have not only approved the episcopacy here settled, but have wished the benefit of it to themselves'; and also he gave great weight to 'the communion which hath always been used between this church and the reformed churches'. Accordingly he, like Taylor, placed charity above rubrics:

And therefore, though I must not take upon me either to justify or to condemn their ordinations, averring on the one side that they are not according to rule, seeing on the other side that they are owned by my superiors; yet I must acknowledge that there are very great reasons to hope and presume, that God accepteth of their ordinations, though not made according to rule, in consideration of the necessity that drove them to it, and of the reformation which they were used to propagate.[1]

Thus under the pressure of a century of acute controversy, the Anglican divines had developed a positive, constructive, and consistent apologetic for episcopacy as retained in the church of England. It was held to be not of dominical but of apostolic appointment, and as *divino jure* only in that sense; as necessary where it could be had, but its absence where historical necessity compelled did not deprive a church of valid ministry and sacraments. It was necessary to the perfection or integrity of a church, though not to its essence; and on the ground of its historic continuance in the church, its restoration in the foreign non-episcopal churches was

[1] *Ibid.* vol. v, pp. 426–30.

much to be desired. But this Janus-prospect of the Anglican apologia caused much misunderstanding amongst reformed churches, which indeed has continued to this day. It is the more important, therefore, to emphasise the *rationale* and representative character of this standpoint. When Archbishop Wake, during the first quarter of the eighteenth century, entered into an eirenical correspondence with Gallican theologians of the Sorbonne concerning the possibility of union between their church and his own, he was at pains to insist on both sides of the Anglican position; and to explain to their incredulous ears how the church of England could maintain its own defence of episcopacy on the one hand, and yet on the other hand allow the presbyterian foreign churches to be true churches. To Pierre François Le Courayer he set forth his interpretation of the paradox. On the one side, he appealed to the writings of Bridges, Sutcliffe, Saravia, and Bilson, to establish the fact that the sixteenth-century Anglicans 'learnedly pleaded the cause of episcopacy and defended the distinction of bishops and presbyters and their succession from the apostles' times and hands'; in which they were followed by their seventeenth-century successors who also 'stood up for the episcopal pre-eminence'. On the other side, he insisted that these same apologists had not 'abandoned the defence of the other reformed churches':

No, by no means. Our writers still continue to affirm that their Orders are not null, though they be not canonical; that their necessity excuses them; and that though we think them defective in that respect that they want an episcopal ordination, yet not so defective as utterly to unchurch them.

In support of his contention, he cited various of the authors above mentioned; especially Andrewes, to whose authority he attached particular weight; and in whose correspondence with Du Moulin (he affirmed) 'you will find one of the most tenacious assertors of the episcopal government, nevertheless far from unchurching all the other reformed churches for want of it'. Ever since the Reformation, indeed, Anglican divines had been divided in sympathy between the Puritan and Anglo-Catholic traditions; and some individuals had gone to extremes on each side. But the *via media* had been generally upheld by the majority of representative theologians.

The sum of all is: that in these particulars our divines have from the beginning gone their several ways; but yet so as not to have either given up our own episcopal succession and consecration on the one hand, or to have utterly condemned the establishment of the reformed churches on the other.[1]

Most particularly, the distinction between the essence and the integrity of the church had proved itself to be a concept of protean potentiality. Whitgift had asserted in 1574 that 'notwithstanding government, or some kind of government, may be a part of the church, touching the outward form and perfection of it, yet is it not such a part of the essence and being, but that it may be the church of Christ without this or that kind of government'.[2] Joseph Hall too had distinguished between 'the true essence of a church' and its 'glory and perfection'; whilst the Romanist writer Thomas Stapleton had likewise proferred an *intrinsic and essential definition of the church* on the one hand, and a *full definition or rather description* on the other; which Bramhall had seized upon with avidity: 'I like Stapleton's distinction well, of the nature and essence of a church from the integrity and

---

1 N. Sykes, *William Wake*, vol. II, pp. 15-17.
2 Whitgift, *Works*, vol. I, p. 185.

perfection thereof.'[1] Thus Anglican apologetic for episcopacy, as necessary where it could be had but its lack
not unchurching those churches deprived of it by
historical circumstances, adopted the principle of episcopal government and ordination as being of the *plene esse*
rather than of the *esse* of the church.

[1] Bramhall, *Works*, vol. II, p. 26. Stapleton, *Relectio* . . . *Principiorum Fidei Doctrin-alium* (1596). 'Controversia: I. Quaestio: 5. De definitione Ecclesiae: Articulus I. Intrinseca autem et essentialis ejus definitio haec esse videtur: Ecclesia est societas Christi nomen profitentium, in unitate fidei et sacramentorum collecta atque legitime ordinata. . . . Plena autem Ecclesiae definitio seu potius descriptio . . . talis est: Ecclesia Christi secundum statum Novi Testamenti est multitudo collecta Christi nomen profitentium, incipiens a Jerusalem, indeque per universum mun-dum dispersa, crescens per omnes gentes, semper illustris et manifesta, mixta bonis et malis, electis et reprobis, fide et sacramentis sancta, origine et successione Apostolica, amplitudine Catholica, connexione et ordine membrorum una, dura-tione perpetua.'

IV

OLD PRIEST AND NEW PRESBYTER

'BLESSED be God,' wrote Joseph Hall in *The Peacemaker*, there is no difference in any essential matter betwixt the Church of England and her Sisters of the Reformation. We accord in every point of Christian doctrine without the least variation; their public Confessions and ours are sufficient convictions to the world of our full and absolute agreement. The only difference is in the form of outward administration; wherein also we are so far agreed that we all profess this form not to be essential to the being of a church, though much importing the well or better being of it, according to our several apprehensions thereof; and that we do all retain a reverent and loving opinion of each other in our own several ways, not seeing any reason why so poor a diversity should work any alienation of affection in us, one towards another; but, withal, nothing hinders, but that we may come yet closer to one another, if both may resolve to meet in that primitive government, whereby it is meet we should both be regulated, universally agreed upon by all antiquity; wherein all things were ordered and transacted by the consent of the Presbytery, moderated by one constant President thereof.[1]

In order to translate these charitable sentiments into actuality, some contacts between the church of England and the foreign reformed churches would need to be made; and it is equally necessary and instructive therefore to examine how the theological principles of Anglican divines, already sketched, found practical expression. From the outset it was clear that the church of England would not surrender its own episcopal government in the interests of the union of Protestants. At the beginning of

---

[1] J. Hall, *Works*, vol. VII, p. 58.

the primacy of Matthew Parker, he was invited by Calvin

to prevail with Her Majesty to summon a General Assembly of all the Protestant clergy, wheresoever dispersed; and that a Set Form and Method (that is, of Publick Service and Government of the Church) might be established, not only within her Dominions, but also among all Reformed and Evangelick churches abroad.

The archbishop submitted this letter to the privy council, and was instructed in his reply

to thank Calvin and let him know that they liked his proposals, which were fair and desirable. Yet as to the Government of the Church, to signify to him that the Church of England would still retain her Episcopacy, but not as from pope Gregory ... but from Joseph of Arimathea ...; yet also renouncing the Romish manner, way and ceremonies of episcopacy, which were either contrary to God's glory or the English monarchy.[1]

The death of Calvin, however, prevented further progress and a council of the Protestant churches did not take place until the Synod of Dort in 1618, at which Bishop Hall was present as one of the English delegation.

When the Belgic Confession was brought into the synod, representing the result of its deliberations, the Anglican divines, whilst approving all its doctrinal tenets, took issue with the introduction of matters of polity and ecclesiastical discipline and therewith the commendation of a parity of ministers. Bishop Carleton of Llandaff, on behalf of himself and his brethren, protested against this and affirmed the Anglican attitude in regard to episcopacy: 'I showed that by Christ a parity was never instituted in the church'; that bishops were appointed by the apostles to succeed them; and 'that this order hath been maintained in the church from the time of the apostles; and herein I appealed to the judgement of antiquity, and

---

[1] J. Strype, *Life of Matthew Parker*, bk. 2, ch. 2, p. 69 (edition of 1711).

to the judgement of any learned man now living and craved to be satisfied if any man of learning could speak to the contrary'. This intervention, he explained, was not intended 'ad harum ecclesiarum offensionem, sed ad nostrae Anglicanae defensionem'. No public answer was vouchsafed to Carleton in the synod; but individual members assured him privately 'that they did much honour and reverence the good order and discipline of the church of England, and with all their hearts would be glad to have it established amongst them; but that could not be hoped for in their state'.[1]

Around the question whether ministers of the foreign reformed churches, presbyterally ordained, were admitted without episcopal reordination to benefices *with cure of souls* in the church of England during the three-quarters of a century dividing the accession of Elizabeth I from the civil war, so much partisan controversy has raged that it is difficult amidst the smoke to discern the authentic historical lineaments of the position. The evidence for such admission consists in part of general statements, and in part of particular instances; and it will be convenient to examine them severally. Dr John Cosin, afterwards bishop of Durham, averred in 1650 that

if at any time a minister so ordained in these French churches, came to incorporate himself in ours and to receive a public charge of cure of souls among us in the church of England, (as I have known some of them to have so done of late and can instance in many other before my time), our Bishops did not re-ordain him before they admitted to his charge, as they would have done if his former ordination here in France had been void.[2]

---

[1] T. Fuller, *Church History*, bk. x, sect. v (ed. J. S. Brewer, 6 vols.), vol. v, p. 471; A. J. Mason, *The Church of England and Episcopacy*, p. 107.

[2] J. Cosin, *Works*, vol. iv, p. 403 (there is no question about benefices without cure of souls, i.e. cathedral prebends and other sinecures).

A similar affirmation was made by Joseph Hall:

I know those, more than one, that by virtue only of that ordination which they have brought with them from other reformed churches, have enjoyed spiritual promotions and livings, without any exception against the lawfulness of their calling.[1]

Cosin and Hall were contemporary with the circumstances they described; but Bishop William Fleetwood, writing during the reign of Anne on the controversy concerning lay baptism, was reciting what he had received as the tradition of the church of England in respect of presbyterian orders conferred in the foreign reformed churches. He argued that if by the phrase 'lawful minister' the church of England

meant thereby only one episcopally ordained, then she must contradict her own orders, and overthrow her own doctrine and design, by admitting and instituting and inducting into parishes such persons as had not been episcopally ordained. But this was certainly her practice during the reigns of King James and King Charles I and to the year 1661. We had many ministers from Scotland, from France, and the Low Countries, who were ordained by presbyters only and not bishops; and they were instituted into benefices with cure, and accordingly baptised the children of their several parishes, and did all other offices of the ministry and yet were never ordained.[2]

Although Fleetwood could not claim personal cognisance of any such ministers (as Cosin and Hall did), yet his contention would have had little force if he had not supposed that its premise, namely the admission of foreign presbyters to livings with cure of souls before the Restoration, would have been generally agreed. A decade later still, Archbishop Wake in the course of his correspondence with foreign divines, both Gallican and Protestant, enquired of the antiquarian Thomas Tanner,

[1] J. Hall, *Works*, vol. x, p. 341.   [2] W. Fleetwood, *Works* (1737), p. 552.

archdeacon of Norfolk and chancellor of Norwich, concerning this same point. On 20 July 1725 Tanner replied that he believed that before 1571

there were in fact some persons admitted not only as Lecturers and temporary curates, but to perpetual benefices, who had not episcopal ordination; but then they were either foreigners, or such of our own countrymen who were ordained abroad during their exile t[empore] R[eginae] Mariae; [and further, that he] did not recollect that he had met with any re-ordination till after episcopacy was abolished by ordinance of the two Houses of Parliament, 1644.

Per contra, he affirmed that between 1571 and the Act of Uniformity of 1662

there were in fact persons admitted to cures of souls, where sacraments to be administered, and to benefices, who were not episcopally ordained. One instance I laid my finger on in Bishop Wren's Consignation Book upon his Visitation in Archbishop Laud's time, 1636.[1]

The case thus mentioned by Tanner was the *locus classicus* of Dr Peter de Laune, who had been minister of the Walloon Congregation in Norwich. According to the biographer of Archbishop Tillotson, de Laune approached Bishop John Overall of Norwich in 1618–19 with a presentation to a living; whereupon the bishop

asked him where he had his orders. He answered that he was ordained by the Presbytery at Leyden. The Bishop upon this advised him to take the opinion of counsel, whether by the laws of England, he was capable of a benefice without being ordained by a Bishop. The Doctor replied, that he thought his Lordship would be unwilling to re-ordain him, if his counsel should say, that he was not otherwise capable of the living by law. The Bishop rejoined, 'Re-ordination we must not admit, no more than a re-baptization; but in case you find it doubtful, whether you be a Priest capable to receive a benefice among us or no, I will do the same office for you, if you desire it, that I

---

[1] *Arch. W. Epist.* 11, f. 200.

should do for one who doubts of his baptism, when all things belonging essentially to it have not been duly observed in the administration of it, according to the rule in Book of Common Prayer, *If thou beest not already etc*. Yet for mine own part, if you will adventure the orders that you have, I will admit your presentation, and give you institution into the living howsoever.

The biographer recorded this episode on the authority of a letter of Overall's secretary, John Cosin himself, then before him as he wrote, based on Cosin's testimony as an eyewitness; and concluded his narrative that 'the title, which this presentation had from the patron, proving not good, there were no further proceedings in it; yet afterwards Dr de Laune was admitted into another benefice without any new ordination'.[1]

Upon the translation of Bishop Francis White indeed from Carlisle to Norwich, a decade after the death of Overall, Archbishop Abbot of Canterbury claimed as his Option on 17 February 1628/9 the rectory of Redenhall, with the chapelry of Harleston thereto annexed, in the deanery of Redenhall and the archdeaconry of Norfolk. During the same year this living fell vacant by the death of Richard More; and Abbot nominated to the earl of Arundel (in whose presentation it lay upon the nomination of the bishop of Norwich) Peter de Laune for institution by the bishop. Accordingly de Laune was instituted by Bishop White on 12 November 1629. In the Consignation Book of Bishop Matthew Wren in 1636 de Laune is described as 'ordinatus presbyter per Doctores et Professores Collegii de Leyden, 26 Junii, 1599'. Accordingly Tanner commented to Wake that 'Bishop White instituted this non-episcopal ordained man; and he seems to have had no trouble on that account either from Bishop White, Corbet, Wren, or Montagu, or upon

---

[1] T. Birch, *Life of John Tillotson*, pp. 170-1 (London, 1753).

Archbishop Laud's Metropolitical Visitation in 1635; for he enjoyed this benefice till after 1642.' It appears highly probable therefore that de Laune did not receive episcopal ordination during his clerical career; but the matter is not capable of positive proof.[1]

A high degree of probability attaches also to the case of Caesar Calandrinus; who, having been brought up in Italy in the Roman church, forsook both, received presbyterian orders abroad, and then came to England and was a member of Exeter College, Oxford, where he graduated B.D. He was instituted to the rectory of Stapleford Abbots in Essex on 20 June 1620 on the

[1] The evidence concerning de Laune is as follows: *The Register of Archbishop Abbot*, vol. II, f. 174–5, records the grant on 17 February 1628–9 by Bishop White to Abbot as his Option of the Rectory of Redenhall. The same register, vol. III, f. 102, records the nomination by Abbot on 7 November 1629 to the earl of Arundel for presentation to Bishop White, of de Laune, described simply as *clericus*. Bishop Wren's Consignation Book of 1636, f. 77, records as rector of Redenhall: 'Mr Petrus de Laune, sacrae theologiae professor. Ordinatus per Doctores et Professores Collegii de Leyden, 26 Junii 1599, Institutus per Franciscum Episcopum Norvic: 12 November 1629.' The record further mentions that the institution was upon the nomination of Abbot and the presentation of the earl of Arundel; and that de Laune received the Archbishop's licence to preach through his Province under the seal of the Faculty Office on 16 August 1632. The entry in the Consignation Book of 1636 is confirmed in Tanner's list of incumbents. But Francis Blomefield's *An Essay towards a Topographical History of the County of Norfolk* (edition 1806, London), vol. v, p. 360, has a footnote to de Laune's name as rector of Redenhall to the following effect: 'Natione Gallus, ecclesieque Gallice intra civitatem Norvic: antistes in sacros diaconatus et presbyteratus ordines juxta morem et ritum ecclesie Anglicanae cooptatus est, ac predicare licentiatus authoritate ordinaria, gradumque magistri in artibus suscepit.' The authority cited is 'Revisio Archid: Norff. A° 1630'. Unfortunately this 'Revisio' is not extant either in the episcopal or civic archives at Norwich. But Tanner's examination of the Consignation Book of 1636 and its evidence, still extant, throw at least considerable doubt on the accuracy of Blomefield. For if de Laune were episcopally ordained between his institution in 1629 and the date of the 'Revisio' in 1630, it is strange, to put the matter at its lowest, that Bishop Wren's Consignation Book of 1636 should have specified the presbyterian ordination at Leyden and made no mention of the subsequent episcopal ordination. Similarly Tanner, both in his letter to Wake and in his manuscript list of incumbents, was unaware of any evidence in his time of the reordination. The probability seems therefore on the side of no episcopal ordination; though the statement of Blomefield casts a doubt on this. There are no extant ordination lists at Norwich for the episcopate of Bishop White. Blomefield also says that de Laune ceased to be rector in 1636, Tanner that he continued 'till after 1642'.

presentation of Charles, prince of Wales; and on the following day he took out Letters Dimissory from Archbishop Abbot to receive the orders of deacon and priest from any bishop.[1] Upon this occasion therefore Marcus Antonius de Dominis, formerly archbishop of Spalato, who had made the same spiritual pilgrimage and had been appointed dean of Windsor in 1618, urged Bishop Thomas Morton of Lichfield to reordain Calandrinus. On 29 June, Morton replied, giving his reasons for declining:

In the case of Caesar Calandrinus, a man well worthy of praise both by his own learning and by your commendation, I would gladly and freely satisfy your letter; but he has brought to me a Form of his Admission into Holy Orders, in which (if I have any skill in Theology) nothing which is necessary to the essentials of holy ordination, remains to be desired. Unless perchance we should wish to deny the power of ordination to the Pastors by whom he was ordained; which indeed cannot be done, as it seems to me, without great and intolerable offence to all the foreign Churches, of which I am not willing to be the agent.

What some maintain is to be feared, namely that unless the custom of our own country be observed, he may not enjoy safely any rectory according to the laws of the realm, is of no importance; if indeed it is the fact, which is also stated in his Form, that the custom of the aforementioned churches is approved by royal authority.

To this letter the bishop added in his own hand the following postscript:

If, however, you think that he ought to be required to have English ordination, I should very much wish to have this caution expressed in the episcopal documents. 'Since it does not

---

[1] *Register of Archbishop Abbot*, vol. II, f. 225b: 'Eodem die concessae fuerunt litterae dimissoriae Caesari Calendrino in Collegio Exon: nuper Alumno, ad recipiendos sacros diaconatus et presbyteratus ordines a quocumque Episcopo [21 June 1620].'

appear to us sufficiently clear from the public documents that he was admitted to Holy Orders'.[1]

That Calandrinus continued after institution without reordination seems clear from a letter of 28 November 1624 from Richard Montagu, the future famous high-church bishop and at that time incumbent of Stanford Rivers, to John Cosin:

Mr Shaw's friends are potent, you know. I believe they may fetch Calandrine about his benefice as not being a priest when he was instituted, according to our English Church. If he were endenized [naturalised] haply Mr Shaw will work upon it. There is no harm in putting this into his head; and, if it may be, by such opportunity to vindicate us from those ministers not priests.[2]

In fact Calandrinus retained his benefice until he became minister of the Dutch Reformed Church, Austin Friars, in London in 1639.

Two swallows indeed do not make a summer; and it would be absurd to pretend that the instances of de Laune and Calandrinus in any way weakened or affected the requirement of episcopal ordination as the rule of ministry in the church of England. Notwithstanding, when the Anglican representatives on a joint committee

[1] J. H. Hessels, *Ecclesiae Londino-Bataviae Archivum*, Tomus Primus (1887), no. 363, pp. 848–9: 'In gratiam Caesaris Calandrini, viri tum eruditione sua tum vestra commendatione laudatissimi, literis vestris lubentissime liberimmeque satisfecerem; sed attulit Ille mihi Formulam Initiationis suae in ordines sacros, in qua (si quid ego in Theologia sapio) nihil quod ad sacrae ordinationis essentiam necessario spectet, desidari posset; nisi forte Pastoribus, a quibus est institutus, potestatem ordinandi derogare velimus; quod sane absque immani, ut mihi videtur, et intolerabili scandalo omnium exterarum Ecclesiarum effici nequit. Cujus equidem author esse nollem. Quod autem Alii obtendunt metuendum esse, ne per leges Regni is Rectoria aliqua secure gaudeat, nisi mos noster patrius observetur, nullius momenti est; siquidem verum est, quod etiam in eadem Formula inseritur, nempe Praedictarum Ecclesiarum consuetudinem Regiae Magestatis authoritate approbatam esse. . . . Si tamen visum vobis fuerit, ordinationem Anglicanam ab illo exigere, magnopere cuperem hanc cautelam in Episcopalibus Instrumentis exprimi nimirum. Quando quidem nobis non satis constet ex actis publicis eum fuisse sacris ordinibus initiatum.'

[2] J. Cosin, *Correspondence*, vol. I, p. 30 (Surtees Society).

of Anglicans and Freechurchmen in 1925 stated, in their 'Second Memorandum on the Status of Existing Free Church Ministry', that 'in the confused times of the sixteenth and seventeenth centuries, exceptions to the rule requiring episcopal ordination sometimes occurred', but that 'they form a very insecure basis of precedent', they did somewhat less than justice both to the historical evidence and to its interpretation.[1] For the alleged 'confusion of the times' was neither intellectual nor theological, since the Tudor and Stuart churchmen in question had a coherent and consistent theory of church polity and order. And the cases of de Laune and Calandrinus were consistent with and illustrative of their conviction that, though episcopacy was necessary where it could be had, its absence owing to circumstances of historical necessity did not invalidate the ministry and sacraments of the foreign reformed churches. Accordingly the instances of the admission of such ministers of presbyterian ordination to benefices with cure of souls in England were simply the translation of precept and principle into practice. Furthermore, the paucity of such cases was the natural consequence of the circumstance that, in those as in other centuries of its history, the church of England recruited its ministry predominantly from 'the English by nation as well as in church discipline'.

The case of John Morrison, ordained presbyter by the General Synod of Lothian and licensed to preach the word and administer the sacraments throughout the province of Canterbury by Archbishop Grindal's vicar-general, is interesting because it raises the question whether the church of Scotland was regarded as a *foreign* reformed church. For the Anglican apologists

[1] G. K. A. Bell, *Documents on Christian Unity*, 2nd series, no. 121, p. 80.

drew a sharp distinction between foreign Protestants who could not have episcopacy, and Dissenters at home who had deliberately rejected a reformed episcopal church or had sought presbyteral ordination abroad. This differentiation indeed was a logical outcome of their emphasis upon necessity, since no such condition existed in England. It was a moot point, therefore, whether Scotland should be included within the foreign or the domestic orbit. Hooker inclined to the former category. Writing of church polity he observed that,

in which respect for mine own part, although I see that certain reformed churches, the Scottish especially and French, have not that which best agreeth with the sacred Scripture, I mean the government that is by Bishops, inasmuch as both these churches are fallen under a different kind of regiment; which to remedy it is for the one altogether too late, and too soon for the other during their present affliction and trouble: this their defect and imperfection I had rather lament in such case than exagitate, considering that men oftentimes without any fault of their own may be driven to want that kind of polity or regiment which is best, and to content themselves with that, which either the irremediable error of former times, or the necessity of the present, hath cast upon them.[1]

Laud, however, held a different view. Replying to Hall, who had submitted to him the draft of his *Episcopacy by Divine Right Asserted*, he commented that 'you do extremely well to distinguish the Scottish business from the state of the foreign churches; but yet as to those churches and their authors, you are a little more favourable than our case will now bear'.[2] Between the primacies of Grindal and Laud indeed many waters had flowed both in Thames and Tweed; and the former's action in licensing a Scottish presbyterian divine to preach and

---

[1] Hooker, *Ecclesiastical Polity*, III, xi, 16.
[2] Laud, *Works*, vol. VI, pt. II, p. 577 (14 January 1639).

administer the sacraments throughout his province would have been anathema to his Caroline successor. On 6 April 1582 William Aubrey, vicar-general, issued to John Morrison a licence in the following well-known terms:

Since, as we understand by testimony worthy of credit, you, the aforesaid John Morrison about five years past in the town of Garvet in the county of Lothian of the kingdom of Scotland, were admitted and ordained to Holy Orders and the sacred Ministry by the General Synod or Congregation of the said county, assembled in the said town of Garvet, by imposition of hands according to the laudable Form and Rite of the Reformed Church of Scotland; and since the said Congregation of the county of Lothian is conformable to the orthodox faith and sincere religion now received and established by public Authority in this realm of England.

We therefore, as much as in us lies and by right we are able, approving and ratifying the Form of your Order and Preferment done in such manner aforesaid, grant and impart, readily in the Lord, to you a Licence and Faculty, with the consent and express command of the Most Reverend Father in Christ, Lord Edmund, by Divine Providence Archbishop of Canterbury, Primate of all England and Metropolitan, to us signified, that in virtue of these Orders received by you, you may freely and lawfully have authority in any convenient places in and throughout the whole Province of Canterbury, to celebrate Divine Offices, minister the Sacraments, and sincerely and purely to preach the Word of God either in Latin or English according to the talent given to you by God, as much as in us lies and of right we may, and so far as the laws of the Realm do allow.[1]

---

[1] J. Strype, *Edmund Grindal*, bk. ii, appendix no. xvii: 'Cum uti ex fide digno Testimonio acciperimus, tu praefatus Johannes Morrison circiter quinque annos elapsos in oppido de Garvet in Comitat: Lothien. Regni Scotiae per generalem Synodum sive Congregationem illius Comitatus in dicto Oppido de Garvet congregatam juxta laudibilem Ecclesiae Scotiae Reformatae Formam et Ritum ad sacros Ordines et sacrosanctum Ministerium per manuum Impositionem admissus et ordinatus fueras. Cumque etiam dicta Congregatio illius Comitat: Lothien Orthodoxae Fidei et sincerae Religionis, in hoc Regno Angliae modo receptae et auctoritate publica stabilitae, sit conformis. Nos igitur Formam Ordinationis et Praefectionis tuae hujus modi, modo praemisso factam, quantum in

The purport of Grindal's action was evident: that a Scottish presbyterian minister—and it is possible that other instances occurred[1]—might be licensed not only to preach and perform divine service, but also to administer the sacraments in the church of England. It was not surprising therefore that nearly a century and a half later, the Gallican divine Le Courayer found this document startling and disconcerting.

C'est une reconnaissance [he wrote to Wake] de la validité de l'Ordination d'un Ministre Écossais ordonné selon le Rit Presbytérien d'Écosse, et une permission à lui de prêcher et d'administrer les Sacramens comme s'il avait été ordonné selon le Rit de l'Église Anglicane. . . . Cette pièce est embarrassante, car cela prouve ce qui parait d'ailleurs, que ce prélat était purement Presbytérien, et ne faisait nulle différence entre les Ordinations des Épiscopaux et celles des simples Consistoires.[2]

In his reply, Wake admitted the fact, but denied the inference:

The Licence granted by Archbishop Grindal's Vicar-General to a Scot-Presbyterian to officiate here in England, I freely own it, is not what I should have approved of, yet dare not condemn. I bless God that I was born and have been bred in an Episcopal Church; which I am convinced has been the government established in the Christian Church from the very time of the Apostles. But I should be unwilling to affirm that where the Ministry is not Episcopal, there is no Church, nor any true

nos est, et de jure possumus, approbantes et ratificantes, Tibi, ut in hujusmodi Ordinibus per te susceptis, in quibuscunque locis congruis in et per totam Provinciam Cantuarien: divina Officia celebrare, Sacramenta ministrare, necnon Verbum Dei Sermone Latino vel vulgari, juxta Talentum tibi a Deo traditum, pure et sincere praedicare, libere et licite possis et valeas, Licentiam et Facultatem, de Consensu et expresso Mandato Reverendissimi in Christo Patris Domini Edmundi, divina providentia Cantuarien: Archiepiscopi, totius Angliae Primatis et Metropolitani, nobis significato, quantum in nobis est et de jure possumus, ac quatenus Jura Regni patiuntur, benigne in Domino concedimus et impertimus.'

1 Dr Gordon Donaldson, in *The Making of the Scottish Prayer Book of 1637*, p. 5, n. 1, observes that he has 'collected particulars of over 30 Scots who were beneficed in the Elizabethan Church'; but no particulars of their ordination are given.
2 N. Sykes, *William Wake*, vol. II, pp. 14-15.

administration of the sacraments. . . . And in the case you mention, who can say how far a Bishop may have power to license a person, not rightly ordained, to officiate in the Church committed to his jurisdiction. . . . And should I (erroneously) think such ordination in some circumstances valid, yet I do not see how that would affect my own orders, which I must always prefer exceedingly before the other. At present our constitution is otherwise settled; nor can any archbishop or bishop license any man to officiate or administer the holy sacraments, especially that of the blessed Eucharist, who is not by an episcopal ordination qualified for it.[1]

Thus Wake refused to disavow, whilst being unable to approve, Grindal's action; accepting the fact, but pointing out that since the Act of Uniformity of 1662 episcopal ordination had been indispensable for ministry in the church of England.

In the licence issued by Grindal's vicar-general, the phrase 'so far as the laws of the realm do allow' is interesting; and has been by some writers referred to the statute of 13 Elizabeth I, cap. 12, 'An Act to Reform Certain Disorders touching Ministers of the Church', which required

that every person under the degree of a bishop, which does or shall pretend to be a priest or minister of God's holy word and sacraments, by reason of any other form of institution, consecration, or ordering than the form set forth by parliament in the time of the late . . . king Edward VI, or now used in the reign of our most gracious sovereign lady, . . . shall in the presence of the bishop or guardian of the spiritualities of some one diocese where he has or shall have ecclesiastical living, declare his assent and subscribe to all the articles of religion, *which only concern the confession of the true Christian faith and the doctrine of the sacraments*, comprised in a book imprinted, intituled Articles whereupon it was agreed by the archbishops and bishops of both provinces, and the whole clergy in the Convocation holden at London in the year 1562.

---

[1] *Biographia Britannica*, vol. vi, pt. ii, p. 4094.

Professor Neale's recent detailed scrutiny of the parliamentary history of this statute has demonstrated that its final form was a compromise conflation of two separate bills, 'for the sound Christian religion' and 'for the order of ministers', respectively.[1] Moreover he has also shown that whilst the occasion of the measure was undoubtedly the anti-Romanist sentiment evoked by the northern rebellion of 1569 and the papal excommunication of 1570, its form was affected by the fact that 'the Commons were quite determined that for radically-minded ministers it must be sufficient to subscribe to some only of the articles'. Hence the restrictive phrase limiting subscription to those articles 'which only concern the confession of the true Christian faith and the doctrine of the sacraments', and expressly excluding therefore those relating to church government. It has been argued that by means of this restriction persons in presbyterian orders obtained institution to benefices in England solely by subscription to the doctrinal articles. But Archbishop Wake in his investigation of the matter concluded that in 1571 'ordinations of presbyterians there had been none in England that ever we had heard of'; whilst of 'ministers ordained abroad by the reformed churches, there were few, if any among us; and those not suspected to need an act of parliament to prove them to be of sound religion'. Furthermore, the statute mentioned specifically deacons and priests, whereas these orders 'were not then known or allowed of in the other reformed churches, who had no such distinction of orders, nor did allow any such deacons as were to officiate in the ministry of the church'. They had indeed their own deacons; 'but not such as we mean, who are to minister in the church'. Accordingly

[1] J. E. Neale, 'Parliament and the Articles of Religion, 1571', *English Historical Review*, lxvii (October 1952), pp. 510–21.

he interpreted the act as applying only to persons ordained before Henry VIII's breach with Rome or during the Marian reaction [1]; and there can be no doubt that this was the purport of the statute in its final form.

Notwithstanding, the learned canonist Bishop Edmund Gibson pointed out to Wake that the act was confined to admission to benefices with cure of souls;

but as to all other promotions, this statute left them in the same state as before; and there seems to have been no other bar to persons ordained by other than bishops, from officiating as curates, except the difficulty of subscribing to the XXXIX Articles.

The 13 of Elizabeth relating only to benefices with cure, archbishop Grindal and Dr Aubrey might perhaps think themselves under no restraint from admitting one to officiate as Curate who had received Orders in Scotland.

It might have been upon the same account that Mr Travers thought he had reason to complain of his being silenced at the Temple church, which is not a benefice with cure. . . . The last act of uniformity [1662] extends the incapacity to be admitted to all ecclesiastical promotions whatsoever, unless the person who desires such promotion shall have been made priest according to the Form prescribed in the Book of Common Prayer, or otherwise by episcopal ordination.[2]

Walter Travers indeed had put himself out of court by deliberately declining episcopal ordination in England during the reign of Elizabeth I and seeking presbyterian orders abroad, when no necessity compelled. But even if the ambiguities of the statute may have permitted a few individuals to obtain a ministerial commission in the church of England when possessed of presbyterian orders conferred out of the kingdom, its purpose was plainly directed to Romish clergy and not to nonepiscopal Protestants.

---

[1] *Arch. W. Epist.* 11, f. 231d. [2] *Ibid.* f. 199.

In the case of the Scottish episcopal consecrations of 1610, the validity of presbyterian ordinations was clearly implied in the action then taken. For when James I sent for the archbishop of Glasgow and the bishops of Brechin and Galloway to London to receive consecration to the episcopate, the first-named, John Spottiswoode, related how

a question in the meantime was moved by Dr Andrewes, bishop of Ely, touching the consecration of the Scottish bishops, who, as he said, 'must first be ordained presbyters, as having received no ordination from a bishop'. The archbishop of Canterbury, Dr Bancroft, who was by, maintained 'that thereof there was no necessity, seeing where bishops could not be had, the ordination given by the presbyters must be esteemed lawful; otherwise it might be doubted if there were any lawful vocation in most of the Reformed churches'. This applauded to by the other bishops, Ely acquiesced.[1]

Spottiswoode was not only contemporary with the incident but an eyewitness; and his testimony is superior to that of Peter Heylyn, who, writing almost a generation later, ascribed to Bancroft the opinion that consecration to the episcopate might be *per saltum* according to the

---

[1] J. Spottiswoode, *History of the Church of Scotland*, vol. III, p. 209 (ed. M. Russell, 1851). T. Hannan ('The Scottish Consecrations in London in 1610', *Church Quarterly Review*, January 1911) argues that the Scottish bishops had never received even presbyterian ordination, because the *First Book of Discipline* considered imposition of hands optional—'we judge it not necessary'. But Dr W. McMillan (*The Worship of the Scottish Reformed Church, 1550–1638*) argues 'that what must have been in view, was the admission of those who were already priests to benefices'. He points out moreover that in 1566 the General Assembly approved the Helvetic Confession, which required ordination 'by the presbyters with public prayer and laying on of hands'. In 1570 the Assembly approved a 'publick and solemne Form of Ordination', which was described in the Ordinal of 1620 as a 'good and commendable order'; and in the *Second Book of Discipline* (prepared in 1578 and accepted in 1581) ordination was to be by prayer and imposition of hands. Dr McMillan therefore contends that 'it seems likely that this simply confirmed existing usage' (pp. 342–5). If the Scottish bishops had not received ordination by imposition of hands, they were notwithstanding described as *Ministri* in the royal mandate of James I for their consecration.

precedents of Ambrose of Milan and Nectarius of Constantinople.[1] The episode was important as evidence that Bancroft here equated the Scottish with the foreign reformed churches as situated in circumstances 'where bishops could not be had', and in which therefore presbyterian ordination must be esteemed lawful, and that Andrewes by his participation in the consecration also acquiesced in this view. This interpretation was adduced by Wake to Le Courayer as evidence that the Anglican bishops at that time

allowed the ordination they had received at home to be sufficient to qualify them for episcopal consecration. . . . It shews what opinion our bishops had of this matter then; and I do not find they changed their principles afterwards. It is plain bishop Andrewes, one of the most scrupulous among them, did not; for his Letters to Du Moulin were written long afterwards, in 1618.[2]

It is common knowledge that the Scottish bishops, though on their return home they consecrated other presbyters to share the episcopal office, did not reordain the parochial presbyters. Nor is it clear even that actual presbyterian ordinations ceased after 1610; since 'as late as 1626 there were some ministers who were admitted without episcopal ordination'.[3] The most famous of the Aberdeen doctors, John Forbes, who was a leading figure on the episcopal side in the controversies of the seventeenth century, was himself ordained by a Dutch presbytery in 1619, though his father was then bishop of Aberdeen. Moreover in 1615 Spottiswoode remarked, amongst 'articles required for the service of the church

---

[1] P. Heylyn, *The History of the Presbyterians, 1563–1647* (Oxford, 1670): 'There was no such necessity of receiving the order of Priesthood, but that Episcopal Consecration might be given without it, as might have been exemplified in the cases of Ambrose and Nectarius' (p. 387).

[2] *Arch. W. Epist.* 11, f. 56, 13d.   [3] W. McMillan, *op. cit.* p. 347.

of Scotland', both 'an order for election of archbishops and bishops' and 'a uniform order for electing of ministers and their receiving'. Hitherto the two forms available were those contained in the Book of Common Order of 1561 and the 'publick and solemne form of ordination' of 1570, which unfortunately has not survived. It is probable that some bishops used the Anglican Ordinal before 1620; but it is evident that current practice was variable. 'The Forme and Manner of Ordaining Ministers', issued by episcopal authority in 1620 but lacking confirmation by the temporal power, was based on the Anglican Ordinal, but with significant differences.

Throughout it omitted all mention of the words 'priest' and 'priesthood'. 'The Praeface', unlike its English contemporary, contained no reference to the threefold orders of ministers as having been in the Church since the apostles' time. It contented itself with recalling that

in the Church of Christ it hath always been holden unlawful for any man, by his own private authority, to preach the word of God, to administer the holy Sacraments, or execute any part of the Spiritual office of a Pastor, except he were first called, tried, and examined, and being found qualified for the function, by public prayer with imposition of hands, orderly admitted to the same. Accordingly hath our Church in divers Assemblies, and specially in the Assembly which was kept at Edinburgh the fifth of March 1570, appointed diligent examination to be made of the learning, qualities, and good conversation of pastors before their entry. And their admittance to be by a public and solemn form of ordination. Wherefore, to the intent this good and commendable order may be kept hereafter in the Church, it hath been thought meet to prescribe a special form of ordaining ministers and consecrating of archbishops and bishops to their places, which in all times hereafter shall be observed by these that have power to ordain or consecrate.

Like the contemporary English form its prefatory rubric required that 'there shall be a sermon made, declaring the duty and office of Ministers, with their necessity in the Church, and how reverently the people ought to esteem of them and their vocation'. The presentation, exhortation, and interrogatories to the candidates were taken from the English Ordinal; but the actual prayer of ordination was adopted almost verbatim from the Book of Common Order. It omitted the form of words used in England at the imposition of hands:

Receive the Holy Ghost; whose sins thou dost forgive, they are forgiven; and whose sins thou dost retain, they are retained; and be thou a faithful dispenser of the word of God and of his holy Sacraments. In the name of the Father, and of the Son and of the Holy Ghost. Amen.

Instead it substituted the following:

In the name of God and by the authority committed unto us by the Lord Jesus Christ, we give unto thee power and authority to preach the Word of God, to minister his holy Sacraments, and exercise Discipline in such sort as is committed unto ministers by the order of our Church; and God, the Father of our Lord Jesus Christ, who has called thee to the office of a watchman over his people, multiply his graces with thee, illuminate thee with his Holy Spirit, comfort and strengthen thee in all virtue, govern and guide thy ministry to the praise of his holy name, to the propagation of Christ's kingdom, to the comfort of his Church, and to the discharge of thy own conscience in the day of the Lord Jesus; to whom with the Father and the Holy Ghost be all honour, praise, and glory now and ever. Amen.

The office contained also its own form of words at the delivery of the Bible: 'This is the Book of Scripture, which thou must study continually, and make the ground and rule of thy doctrine and living.'

Together with this office, there was a 'Forme and

Manner of consecrating an Archbishop or Bishop', which provided for 'a sermon touching the office and duty of a bishop'; and embraced the interrogatories and the *Veni Creator* from the Anglican order. In the prayer spoken by the archbishop before the imposition of hands there was specific mention of the office to which the candidate was consecrated, in the form of 'this thy servant, whom we are now to receive unto the office of a Bishop within thy house'. At the laying on of hands the chief consecrator said as follows:

We, by the authority given us of God, and of his Son the Lord Jesus Christ, give unto thee the power of Ordination, imposition of hands, and correction of manners, within the diocese whereunto thou art, or hereafter shall be, called. And God Almighty be with thee in all thy ways, increase his graces unto thee, and guide thy ministry to the praise of his holy name, and the comfort of his Church. Amen.[1]

It is to be observed further that no form was provided for the ordering of deacons; and it is probable that the ordination of deacons commenced only in 1637. It was natural, therefore, that in 1636 Bishop Wedderburn of Dunblane should point out to Laud 'the two great reasons why the Book of Ordination ... is short and deficient'; namely, 'that in the admission to priesthood the very essential words of conferring orders were left out', and that 'the order of deacon is made but as a lay office'. Notwithstanding these defects, the Scottish episcopal church and its ministry were accepted as sufficient by contemporary English bishops; and in the Bidding Prayer prescribed in the Canons of 1604, the people were exhorted to pray 'for Christ's holy, catholic Church, ... and especially for the Churches of England, Scotland, and Ireland', without any difference or inequality being

[1] G. W. Sprott, *Scottish Liturgies of the Reign of James VI*, pp. 111–29. (1901 edition)

implied between these three several branches of the catholic church.

Throughout the Anglican references to foreign reformed churches there recurs the refrain of historical necessity, which had caused them unwillingly and involuntarily to abandon episcopacy. This, however, was challenged directly by Jeremy Taylor. In considering the argument from necessity he allowed that,

indeed if the case were just thus, it was very hard with good people of the transmarine churches; but I have here two things to consider: First, I am very willing to believe that they would not have done anything either of error or suspicion but in cases of necessity. But then I consider that M. Du Plessis, a man of honour and great learning, does attest that at the first reformation there were many archbishops and cardinals in Germany, England, France, and Italy that joined in the reformation, whom they might, but did not, employ in their ordinations; and what necessity then can be pretended in this case, I would fain learn, that I might make their defence. . . . Secondly, I consider that necessity may excuse a personal delinquency, but I never heard that necessity did build a church. . . . Thus the case is evident, that the want of a bishop will not excuse us from our endeavours of acquiring one; and where God means to found a church, there He will supply them with those means and ministers which Himself hath made of ordinary and absolute necessity. And therefore if it happens that those bishops which are of ordinary ministration amongst us prove heretical, still God's church is catholic, and, though with trouble, yet orthodox bishops may be acquired. . . . So did the reformed churches refuse ordinations by the bishops of the Roman communion. But what might they then have done? . . . those good people might have had order from the bishops of England or the Lutheran churches, if at least they thought our churches catholic and christian.[1]

It was indeed widely agreed that the medieval papacy had brought episcopacy into such discredit that many

[1] J. Taylor, *Works*, vol. v, pp. 119–21.

leading reformers saw no means of effecting the necessary reforms save by jettisoning the episcopal order. Even Saravia, for example, confessed the truth of this, whilst deploring the abandonment of episcopacy.[1] Joseph Hall likewise allowed that the continental reformed churches 'were forced to discard the office as well as the men; but yet the office because of the men, as popish, not as bishops'; and Francis Mason, in the 'Epistle Dedicatorie' to his defence of the episcopal succession in the church of England, contrasted the good fortune of that church in this respect with the circumstances of other reformed churches, 'constrained by necessity to admit extraordinary fathers, that is, to receive ordination from presbyters, which are but inferior ministers, rather than to suffer the fabric of the Lord Jesus to be dissolved'.[2] Moreover a valuable essay (though its value is historical rather than apologetic) on 'Feudal Episcopacy' in a recent symposium, *The Apostolic Ministry*, affords abundant justification for the inability of the reformers to recognise the authentic lineaments of an apostolic succession underneath the strange metamorphoses of the episcopate from Gregory the Great to Julius II.[3] Likewise, in the political conditions of the sixteenth century, successful defiance of the papacy and reform of the church were impracticable without the active championship of the godly prince, whether emperor, king, prince, or municipal council; and in this respect also

[1] H. Saravia, *Diversi Tractatus*, Prologus: 'hodie autem tyrannidis Episcopi Romani et satellitum ipsius odio factum est, ut haec nomina in controversiam vocentur, idque a diversis, diversa ratione. ... Antichristus Romanus cum suis Episcopis, Archiepiscopis, Patriarchis et Metropolitanis, sic Christi Ecclesiam afflixit, ut sub his nominibus credatur latere tyrannis. Semel ictus a scorpione, sub quovis lapide credit latere scorpionem, et morsus a cane, quemvis pavescit canem.'

[2] F. Mason, *Of the Consecration of Bishops in the Church of England*, 1613, Epistle Dedicatorie to Archbishop Abbot (p. 2).

[3] T. M. Parker, 'Feudal Episcopacy' in *The Apostolic Ministry* (ed. K. E. Kirk, 1946).

circumstances differed widely from the Empire to England, from France to Scotland, and from the imperial cities of Germany to Zurich and Geneva. Thus George Downham, asking 'why in other churches the learned men have not restored bishops', gave this reason:

for that they could not, either because the popish bishops were still countenanced by the civil magistrate, as in France; or because the form of civil government being after the expulsion of the bishop changed into a popular state, could no more endure the government of a bishop than Rome after the expulsion of Tarquinius, the regiment of a king.[1]

The fortunes of the reforming movement depended directly and immediately on the policy of civil rulers; and full weight in assessing the plea of necessity must be given to local conditions governing the attitude of kings and bishops. The varying fortunes of reform in England under the Tudors, or of episcopacy in Scotland under the Stuarts, or of both in the Scandinavian kingdoms illustrated sufficiently this point. Only in England and Sweden was royal resolution combined with episcopal subservience in sufficient measure to ensure the continuity of episcopacy side by side with reform of doctrine and liturgy; and elsewhere only the *Unitas Fratrum* preserved their episcopal succession through centuries of storm and stress.

But it would be as unrealistic as unveracious not to recognise also that the maintenance of episcopal continuity was subordinated by the reformers to the achievement of purity of doctrine, and was regarded as itself of secondary importance. A modern Lutheran scholar has written that

Luther never tried to find ways of keeping it. When he had the opportunity of establishing Lutheran bishops in Naumberg and Merseberg, he did not try to get other bishops to ordain

[1] G. Downham, *Defence of a Sermon*, p. 166.

them. . . . I cannot believe that Luther really could not have found some few consecrated bishops who were willing to ordain Lutheran bishops if he had really tried to find them. Could what was possible in Sweden have been quite impossible in much larger Germany, if Luther had really tried it? And if all German bishops and their suffragan bishops or Weihbischöfe, an enormous number, had refused unanimously, could he not have asked foreign bishops? A still more relevant consideration is to hand. Luther's Roman bishop had been the bishop of Brandenburg. The Roman bishop of Brandenburg, Matthias von Jagow, became officially a Lutheran in 1529 and lived until 1545. The 'consecration' of Amsdorf as bishop of Naumberg was in 1542, and that of George von Anhalt as bishop of Mersburg in 1544. Was it not very probable that Luther should have tried to get Matthias von Jagow to officiate at these consecrations? [1]

Against this conclusion must be set the contention of other scholars that Luther hoped to maintain a reformed and evangelical episcopate as the government of his churches; and that as late as 1530 he cherished hopes of preserving the episcopal constitution for the whole of Germany under a primate, had not the refusal of the archbishop of Mainz and most of the bishops made this impossible. [2] Similarly in the 'Apologia for the Confession of Augsburg' it was insisted that

we have often testified that we desired very anxiously to preserve the ecclesiastical polity and the grades of ministry in the Church, constituted though they are by merely human authority. For we know that the ecclesiastical discipline has been constituted by the Fathers as useful and good, in the manner described by the ancient canons. But the bishops either compel our priests to reject and condemn the teaching which is contained in our Confession, or they kill those miserable and innocent men. [3]

[1] H. P. Kramm, 'The Pastor Pastorum in Luther and early Lutheranism' in *And Other Pastors of Thy Flock*, pp. 130–1 (ed. F. Hildebrandt, Cambridge, 1947).
[2] Karl Holl, *Gesammelte Aufsätze*, I, Luther, pp. 375–80.
[3] Apology for the Confession of Augsburg, Article XIV.

Likewise of the consecration in Denmark by John Bugenhagen in 1537 of seven Lutheran superintendents of the reformed church of that kingdom, it has been affirmed that

it was not, on the one hand, a case in which no true episcopal consecration could be had; in all probability a very slight pressure would have brought the older bishops to consecrate Gyldenstjerne, Rønnov, and the others who might have carried the ancient succession on. Nor was it, on the other hand, a case of deliberate preference for presbyterian ordination, as in some countries; the men now set apart—or almost all of them—were to have sole authority to ordain. The act was distinctly intended to mark a new beginning.[1]

In 1536 indeed King Christian III, having secured the crown after a civil war of two years and being a sincere Lutheran, had deposed and imprisoned all the Danish bishops. Economic motives joined hands with a desire to 'uphold the true doctrine of our Lord Jesus Christ, now so corrupted, together with sound and true Christian worship', to create a pastoral episcopate whose powers should relate to spiritual government only, and who were designed to be 'bishops or superintendents who can instruct, teach and preach the holy Gospel, God's Word, and the Holy Christian Faith to the people at large'. Accordingly on the day of the royal assent to the *Ordinatio Ecclesiastica*, 2 September 1537, Bugenhagen consecrated the seven new superintendents or bishops; and with them the bishop-elect of Bergen, Geble Pedersson, one of the two pre-Reformation Norwegian bishops allowed to continue in office in that church. The intention was clearly to continue the succession of *episcopi seu superintendentes*, and the action was in harmony

---

[1] E. H. Dunkerly, *The Reformation in Denmark*, p. 78; quoting A. J. Mason in *The Church Quarterly Review*, April 1891, p. 186.

with the Schmalkaldic Articles, which recognised, according to the theory of Jerome and its defenders during the middle ages, the identity of order between bishop and presbyter, and the justification for consecration by presbyters where the bishops were hostile to the reformed faith.[1] Thus in Denmark and its dependent territories, the *successio localis* and the *successio doctrinalis* were preserved, at the cost of losing the *successio personalis*. Professor Einar Molland has summarised the matter thus:

As to the manner of consecration, we regard the formal continuity of ordination throughout the history of the church as desirable, but not as a *conditio sine qua non* for the validity of the ministry and of the sacraments. In cases where the church has to choose between the right Gospel and the rightly-interpreted and rightly-administered sacraments on the one hand, and on the other hand the formal continuity of ordination, she must choose the Gospel and the sacraments. The Anglican church has not been faced with this choice. But the Lutheran churches have been in this situation. . . . This was their choice. Should they have preferred the formal apostolic succession?[2]

In regard to the reformed churches, it has been observed already that Calvin did not object in principle to episcopacy, but rather believed himself to be restoring the New Testament *episkopos* in the person of his *pastor*; and the learned Joseph Bingham concluded of the French Huguenots that their abandonment of that order arose from necessity rather than from choice:

[1] B. J. Kidd, *Documents Illustrating the Continental Reformation*, nos. 132, 132a: The Recess of the Diet of Copenhagen and Ordinatio Ecclesiastica, pp. 325–34. *Ibid.* no. 128: The Schmalkaldic Articles: 'De potestate Episcoporum: Sed quum iure divino non sint diversi gradus episcopi et pastoris, manifestum est ordinationem a pastore in sua ecclesia factam iure divino ratam esse. Itaque quum episcopi ordinarii fiunt hostes ecclesiae aut nolunt impertire ordinationem, ecclesiae retinent ius suum.

[2] *Union of Christendom*, sect. IV: From the Scandinavian Standpoint, by E. Molland, pp. 18–19 (S.P.C.K. & Church Literature Association, 1940).

But it was their misfortune at first, that they could not have it, though their inclinations led them to embrace it. For no sooner did the popish party hear of the least suspicion of any bishops' leaning towards the Protestant cause, but immediately the whole power both of France and Rome was armed against them. . . . By this we see, it was not any aversion the French Protestants had to episcopacy in general, but rather the iniquity of the times, that hindered bishops from being settled amongst them. . . . All which proves that, though the French Protestants were willing to justify their own government as an allowable thing among themselves; yet they were far from crying down episcopacy as antichristian, or pulling down bishops merely to set up themselves. . . . The truth is, Calvin and Beza and the French church set up such a government and discipline at the reformation as the state of their affairs would bear; but they never absolutely condemned episcopacy, or thought their own model ought to be a rule to other churches.[1]

The staunchness of Anglican divines in thus allowing the plea of historical necessity to the foreign reformed churches may have sprung not only from a sympathetic appreciation of the difficulties of their actual situation, but also from a vivid recollection of the danger they themselves had run of being compelled to make the same hard choice between purity of doctrine and worship and the maintenance of the *successio personalis*; and from the corporate historical memory of the two occasions in which the church of England had come near to losing the episcopal succession by the same harsh necessity. For if Mary Tudor had reigned for twenty-five years instead of five, English Protestants both at home and abroad might have been compelled to organise their churches permanently without bishops; and even when the accession of Elizabeth I delivered them from this strait, the refusal of all the surviving Marian bishops save one to take the oath of supremacy to her created a complex

1 J. Bingham, 'The French Church's Apology for the Church of England' (*Works*, vol. IX, pp. 219–22).

of problems in relation to the consecration of Matthew Parker to the see of Canterbury, which were solved only by the insertion in the royal mandate of 6 December 1559 of the famous *Supplentes* clause:

Supplying by our supreme royal authority, of our mere motion and certain knowledge, whatever either in the things to be done by you pursuant to our aforesaid mandate, or in you, or any of you, your condition, state, or power for the perform-ance of the premisses, may or shall be wanting of those things which, either by the statutes of this realm, or by the ecclesi-astical laws, are required or are necessary on this behalf, the state of the times and the exigency of affairs rending it neces-sary.[1]

This was evidently a revolutionary measure to meet a situation of emergency; and less than a century later the Interregnum presented a similar dilemma. With epis-copacy proscribed at home, and the church of England reduced to a little city of Zoar of exiles abroad, ground between the upper and nether millstones of popery and presbyterianism, its extinction seemed imminent. Indeed if Cromwell had lived another decade—and he was not sixty years of age when he died—the preservation of the episcopal succession would have been precarious to the point of impossibility. Throughout the Commonwealth anxious correspondence passed between the Anglican exiles and the bishops at home, concerning the perpetu-ation of the succession; and even a year after the Pro-tector's death, Edward Hyde wrote despairingly of the church:

The conspiracies to destroy it are very evident; and if there can be no combination to preserve it, it must expire. I do assure you,

---

1 'Supplentes nihilominus, suprema auctoritate nostra regia, ex mero motu ac certa scientia nostris, si quid aut in his quae juxta Mandatum nostrum praedictum per vos fient, aut in vobis aut vestrum aliquo, conditione, statu, facultate vestris ad praemissa perficienda, desit aut deerit eorum quae per statuta hujus regni aut per leges ecclesiasticas in hac parte requiruntur aut necessaria sunt, temporis ratione et rerum necessitate id postulante.'

the names of all the bishops who are alive, and their several ages, are as well known at Rome as in England; and both the Papist and the Presbyterian value themselves very much upon computing in how few years the church of England must expire.[1]

It was natural that Anglicans, who had lived through such dangers to their own episcopacy, should take seriously and sympathetically the argument from in-eluctable historical necessity.

The seventeenth century indeed presented alternations of fortune as kaleidoscopic as catastrophic, both to episcopacy and presbyterianism, and in Scotland no less than in England. The alliance of Scottish episcopacy with the Stuart monarchy led to its fall in 1638; and in turn this fate was visited upon the English episcopate during the civil war between crown and parliament. For the parliamentary party needed military allies; and the help of the Scots was purchased at the price of the summons of the Westminster Assembly in 1643, charged with the reformation of religion in England 'according to the Word of God and the example of the best reformed churches'. Once more a golden opportunity was missed; for the synod, instead of seeking the conversion of pre-lacy into a constitutional episcopacy attempered unto presbytery, chose to abolish root and branch both the episcopal polity and the Book of Common Prayer; thereby extirpating the traditional Anglican order and provoking an abiding resentment against presbyterian-ism and its Scottish parentage.[2] All that had been said contumeliously of episcopacy in Scotland was to be

[1] R. S. Bosher, *The Making of the Restoration Settlement*, p. 97 (1951).

[2] T. Pierce, *The New Discoverer Discovered by way of Answer to Mr Baxter* (1659): 'Now had you sworn in taking the Scottish Covenant, to change the *name* of a Bishop and there had stopped, you might have cited the *Peacemaker* [of Bp Hall] with much more reason than you now do. But you swore to endeavour the extir-pation of the *thing*, of Church government itself by law established' (p. 222).

repaid with interest by English episcopalians of Scottish presbytery. Joseph Hall's *Episcopacy by Divine Right Asserted*—a strange and unexpected work from his pen—was provoked in 1637 by the spectacle of the renunciation of his episcopal function by Bishop Graham of Orkney. 'Good God, what is this, that I have lived to hear? That a Bishop in a Christian Assembly should renounce his episcopal function, and cry mercy for his now-abandoned calling?' [1] Much fiercer was the tone of Bramhall's 'Fair Warning to take heed of the Scottish Discipline, as being of all others most injurious to the Christian magistrate, most oppressive to the subject, and most pernicious to both', which was printed abroad in 1649, and fulminated against the overthrow of episcopacy in England and its replacement by presbyterianism. In it Bramhall denounced the Scottish attempt

to compel foreign churches to dance after their pipe, . . . and by force of arms to turn their neighbours out of a possession of above fourteen hundred years to make room for their Trojan horse of ecclesiastical discipline. [Further, he affirmed that] if it were not for this Disciplinarian humour . . . I doubt not but all reformed Churches might easily be reconciled. Before these unhappy troubles in England, all Protestants, both Lutherans and Calvinists, did give unto the English Church the right hand of fellowship.[2]

Accordingly, when at the restoration of Charles II episcopacy and the Book of Common Prayer were re-instated in England, not only was this form of polity reimposed upon Scotland, but care was taken to close all former loopholes in respect both of ordination and subscription. The Preface to the Ordinal was revised so as to require henceforth that

no man shall be accounted or taken to be a lawful Bishop, Priest, or Deacon in the Church of England, or suffered to

[1] Hall, *Works*, vol. x, p. 145.   [2] Bramhall, *Works*, vol. III, pp. 241, 243.

execute any of the said functions, except he be called, tried, examined and admitted thereto, according to the form hereafter following, or hath had formerly Episcopal Consecration or Ordination.

Similarly the Act of Uniformity of 1662, in addition to requiring a declaration of 'unfeigned assent and consent to all and everything contained and prescribed' in the revised Book of Common Prayer, and an abjuration of the Solemn League and Covenant, enacted that episcopal ordination should be indispensable for all present and future holders of any ecclesiastical office whatsoever in the church of England:

Provided always and be it enacted, that from and after the feast of St Bartholomew ... in the year of our Lord 1662, no person who is now incumbent and in possession of any parsonage, vicarage, or benefice, and who is not already in holy orders by episcopal ordination, or shall not before the said feast day of St Bartholomew be ordained priest or deacon according to the form of episcopal ordination, shall have, hold or enjoy the said parsonage, vicarage, benefice with cure, or other ecclesiastical promotion within this kingdom of England or the dominion of Wales, or the town of Berwick-on-Tweed; but shall be utterly disabled and *ipso facto* deprived of the same, and all his ecclesiastical promotions, as if he was naturally dead. . . .

And it be further enacted ... that no person whatsoever shall henceforth be capable to be admitted to any parsonage, vicarage, benefice or other ecclesiastical promotion or dignity whatsoever, nor shall presume to consecrate and administer the holy Sacrament of the Lord's Supper, before such time as he shall be ordained priest according to the form and manner by the said book prescribed, unless he have formerly been made priest by episcopal ordination.

This statute thus laid down the same conditions for ministers of the foreign reformed churches as for Protestant dissenters at home wishing henceforth to exercise the ministry of the church of England. No Lutheran or Reformed pastor might be admitted to Anglican benefices, with or without cure of souls, until he had received episcopal ordination. The Act marked indeed the parting of the ways, and inaugurated a new relationship betwixt Old Priest and New Presbyter.

V

THE PARTING OF THE WAYS

'Though our constitution suffers no man to minister the Sacrament of the Lord's Supper who is not in Priests' Orders,' wrote Archbishop Wake in 1719 to William Beauvoir, chaplain to the British ambassador in Paris:

nor otherwise to officiate in the Church who has not the Order of Deacon by episcopal ordination; yet no one when he receives these Orders, renounces his own which he had before taken, either in the foreign Churches abroad, or even by our own dissenting ministrations at home. Nay, till the last Act of Uniformity, Casaubon, Vossius, and many other foreign divines were actually preferred in our Church, and had no other besides their own Orders.

It was evident that the outstanding innovation of the Anglican restoration settlement was the unvarying requirement of episcopal ordination for ministry in whatever capacity in the church. Its first effects were seen accordingly in the method employed for the reintroduction of episcopacy into the church of Scotland as a consequence of the return of the Stuart monarchy. Four divines were sent to England to receive consecration, Sharp to be consecrated to St Andrews, Leighton to Dunblane, Fairfoul to Glasgow, and Hamilton to Galloway.

When the time fixed for the consecration of the bishops of Scotland came on [wrote Burnet], the English bishops finding that Sharp and Leighton had not episcopal ordination as priests and deacons (the other two having been ordained by bishops before the wars), they stood upon it that they must be ordained first deacons and then priests. Sharp was very uneasy at this, and remembered them of what had happened when king James had set up episcopacy. . . . But the late war and the disputes during that time had raised these controversies higher, and brought men to stricter notions and to maintain them with more fierceness. The English bishops did also say, that by the late act of uniformity that matter was more positively settled than it had been before; so that they could not legally consecrate any, but those who were, according to that constitution, made first priests and deacons. They also made this difference between the present time and king James'; for then the Scots were only in an imperfect state, having never had bishops among them since the Reformation; so in such a state of things in which they had been under a real necessity, it was reasonable to allow of their orders, how defective soever; but that of late they had been in a state of schism, had revolted from their bishops, and had thrown off that order; so that orders given in such a wilful opposition to the whole constitution of the primitive church was a thing of another nature. . . . Sharp stuck more at it than could have been expected from a man that had swallowed down greater matters. Leighton did not stand much upon it. He did not think orders given without Bishops were null and void. He thought the forms of government were not settled by such positive laws as were unalterable; but only by Apostolical practices, which, as he thought, authorised Episcopacy as the best form. Yet he did not think it necessary to the very being of a Church. But he thought that every Church might make such rules of ordination as they pleased, and that they might reordain all that came to them from any other Church; and that the reordaining a Priest ordained in another Church imported no more, but that they received him into orders according to their own rules; and did not infer the annulling the orders he had formerly received. These two were upon this privately ordained Deacons and Priests. And then all the four were consecrated publicly in the Abbey of Westminster.[1]

As in 1610, so in 1661, the reasons for the course of action taken were of equal importance with the action

[1] G. Burnet, *History of My Own Times*, bk. II, anno 1661.

itself. At the former date, the church of Scotland had been accorded quasi-recognition as a foreign reformed church, labouring 'under a real necessity'. At the latter time, it was regarded as being 'in a state of schism', and that of its own deliberate contrivance. Moreover, the episodes of the civil war, and particularly the prevalence of presbyterian ordinations both in England and Scotland during the Interregnum, had necessitated the erection of an insuperable fence against the possibility of non-episcopal ministers being allowed to officiate in the church of England; of which the act of uniformity was the expression. When, therefore, Bramhall found in his Irish diocese some ministers in presbyterian orders, including some ordained in Scotland, he informed them that they were not qualified

for any preferment in the Church. Upon this, the question arose, 'Are we not Ministers of the Gospel?' To which his Grace answered: That was not the question; at least, he desired for peace sake, that might not be the question for that time. 'I dispute not', said he, 'the value of your ordination, nor those acts you have exercised by virtue of it; what you are, or might be, here when there was no law, or in other Churches abroad. But we are now to consider ourselves a national Church limited by law, which among other things takes chief care to prescribe about ordination; and I do not know how you could recover the means of the Church, if any should refuse to pay you your tithes, if you are not ordained as the law of this Church requireth; and I am desirous that she may have your labours, and you such portions of her revenues as shall be allotted to you, in a legal and assured way.

The means which he employed were illustrated by the clauses which he inserted into the letters of orders granted by him to Mr Edward Parkinson, whom he reordained conditionally:

Not annulling the former orders (if he had received any such), nor deciding as to their invalidity, much less condemning all the sacred orders of the foreign Churches (which we leave to their own Judge), but only supplying whatever may previously have been lacking according to the requirement of the canons of the Church of England, and providing for the peace of the Church, so that occasion of schism may be taken away, and the consciences of the faithful satisfied, and that none may doubt concerning his ordination, or reject his presbyteral acts as being invalid.[1]

When the newly-consecrated Scottish bishops returned home, they consecrated six further bishops, but without previously ordaining them deacon and priest; nor was any attempt generally made to reordain the existing parochial presbyters. Indeed it is uncertain which forms of ordination were used between the Restoration and the Revolution in Scotland; for the interpretation of the phrases 'according to the order of the Church of Scotland' and 'juxta morem ritum antique et catholice ecclesie Scoticane' is obscure; whilst so late as 1680 Archbishop Patterson of Edinburgh observed that 'there is no form of ordination appointed to this day'. It may well be that the Scottish Ordinal of 1620 and the English Ordinal were both in use.[2]

Amongst the foreign reformed churches also, the Anglican requirement of episcopal ordination, and therefore of reordination of their presbyters, was only understood with difficulty. The chaplain and secretary to the English envoy to the Swiss Cantons, Mr J. C. Werndly, wrote in 1706 to Bishop Compton of London:

1 Bramhall, *Works*, vol. 1, pp. xxiv, xxxvii: 'Non annihilantes priores ordines (si quos habuit) nec invaliditatem eorundem determinantes, multo minus omnes ordines sacros Ecclesiarum forinsecarum condemnantes, quos proprio Judici relinquimus, sed solummodo supplentes quicquid prius defuit per canones Ecclesiae Anglicanae requisitum, et providentes paci Ecclesiae, ut schismatis tollatur occasio, et conscientiis fidelium satisfiat, nec ulli dubitent de ejus ordinatione, aut actus suos presbyteriales tanquam invalidos aversentur.'

2 G. Donaldson, 'Scottish Ordinations in the Restoration Period', *Scottish Historical Review*, October 1954.

I have been asked two chief questions that have somewhat puzzled me, and I humbly crave your lordship's directions about the same; viz, (1) In case the Nonconformists were willing to be re-united, whether or not they would be required to swear, that they believe episcopacy to be absolutely *de jure divino*? (2) Why are such priests as are ordained by Roman Catholic bishops admitted to the sacred offices in the Church of England, when the French and other foreign ministers are not admitted without a Re-ordination, though they were ordained by a Protestant Synod?[1]

Archbishop Wake, whose policy was to encourage theological students from the foreign reformed churches studying in England as well as ministers ordained in those churches, to receive episcopal ordination before returning home, also found his action difficult of explanation. In the case of Mr James Horner he confessed to Père Le Courayer, his Gallican correspondent:

I have ordained Mr Horner both deacon and priest; and thereby received him into the ministry of the Church of England. This is a work that gives the most offence of any to the other Reformed Churches; but I must agree with you that I know no government older than Calvin's time, but what was episcopal, in the Church of Christ.[2]

The principal defence offered to assuage such scruples was to explain the requirement of episcopal ordination as both the result of the act of uniformity and as a domestic rule of the church of England which involved no judgment on the validity of the presbyterian orders of the foreign reformed churches.

This was the contention of M. Claude Grosteste de la Mothe, minister of the French church of the Savoy, who assured his compatriots that the practice of reordination was

---

[1] Rawlinson MSS. (Bodley), 982, f. 47.
[2] *Biographia Britannica*, vol. VI. pt. 11, p. 4094b.

en vertu d'une loi civile, ce qui n'empêche nullement qu'ils ne disent que l'ordination des Églises Étrangères est valide. C'est ainsi que la plupart des théologiens Anglais s'expliquent. D'autres adjoûtent que le gouvernement des Églises Étrangères étant defectueux, leurs ministres quoi qu'ils soient de vrais ministres, sont obligés de rectifier ce défaut quand ils se trouvent dans un royaume où cela peut aisément. Leur ministère était bon dans un pays où ils ne pouvaient faire mieux, mais la Providence les ayant transportés dans un royaume où ils ont plus de liberté, c'est à eux à en profiter, en donnant à leur ministère une plenitude de perfection. Que l'on choisisse telle des deux réponses que l'on voudra, il sera évident que la seconde ordination que l'on donne en Angleterre aux ministères étrangères, ne suppose point de nullité dans la première. ... Si on joint à cette considération que le ministère étranger a besoin pour parvenir à sa plenitude d'être secouru par l'ordination épiscopale, on suppose seulement que le ministère est imparfait, mais on reconnait qu'il a toute la vérité et toute l'essence du ministère.[1]

Similar considerations influenced the famous English divine John Humfrey, who, having been ordained by a Classis of presbyters in 1649, was persuaded in 1661 by Bishop Pierce of Bath and Wells to receive episcopal ordination, and published a defence of his action. Shortly, however, he repented, renounced his Anglican orders, and was deprived of his vicarage of Frome Selwood in 1662. Thereafter he became minister of various Independent congregations in London, where he continued to exercise his ministry till his ninety-ninth year. In his vindication, entitled *The Question of Re-ordination*, published in 1661, he argued:

I will distinguish then between what Ordination is required to the setting apart a man to the office of a Minister in the sight of God, and what is requisite to the making him received a Minister among men, and give him authority (or full repute)

[1] C. G. de la Mothe, *Correspondence Fraternelle de l'Église Anglicane avec les autres Églises Reformées et Étrangères*, p. 83 (The Hague, 1705).

to execute that office in the church or place where he shall be called. I believe (as before) that Ordination by the Presbytery only (sufficing but a little while ago to both,) suffices still to the former, (supposing Ordination goes so far). But we all begin to know also that ordination now by a Bishop is necessary to the latter; and consequently, though I have been ordained before by the Presbytery, this hinders not, but that I may be ordained again by the Bishop; because I seek not to be ordained by him to make me a Minister again, which I am *in foro Dei* already, but to have Authority (as to men) to use my Ministry, and be received as such, (which I cannot else) *in foro Ecclesiae Anglicanae.* ... In short, there is my Ministry, and the use of my Ministry in the English Church. My first ordination (as we suppose) hath given me the one; yet is the latter not superfluous, because it conduces (and that legally and regularly) to the other.[1]

Furthermore, a parallel was drawn between this requirement of the church of England and the traditional practice of some of the foreign reformed churches. Thus Whitgift, in refusing to accept the argument of Walter Travers that his presbyterian ordination received in the Low Countries could not be repeated, had rejoined that

the French churches practise otherwise, neither will they admit any of our ministers, ordained according to the laws of this church, to exercise his function among them, without a new kind of calling according to their platform.[2]

The same was affirmed by Jeremy Taylor, who stated that

it is their constant and resolved practice at least in France, that if any returns to them they will reordain him by their presbytery, though he had before episcopal ordination; as both their friends and their enemies bear witness.[3]

After the act of uniformity of 1662, Joseph Bingham

---

[1] John Humfrey, Minister, *The Question of Re-ordination, whether, and how a Minister ordained by the Presbytery, may take Ordination also by a Bishop; Published for the sake of the many concerned and perplexed about it at this season, without strife, for the promotion only of the Holy Gospel and peace*, pp. 18–20 (London, 1661).

[2] J. Strype, *Life of Whitgift*, vol. III, p. 183.   [3] J. Taylor, *Works*, vol. V, p. 119.

specifically defended its requirement by reference to Geneva and France, maintaining that

there is nothing in it contrary to the principles or practice of Geneva, nor perhaps of the whole French church ... wherefore, if it be lawful at Geneva for a minister to receive a new ordination, because the laws require it, I do not see what can make it unlawful in England to submit to the same thing, in compliance with the law, when men have no other regular way to settle themselves in any cure; let their opinion of their former ordination be what it will, which comes not into the present dispute. For, even supposing their former ordination to be valid, I show, they may submit to a new ordination without sin; and if they will be peaceable, they ought to do it after the example of Geneva.[1]

But although such explanations eased the yoke, they did not explain the differential treatment accorded to Roman priests over Protestant presbyters; and during the negotiations in the reign of Queen Anne for a union of the Lutheran and Reformed churches in the dominions of the king of Prussia, through the mediation of the church of England, the Prussian minister in London, M. Bonet, warned his fellow-countrymen that Anglican opinion attached greater importance to episcopacy than to liturgy and ceremonies:

La conformité qu'on peut souhaiter par deçà regardera moins un changement dans la liturgie et dans le rituel, que dans le gouvernement ecclésiastique; on est ici pour l'épiscopal, qu'on regarde du moins comme d'institution Apostolique. La plus part du clergé ici est dans la prévention, qu'il y a une succession non interrompue depuis les apôtres jusques à présent; et suivant cette supposition ils prétendent qu'il n'y a point de bon gouvernement ecclésiastique que celui où il se rencontre des évêques de cet ordre, ni des véritables ministres de l'Évangile, que ceux qui ont été ordinés par des évêques. Et si d'autres ne vont pas si loin, ils font toujours une grande différence entre les

---

[1] J. Bingham, *Works*, vol. ix, pp. 296–7.

ministres de l'Évangile qui ont reçue l'imposition des mains d'un évêque, ou d'un synode composé des ministres ordinaires.[1]

In this report M. Bonet presented a more rigid view than that set forth by M. de la Mothe; for the reign of Anne witnessed a high-church revival after the somewhat chilling rule of William and Mary. But throughout this negotiation for the bestowal of a valid episcopate on the Protestant churches of Prussia, together with a liturgy closely modelled on the Anglican Book of Common Prayer, it was significant that the leaders in England were all high-churchmen; one of whom, George Smalbridge, afterwards bishop of Bristol, expressed the opinion that

> we should be importunate with them to receive episcopacy; and if, after being called upon and shewn that the reception of it is practicable, they will still obstinately refuse to embrace it, we shall not be obliged to entertain the same charitable opinion of them, which we and those who have gone before us have hitherto done.[2]

This frank statement was equally important as testimony of the general allowance made by high-churchmen for the foreign reformed churches traditionally in the past, and as evidence of a desire to make an end to temporising and pleas of ineluctable historical necessity by pressing upon them the duty of restoring episcopacy, now that it could be had from an unimpeachably reformed source in the church of England.

With respect to the theory of episcopacy to which Anglicans were committed by their insistence on episcopal ordination for ministry in their church, Dr William Nicholls, rector of Selsey and canon of Chichester, who

---

[1] T. Sharp, *Life of John Sharp*, ii, appendix ii, no. viii. Cited in N. Sykes, *Daniel Ernst Jablonski and the Church of England*, p. 20 (S.P.C.K., 1950).

[2] N. Sykes, *op. cit.* p. 16, citing Ballard MSS. (Bodleian Library), vii, f. 16 (1708).

maintained a vigorous and extensive correspondence with foreign divines, explained to Professor Pictet of Geneva that no belief that episcopacy was *divino jure* was required:

> You think, most learned sir, that whoever is ordained amongst us, is obliged by the obligation of an oath to accept episcopacy as ordained by divine right. What private individuals think on this matter is of little importance; but no such subscription is required by public authority. We do indeed subscribe that the Anglican Liturgy contains nothing contrary to the Word of God. But there is nothing in that Liturgy nor in its rubrics which asserts in so many words the divine right of episcopacy. In the Preface to the formularies of Ordination it is merely stated that 'It is evident unto all men diligently reading Holy Scripture and ancient Authors, that from the Apostles' time there have been these Orders of Ministers in Christ's Church: Bishops, Priests, and Deacons.' Even this clause, which does not affirm the divine right of episcopacy, is not read in Church, nor is it the Liturgy itself but only a Preface to this Office of the Liturgy.[1]

In even more positive terms did Archbishop Wake assure Professor Turrettini of Geneva that he believed

> the Church of Geneva has no exceptions against either our Liturgy or our Thirty-Nine Articles, even the 36th not excepted; which only asserts the validity of our Book of Ordination, but does not affirm the necessity of the three Orders which we retain in our Church.[2]

---

[1] Tenison MSS. 676, Pars Prima, f. 1, Nicholls to Pictet 10, Kal. Dec. 1708: 'Arbitraris Tu, vir doctissime, quod quilibet apud nos ordinandus est, debet agnoscere subscriptionis religione, episcopatum esse jure divino constitutum. Quid privati homines de hac re sentiant parum interest; sed nulla talis subscriptio a publica authoritate requiritur. Nos quidam subscribimus Liturgiam Anglicanam nihil continere Verbo Dei contrarium. Sed nihil est in Liturgia ipsa vel in Rubricis, quod Jus Divinum episcopatus verbis directis asserat. Tantum dicitur in Praefatione ante formulas Ordinationis: Notum est omnibus diligenter Sacram Scripturam et antiquos Authores Legentibus, ab Apostolicis usque temporibus, tres ministrorum gradus in Christi Ecclesia fuisse, Episcopos, Presbyteros, et Diaconos. Jam hac clausula, uti jus divinum episcopatus minime ponit, ita nunquam in Ecclesia legenda est, nec tam ipsa est Liturgia quam cujusdem in Liturgia officii praefatio.' [2] Geneva MSS. Inventaire, 1569, f. 85, 5 Dec. 1720.

Furthermore, in a Form of Service for the reception of converts into the Church of England, drawn up by Convocation in 1714, if the candidate had been a teacher in a nonconformist congregation, he was only required to 'allow and approve of the orders of bishops, priests, and deacons as what have been in the church from the time of the Apostles'.[1]

After the Restoration, however, the church of England was faced by a new problem in its domestic history, namely the conferment of presbyterian ordination in this country during the Interregnum. Before the civil war the only cases of persons in presbyterian orders claiming to minister in the church of England had been presbyters of the foreign reformed churches themselves, or Englishmen allowably ordained abroad during the Marian persecutions, or not allowably having sought foreign presbyterian ordination since 1559. During the Interregnum, however, the church of England had been first disestablished and then proscribed, and presbyterian ordination had been allowed by law. By the act of uniformity of 1662, therefore, all ministers of the restored church of England were required to receive episcopal ordination; and St Bartholomew's Day of that year saw the exodus of many incumbents intruded during the Commonwealth. But their ejection did not put an end to consideration of the possibility of such a reconciliation of the episcopal and presbyterian traditions as might yet result in a comprehensive established church. During the Interregnum indeed John Gauden, a conformist Anglican who was to become bishop successively of Exeter and Worcester after the Restoration, had entered into correspondence with Nicholas Bernard, sometime chaplain and librarian to Archbishop Ussher

[1] E. Cardwell, *Synodalia*, vol. II, p. 802.

and afterwards chaplain and almoner to Cromwell, about the possibility of *rapprochement*. Gauden began by recording his impression that

the minds of ministers . . . be moved towards a fraternal accord, [including] even episcopal men, whose antipathies seemed irreconcilable, [but who in 1656 were] upon a very calm temper. [He hoped] that the succession of ministerial order and authority might be preserved most unquestionable by the happy accord of bishops and presbyters; [and that] there might be presidency and counsel in the government of the church.

In a second letter he was still more optimistic

of beating our swords into ploughshares, since I find the animosities and distances of the episcopal and presbyterian parties much abated; who having little advanced their private or public interests by their scufflings about government and discipline, begin now to see, that their joint concernment as to the honour and succession of their ministerial function depends much upon their fraternal harmony and union.

As bases of concord were suggested

a bishop or president . . . among the presbyters chosen by them, *durante vita benegesta*; that nothing should be done in ordination or other great actions without the president and the major part of the presbyters; . . . and that actions passed in common should be under no divided notion, but as united in a joint society. [Furthermore,] the succession of presidential or episcopal power should be orderly derived or transmitted from those bishops now remaining, [so that] there might be no interruption or intercalation in point of succession; [lest otherwise] we are like to leave to posterity not a seamless coat but scarce such rags and parcels as will cover their nakedness.

Gauden admitted candidly that the English episcopacy had been 'somewhat warped by secular policies and private men's frailties from the primitive pattern and simplicity'; and therefore he favoured Ussher's project. In his third letter he expressed the hope that the agreed form of church polity might combine the three elements of episcopal presidency, counsel of the presbyters, and consent of the people:

I am of opinion that it is not only easy, but the best and safest way, to reconcile these three in one, so as no part should have cause to complain with any modesty or charity.

In conclusion he earnestly advocated

a fair conciliation, as it did of old, when nothing was done without the consent of the presbytery or common council, yet by the moderation and under the presidency of one, whom they chose to be chief among them, according to the pattern received from the first times.

But nothing could be done to effect this constitutional church reform except by the initiative of Cromwell as Lord Protector, and Gauden's hopes remained therefore unrealised; nor were they destined to realisation at the Restoration church settlement.[1]

Notwithstanding the severe setback to presbyterian hopes in 1662, Richard Baxter with Drs Bates and Manton entered into a series of conferences in 1668 with Bishops Wilkins and Reynolds and Drs Burton, Tillotson, and Stillingfleet; at which the form of subscription required of ministers, sundry changes desired by the presbyterians in the Book of Common Prayer, and the optional use of the 'nocent ceremonies' were discussed. But, as Baxter observed, 'the grand stop in our treaty was about re-ordination'; upon which Wilkins, albeit he was brother-in-law to Oliver Cromwell, insisted that 'those consciences must be accommodated who took them for no ministers who were ordained without bishops'. The Anglicans therefore proposed

that such persons as in the late times of disorder have been ordained by Presbyters, shall be admitted to the exercise of the

---

[1] John Gauden to Nicholas Bernard, 1656, *State Papers of John Thurloe* (ed. Thomas Birch), vol. v, pp. 598–601 (London, 1742).

ministerial function by the imposition of the hands of the Bishop with this or the like form of words: 'Take thou authority to preach the Word of God and to minister the Sacraments in any Congregation of the Church of England where thou shalt be lawfully appointed thereunto.'

Baxter objected that the presbyterians could not consent to anything which seemed to signify reordination; and offered the alternative that ministers

ordained only by meer Presbyters ... shall be instituted and authorized to exercise their Ministry (and admitted to Benefices) therein, in such manner and by such persons as by his Majesty shall be thereto appointed, by this form and words alone (Take thou authority etc.) provided that those who desire it, have leave to give in their professions that they renounce not their Ordination, nor take it for a nullity, and that they take this as the Magistrates' License and Confirmation, and that they be not constrained to use any words themselves which are not consistent with this profession.

Since Wilkins in his turn would not accept this formal statement concerning the validity of presbyterian ordination—'where', noted Baxter, 'was our greatest stop and disagreement'—it was finally agreed that

instead of the liberty to declare the validity of our ordination, which would not be endured, ... the terms of Collation should be these: 'Take thou Legal Authority to preach the Word of God, and administer the holy Sacraments in any Congregation of England, where thou shalt be lawfully appointed thereunto': That so the word *Legal* might shew that it was only a general Licence from the king that we received, by what minister soever he pleased to deliver it. And if it were a Bishop, we declared that we should take it from him but as the king's Minister.[1]

At a later date, in 1675, when these abortive discussions were renewed, Baxter put forward his draft of 'An

[1] *Reliquiae Baxterianae* (ed. Matthew Sylvester, London, 1696), pt. III, pp. 25, 35, 34 *bis*.

Act for the Healing and Concord of his Majesty's Subjects in matters of Religion', which included the following provision concerning ordination:

That all such persons as before this time have been ordained as Presbyters by Parochial Pastors only, and are qualified for that office as the Law requireth, shall receive power to exercise it, from a Bishop by a written Instrument (which every Bishop in his diocese is hereby impowered and required to grant) in these words and no other: 'To A. B. of C. in the Country of D. Take thou authority to exercise the Office of a Presbyter, in any place and Congregation in the King's Dominions whereto thou shalt be lawfully called.' And this practice sufficing for present concord, no one shall be put to declare his judgement, whether this, or that which he before received, shall be taken for his Ordination, nor shall be urged to speak any words of such signification; but each party shall be left to judge as they see cause.[1]

Although these conferences led to no practical result, there were interesting echoes of their discussions in the proposals made in 1689 by the royal commissioners, appointed to present both to Convocation and Parliament a project for the Comprehension of Presbyterians and Episcopalians in the Church of England. For the commissioners proposed to insert the following prefatory provisions to the Ordinal:

Seeing the Reformed Churches abroad are in that imperfect state that they cannot receive ordination [marginal addition: *at home*] from Bishops. It is humbly proposed whether they may not be received by an Imposition of a Bishop's hands [*elsewhere*] in these or such like words: 'Take thou authority to preach the Word of God and to minister the Holy Sacraments in this Church as [*where*] thou shalt be lawfully appointed thereunto.'

Whereas it has been the constant practice of the ancient Church to allow of no ordinations of Priests (that is, Presbyters) or Deacons without a Bishop, and that it has been likewise the constant practice of this Church ever since the Reformation to allow none that were not ordained by Bishops, where they could

---

[1] *Reliquiae Baxterianae* (ed. Matthew Sylvester, London, 1696), pt. III, p. 159.

be had; yet in regard that several in this kingdom have of late years been ordained only by Presbyters, the Church being desirous to do all that can be done for peace, and in order to the healing of our divisions, has thought fit to receive such as have been ordained by Presbyters only, to be ordained according to this Office, with the addition of these words in these following places:

Archdeacon: Reverend Father in God, I present unto you these persons present to be admitted to the Order of Priesthood, *if they have not been already ordained.*

Bishop: Good people, these are they whom we purpose, God willing, to receive this day unto the holy office of Priesthood, *if they have not been already ordained.*

Bishop: Receive the Holy Ghost for the Office and Work of a Priest in the Church of God, now committed unto thee by the imposition of our hands, *if thou hast not been already ordained.*

By which, as she retains her opinion and practice which makes a Bishop necessary to the giving of Orders, where he can be had, so she does likewise leave all such persons as have been ordained by Presbyters only the freedom of their own thoughts concerning their former ordinations. It being withall expressly provided that this shall never be a precedent for the time to come; and that it shall only be granted to such as have been ordained before the   day of   : The Letters of Orders are to be given them in so much of the Form as was used in Ireland upon the return of king Charles II to his kingdoms by Bramhall, archbishop of Armagh.[1]

Although the commissioners' proposals were never debated in Convocation, owing to the unfavourable reception which it was anticipated they would encounter, their provisions regarding ordination were important as stating the historic tradition of the church of England in relation to the foreign reformed churches, and as reflecting contemporary opinion amongst men of latitude.

[1] Lambeth Palace Library: The Book of Common Prayer with the emendations proposed in 1689, inserted in the handwriting of Thomas Tenison. Secker MSS. 12.

During the quarter of a century between the Restoration and the Revolution, there was much discussion also both in England and Scotland of projects for the coalescence of episcopacy and presbyterianism as forms of church polity, with particular reference to the suggestions of Archbishop James Ussher. Before the outbreak of the civil war, Ussher had published his *Reduction of Episcopacy unto the form of Synodical Government received in the Ancient Church* as a means of composing differences in England. By it he proposed: first, that in every parish there should be a weekly session of the incumbent together with the churchwardens and sidesmen, to reprove and if necessary to excommunicate scandalous members of the congregation; secondly, that there should be a restoration of suffragan bishops, equal in number to the rural deaneries and representing the *chorepiscopi* of the ancient church, who should assemble a monthly meeting of all their incumbents, to deal with stubborn offenders who were impervious to parochial reproof, and to consider the doctrine and conversation of ministers of their areas; thirdly, that a diocesan synod meeting once or twice a year, consisting of suffragan bishops and parochial incumbents (either as a whole or by representation), and presided over by the diocesan bishop, should consider matters referred to it by the ruridecanal synods, and 'all matters of government' relating to the whole diocese; and fourthly, that there should be a provincial synod, composed of all diocesan and suffragan bishops together with representatives of the parochial clergy of each diocese, presided over by the primate of either province, and dealing with affairs of the greatest import; which, if its sessions were held triennially and coincided with the meeting of parliament (according to the recent triennial act), might unite the two provincial synods into one national synod: 'wherein all appeals from inferior synods might be received, all their acts examined; and all ecclesiastical constitutions which concern the state of the church of the whole nation established'.

In the exacerbated temper of the time, Ussher's proposals did not command the support of the Long Parliament, nor subsequently of the Westminster Assembly, which, thanks to the Solemn League and Covenant, proceeded to the proscription of episcopacy rather than to its reform; and this twin failure was of pregnant consequence for the future ecclesiastical history of both England and Scotland. For although on the return of Charles II the English presbyterians led by Baxter declared their readiness to accept 'the true, ancient, primitive episcopacy or presidency as it is balanced or managed by a due commixtion of presbytery therewith', and offered Ussher's scheme specifically 'as a groundwork towards accommodation and fraternal agreement in this point of ecclesiastical government', the episcopalians were determined to be revenged for the dispossession of their church during the interregnum and refused compromise. The Restoration church settlement, therefore, both in England and Scotland, was characterised by the assertion of episcopacy and the purging of the churches of recalcitrant ministers. Baxter notwithstanding in his conferences with Anglican divines continued to advocate comprehension on the basis of 'the settling of church government according to that of Archbishop Ussher's model'.

It was in Scotland, however, that the saintly and moderate Robert Leighton, successively bishop of Dunblane and archbishop of Glasgow, sought to realise practically this ideal of 'episcopacy attempered unto presbytery', in accordance with his conviction that 'episcopal government, managed in conjunction with presbyters in presbyteries and synods, is not contrary either to the rule of Scripture or the example of the primitive church, but most agreeable to both'. Accordingly he proposed the following heads of accommodation: that the church should be governed by the bishops and clergy together in their synods; that bishops should act therein only as presidents and should be determined by the majority of their presbyters, both in matters of jurisdiction and ordination; that the presbyterian ministers should be allowed to declare that they submitted to the presidency of the bishop only for peace's sake; that bishops should not claim a negative vote upon the decisions of their presbyters in synods; that they should ordain ministers to parishes with the concurrence of the presbytery and the approbation of the people; and that provincial synods should meet triennially at least, with power to receive complaints against the bishops and to censure them. Although this scheme overthrew the parity of ministers on the one hand, it also, as Burnet observed, 'left little more than the name of a bishop' on the other hand. Nevertheless, in a series of conferences held in 1670–1, Leighton went further in concession, proposing:

[first], that if the dissenting brethren will come to Presbyteries and Synods, they shall not only not be obliged to renounce their own private opinion concerning church government, or swear to subscribe anything contrary thereto, but shall have liberty at their entry to the said meetings to declare it, and enter it in what form they please; [secondly], that all church affairs shall be managed and concluded in Presbyteries and Synods by the free vote of the Presbyters, or the major part of them; [thirdly], if any difference fall out in the Diocesan Synod between any of the members thereof, it shall be lawful to appeal to a Provincial Synod or their Committee; [fourthly], that Intrants being law-

fully presented by the Patron and duly tried by the Presbytery, there shall be a day agreed upon by the Bishop and Presbytery for their meeting together for their solemn Ordination and admission, at which there shall be one appointed to preach, and that it shall be at the parish church to which they are to be admitted . . .; [fifthly, that legal security should be given for these provisions about presbyteries and synods and the freedom of speech therein; and sixthly,] that no Intrant shall be obliged to any Canonical Oath or Subscription to the Bishop; and that his opinion as to that government shall not prejudge him in this, but that it shall be free for him to declare it.[1]

These mediating proposals satisfied neither side; for Sharp 'cried out that episcopacy was to be undermined', and Hutchinson on behalf of the dissenting presbyterians declared that they were 'not free in conscience to close with the propositions' as satisfactory. In fact, the temper engendered by the Restoration settlement was antipathetic to reconciliation; and accordingly at the revolution both comprehension failed of realisation in England, and in Scotland the relics of episcopacy were cast out of the established church and presbyterianism restored without limitation.

Although the causes of the abolition of episcopacy and the restoration of presbyterianism in Scotland in 1689 were chiefly political, namely the refusal of the Scottish bishops to forswear allegiance to James II and to accept William III, their religious consequences were abiding. During the generation dividing the Restoration from the revolution, no attempt had been made in Scotland to impose the English liturgy. The revised Book of Common Prayer was used in the royal chapel at Holyrood, and by Gilbert Burnet in his parish of Salton, but hardly anywhere else. The liturgical differences between

---

[1] Burnet, *History of My Own Times*, bk. II, sub annis 1669, 1670. D. Butler, *Life and Letters of Robert Leighton*. The *Remains* of Leighton (ed. W. West).

episcopalian and presbyterian centred in the use by the former of the Lord's Prayer, the Doxology, and perhaps the Creed; and for a time even after the revolution these were the principal distinguishing marks of episcopalian and presbyterian congregations. But as the episcopal minority were driven to seek financial and political support from their brethren of the church of England, so also they came to adopt the English Book of Common Prayer. After 1690 the vicissitudes in ecclesiastical polity in the church of Scotland which had characterised the previous century and a quarter came to an end.

In England also the failure of the comprehension project led to an accentuation of the breach between Anglicans and the Protestant Dissenters. Almost the only important survival from the recent past was the custom of occasional communion. In its origins this practice was purely religious and eirenical, and without political reference or significance. When Edmund Calamy led a deputation of Dissenters to impress on Burnet in 1702 their grounds of opposition to the Occasional Conformity Bill (which he was inclined to regard with some degree of favour), they told him that occasional communion

had been used by some of the most eminent of our ministers ever since 1662, with a design to shew their charity towards that church, notwithstanding they apprehended themselves bound in conscience ordinarily to separate from it; and that it had long been practised by a number of the most understanding people among them, before the doing so was necessary to qualify for a place. We reminded him that Mr Baxter and Dr Bates had done it all along ... and added that should the bill then depending pass into law, it ... would bid fair to destroying that little charity yet remaining among us, and make the breach between the two parties wider than ever.[1]

[1] E. Calamy, *A Historical Account of My Own Life*, vol. 1, p. 473.

To the names of Baxter and Bates could be added John Howe, who

had openly declared for this occasional conformity, before communicating with the established church was a necessary qualification for a place in the magistracy [and was further of opinion that] though to that former sort of communion there hath for many years bypast been superadded the accidental consideration of a place or office attainable hereby, no man can allow himself to think that what he before counted lawful is by this supervening consideration become unlawful.

In this practice most of the leading Dissenting ministers joined, as Howe affirmed:

Most of the considerable ejected London ministers met, and agreed to hold occasional communion with the now re-established church—not quitting their own ministry, or declining the exercise of it as they could have opportunity. And as far as I could by enquiry learn, I can little doubt this to have been the judgment of their fellow-sufferers through the nation in great part ever since.[1]

The continuance of this healing custom and its welcome from the Anglican side were testified to not only by whig prelates such as Archbishop Tenison and bishops Patrick and Burnet, but also by the high-church tory Archbishop Sharp of York, who assured the Dissenter Ralph Thoresby of Leeds of his approval of his communicating monthly at St John's parish church, and censured the criticism of his action by some of his fellow-nonconformists as showing 'what schismatical principles some of the Dissenters are acted by'.[2]

---

[1] E. Calamy, *Life of John Howe*, vol. I, pp. 68, 70. R. F. Horton, *John Howe*, p. 83.

[2] *Letters of Eminent Men to Ralph Thoresby*, vol. I, p. 320. Cf. T. Pierce, *The New Discoverer Discovered*: 'Notwithstanding the heinous and horrid things which you have done and we suffered, God and the world is our witness, we do not shut you out from our Communion ... if you, by name [Richard Baxter], should have occasion to pass this way and present yourself with other guests, at the Holy Supper of the Lord, no man on Earth would be more welcomed.'

But although the latitudinarian temper of the eighteenth century was favourable to the continuance of such practices, it did nothing positively to further the design of 'comprehension'. From the Dissenters' side Philip Doddridge and Dr Chandler made eirenic approaches to Archbishops Herring and Secker and to Bishop Sherlock. Chandler indeed went so far as to offer that, whilst none of his presbyterian brethren would renounce their ordination, yet 'if their lordships meant only to impose hands on us, and by that rite recommend us to public service in their society or constitution, that perhaps might be submitted to'. Herring welcomed the suggestion, describing comprehension as 'a very good thing, he wished it with all his heart' and even thought 'this was a proper time to make the attempt'; but his naturally timorous nature and his maxim *quieta non movere* prevented his making any practical effort to act on Chandler's proposal, or on an alternative idea of Doddridge. The latter indeed advocated

a sort of medium between the present state and that of a perfect coalition, which was that of acknowledging our churches as unschismatical by permitting their clergy to officiate among us, if desired, which he must see had a counterpart of permitting Dissenting ministers occasionally to officiate in churches. It struck him much as a new and very important thought; and he told me more than once, that I had suggested what he should lay up in his mind for further consideration.[1]

Even Secker, though agreeing with Doddridge

heartily in wishing that such things as we think indifferent and you cannot be brought to think lawful, were altered or left free in such a manner that we might all unite, [and assuring him that he had] no reason to believe that any one of the bishops wishes otherwise, and I know some that wish it strongly ... nor

[1] *The Correspondence and Diary of Philip Doddridge* (ed. J. D. Humphreys), vol. v, pp. 42, 75.

perhaps were the body of the clergy ever so well disposed to it as now, [nevertheless added as a final word:] but still I see not the least prospect of it.[1]

The atmosphere of the new dynasty indeed

> When George in pudding-time came o'er
> And moderate men looked big, Sir,

was averse to bold and venturesome projects, in church no less than in state; and the official toleration granted to orthodox Protestant Dissenters in 1689 led to a relaxation of their efforts, whilst they were seriously weakened by the theological controversies which shortly divided them. It is to the relations of the church of England with the foreign Protestant churches therefore that attention must be turned in order to estimate the results of the revolution of 1688 on ecclesiastical projects of union.

[1] *Ibid.* vol. IV, p. 272.

VI

'THE TIMES OF IGNORANCE'

'Our case as to a full satisfaction of communion with the foreign churches', wrote Archbishop Wake to Arthur Charlett on 4 June 1707

is in my opinion very different from theirs with respect to us. They cannot except against our ministry nor the validity of the ordinances which may be supposed to depend upon it. Our clergy are certainly duly ordained, whatever theirs are who want episcopal ordination. And though the case be vastly different between communicating with the Protestants abroad and our Separatists here at home, yet I believe no one who could have the opportunity of an episcopal church even in foreign countries, would make any doubt whether he should choose to partake of some of the Gospel ministrations with that or with those of the presbyterian way. My charity leads me to think, and hope and judge the best of them. But yet I cannot think them so conformable to, at least, the apostolical pattern and establishment, as if they were settled on the same episcopal constitution as our church is.[1]

This differentiation between the foreign Protestants and domestic Dissenters was characteristic of the position of churchmen of Wake's times; as was his preference when abroad for an episcopal to a presbyterian ministry and sacraments. Even Gilbert Burnet combined occasional communion with the foreign reformed churches with regular communion with the church of England:

I was myself an occasional conformist in Geneva and Holland. I thought their churches were irregularly formed, under great defects in their constitution, yet I thought communion with

[1] Ballard MSS., III, f. 83.

142

them was lawful, for their worship was not corrupted; but at the same time I continued my communion with our own church according to the Liturgy of this church with all that came about me. And if the designs of some of the promoters of this Bill [the Occasional Conformity Bill] should be brought about, and I driven beyond sea . . . I in that case would communicate with the foreign churches, but would likewise gather all of this church about me and still continue to worship God according to the Liturgy to my life's end. So I think occasional conformity with a less perfect church may well consist with the continuing to worship God in a more perfect one.[1]

There was indeed a well-established tradition of the welcoming to communion in the church of England of foreign Protestants, both Lutheran and Reformed, when visiting England. Bishop John Davenant of Salisbury, a delegate to the Synod of Dort, had written of the Saxon and Helvetian churches that 'surely, as concerning us, although we consent not with them in all points and titles of controversial divinity, yet we acknowledge them brethren in Christ and protest ourselves to have a brotherly and holy communion with them'.[2] The translation of these general sentiments into practice was reflected in the attitude of Bishop Peter Gunning of Ely, whose chaplain claimed that

there is not one settled church established by public authority that he is not at concord withal, and holds Christian communion, and would actually embrace and receive to his prayers and sacraments, and count as members of the same mystical body whereof Christ is the head, though he does not agree with them in their errors and singularities, and only differs from them where they depart from the scripture and the catholic church.

Amongst the churches 'which do approve of our

1 Cobbett, *Parliamentary History*, vol. VI, col. 164 *seq.*
2 J. Davenant, *Exhortation to Brotherly Communion betwixt the Protestant Churches*, p. 33 (1614 edition).

communion and are upon occasion admitted to it', there were specified:

First, does not his Highness the Prince of Orange and his noble and honourable retinue join in communion with us, as often as they have occasion to come over hither; and are not any of their ministers and others of the Dutch churches publicly permitted to come to our communion? And do we not thereby own them for Christians and fellow-members of the same catholic church? And do they not thereby own us for the like? . . . If at any time the French Protestants come over to our country, do we not likewise profess our concord with them in the substantial principles of the Christian religion? Come we likewise to consider the remains of the ancient Bohemians, do we not hold all friendly communion with them? . . . The same charity and concord is always shewn to the Lutheran churches, some of whom have often communicated with the lord bishop of Ely. . . . The like concord I can show with the Helvetian, Hungarian, and Transilvanian churches, and all that profess the catholic faith.[1]

Further, John Cosin, bishop of Durham after the Restoration, during his exile in Paris in the commonwealth times,

never refused to join with the Protestants either here or anywhere else in all things wherein they join with the church of England. Many of them have been here at our church, and we have been at theirs. . . . I have baptized many of their children at the request of their own ministers. . . . Many of their people . . . have frequented our public prayers with great reverence, and I have delivered the holy communion to them according to our own order, which they observed religiously. I have married divers persons of good condition among them; and I have presented some of their scholars to be ordained deacons and priests here by our own bishops, . . . and the church at Charenton approved of it; and I preached here publicly at their ordination. Besides I have been (as often as I had spare time from attending to our own congregation) to pray and sing psalms with them, and to hear both their weekly and the Sunday sermons at Charenton.[2]

[1] W. Saywell, *Evangelical and Catholic Unity* (*A Vindication of Peter, Lord Bishop of Ely*), pp. 300, 302-4.   [2] J. Cosin, *Works* (L.A.C.T.), vol. IV, pp. 397-8.

Strikingly similar was Wake's account of his own custom during his residence in Paris as chaplain to the British ambassador, Lord Preston:

As to our practice abroad, we went ordinarily every other Sunday to Charenton, but none of us ever received the Holy Eucharist there. In this they were more free with us. I have given the Sacrament to some of their ministers publicly in their own chapel, and to Monsieur Menard in particular while he was actually one of the pastors of the church at Charenton. By certificates from their ministers and antients (without which I never did it) I have many times both baptized their children and buried their dead. And I never heard any exception taken against it. How ready those of Geneva were to consent to the bishop of Sarum's officiating openly in one of their churches and giving the Holy Sacrament to our English in that city, you have doubtless heard.[1]

It was indeed precisely upon the basis of this accepted tradition that Wake rested his argument for a corresponding practice between members of the Anglican and Gallican churches:

The surest way will be to begin as well and go as far as we can in settling a friendly correspondence one with another; to agree to own each other as true brethren, and members of the catholic, christian church; to agree to communicate in everything we can with one another. . . . The Lutherans do this very thing. Many of them communicate not only in our prayers, but in the communion with us; and we never enquire whether they believe consubstantiation, or even pay any worship to Christ as present with the elements, so long as their outward actions are the same as our own, and they give no offence to any with their opinions.[2]

Such were the customs established before the revolution of 1688. Moreover during the high-church revival in the reign of Anne, cordial relations were maintained

1 Ballard MSS., III, f. 40, 21 April 1707.
2 N. Sykes, *William Wake*, vol. I, p. 292.

with the foreign reformed churches; and it was as important as significant that the lead in these matters was taken by avowed high-churchmen. Prominent in the assertion of the principles of high-churchmanship was the university of Oxford, the very seat of Anglican orthodoxy and loyalty. Accordingly when, in an ephemeral academic exercise entitled *Strenae Oxonienses* in 1705 the church of Geneva detected aspersions upon itself, a formal protest was sent by the professors and pastors to Bishop Compton to be forwarded to the university. In particular the Genevese insisted emphatically that they were

so far from having any dislike to the church of England that on the contrary we have always had a singular esteem for her. Nor have any of us, when we have been in England, avoided her Congregations and Communion. . . . Our Rites are such as the Government of the State and the exigence and necessity of our affairs have required; but we neither condemn nor despise those that are different from our own.[1]

To this representation the university made a formal answer, 'in a full assembly of all the doctors, regents, and non-regents', on 12 February 1706, which expressed exactly the standpoint of contemporary high-churchmen:

Our opinion has always been the same with yours concerning the lawfulness of different Rites in different Churches. You will find it to be the doctrine of our Liturgy and of our Articles, that each particular Church hath a right to prescribe ceremonies to its own peoples; and that one Church ought not to condemn another for using Rites different from its own.

---

[1] 'Tantum abest ut ab Ecclesia Anglicana animus noster alienus sit, ut potius semper eam magni fecerimus, nec ullus nostrum dum in Anglia versatus est, ab ejus coetibus *aut synaxi* recesserit. . . . Eos Ritus quidem habemus quales Reipublicae gubernatio et necessitas postularunt; verum a nostris dissimiles nec rejicimus nec in contemptum adducimus.' (*Literae a celeberrimis Pastoribus et Professoribus Ecclesiae et Academiae Genevensis ad Universitatem Oxoniensem transmissae una cum Responsio ejusdem Universitatis Oxon.*)

We are far from being so uncharitable or rigorous in our judgement as peremptorily to condemn those Reformed Churches and to esteem them utterly destitute of Lawful Pastors and of Sacraments duly administered, which, by an irresistible necessity, have much against their will been compelled to swerve from the ancient form of Episcopal Government. Our most celebrated divines are far from passing such censure upon your church, who, whilst they have been abroad, have willingly joined with you in your Sacred Offices. . . . It were indeed to be wished that the ancient form of Church Government by Bishops, which the Apostles, who were instructed by Christ himself, the Author of our Faith, and who were endowed with an extraordinary measure of the Holy Ghost, did institute, might still obtain throughout the whole Christian world. This ancient government, first founded by a more than human authority, and by the Divine Providence derived without interruption from the times of the Apostles to the present age, we, by the special goodness of God, do still retain. . . . The Protestant Interest would certainly be in a more flourishing condition than it now is, if those who hold fast the same primitive Faith, did also agree in retaining the same primitive discipline; and the war in which we are engaged against the tyranny of the Pope, would be carried on with much greater success, if, whilst we oppose the impious and most detestable innovations of the Romish church, our forces were all joined together under the same ancient and Apostolical Form of Government.[1]

1 'De Rituum apud Ecclesias diversas varietate quae Vestra est, Viri Illustrissimi, eadem et nostra semper fuit sententia. Id enim in Liturgia nostra, id in Religionis Articulis expressum reperietis; fas esse unicuique Ecclesiae in ritibus praescribendis jus suum in suos exercere; nefas esse ut altera alteram incuset, quod ritus a suis discrepantes receperit. Alienissimum est a nostra charitate Ecclesias illas Reformatas, quae, ineluctabili necessitatis lege adactae, a primaeva Episcopalis regiminis forma haud sponte sua recesserunt, tanquam legitimis Pastoribus aut Sacramentis rite administratis penitus destitutas, rigida nimis censura damnare; a judicio hoc de Ecclesia vestra ferendo longe semper abfuerunt a Theologis nostris celeberrimi, qui peregre commorantes Sacris vestris lubenter interfuerunt. . . . Id sane optandum erat, ut antiqua illa Ecclesiae per Episcopos gubernandae ratio, quam Apostoli a Christo ipso, fidei nostrae Auctore, edocti et pleniori Sancti Spiritus mensura perfusi instituerunt, per universum orbem Christianum etiamnum vigeret. Hanc Nos disciplinam auctoritate plusquam humana fundatam, ac divina providentia per omnia quae ab Apostolorum usque temporibus fluxerunt saecula ad Nos transmissam, non sine singulari Dei bene-

It was in accordance with this tradition, as exemplified by the Genevan assertion of the custom of their churchmen when in England to present themselves at the holy communion, that in 1709 during the parliamentary debates on a bill for the naturalisation of foreign Protestants, high-church opinion as stated by Bishop Stratford of Chester in the House of Lords pressed as a condition of such naturalisation that these Protestants be required to 'receive the Sacrament according to the Church of England', and protested against the alternative, proposed and carried by the whigs, of communion 'in any Protestant church' in this kingdom.

Equally typical of high-church conviction was the contemporary negotiation for an union of the Lutheran and Reformed churches in the dominions of the king of Prussia on the basis of an episcopate bestowed by Anglican bishops and a German version of the Book of Common Prayer. This project was conceived by Dr Daniel Ernst Jablonski, bishop of the *Unitas Fratrum*, and court-preacher at Berlin; who during his residence in England between 1680 and 1683 had formed a cordial appreciation of and affection for the Anglican liturgy and polity, which inspired the oecumenical ideals of his long life.[1] To this end he drew into correspondence some of the principal high-churchmen of the reign of Anne: Archbishop Sharp of York, Dr George Smalridge, canon and dean of Christ Church and subsequently

---

ficentia retinemus. . . . Faelicius certe Reformatorum Res procederent, si qui eandem primaevam fidem tenent, eandem etiam primaevam Disciplinam amplecterentur; et meliori successu bellum Papali tyrannidi inductum gereretur, si contra impias, piisque omnibus detestandas Pontificiorum innovationes, conjunctis, sub antiqua Apostolici regiminis forma copiis militaremus.' (*Responsio*, 12 February 1706.)

[1] N. Sykes, *Daniel Ernst Jablonski and the Church of England: A study of an Essay towards Protestant Union* (London, S.P.C.K., 1950); E. Benz, *Bischofsamt und apostolische Sukzession im deutschen Protestantismus* (Stuttgart, 1953).

bishop of Bristol, and Dr John Robinson, bishop of Bristol. Smalridge commended the scheme to Sharp as one 'which may tend so much to the glory of God and the good of his church', and 'in which the honour of your own church and the edification of foreign churches seem to be so much interested'. The northern primate lent it enthusiastic support; whilst Francis Atterbury, the leading protagonist of the lower house of Canterbury Convocation in its controversy with the upper house, likewise gave it his blessing; so that the lower house, taking note 'of the present endeavours of several re-formed churches to accommodate themselves to our li-turgy and constitution', desired the counsel of the bishops

in what manner it may be proper for this convocation, with Her Majesty's leave and encouragement, to express their great satisfaction to find them in such good dispositions, and their readiness to maintain and cherish such a fraternal corres-pondence with them, as may strengthen the interest of the reformed religion against the common enemy.

This readiness of high-churchmen to enter into negoti-ation with foreign Protestants for the restoration of epis-copacy and a version of the Anglican liturgy was emphasised by the aloofness and coldness of the low-church Archbishop Tenison of Canterbury; so that the queen's secretary of state, St John, was at pains to assure the Prussian court that his grace's attitude was 'directly contrary' to the 'general inclination and avowed sense' of the English clergy, who were anxious to 'join with the bishops in promoting a closer correspondence between the two churches'. Although political differ-ences frustrated the hopes of the bishops and clergy, their zeal was beyond doubt.

The reply of the university of Oxford to the Genevan complaint seemed to Wake not only 'well-drawn', but

also such as 'ought not to give any just offence to any';
unless indeed to the non-jurors, apropos of whom he
asked the master of University College slyly, 'How will
Mr Dodwell and his friends like your free declaration
of your opinion concerning the foreign churches who
want bishops, and by that means have no ministry, no
sacraments, such as you allow those of Geneva to have?'[1]
Moreover it gave him an excellent jumping-off ground
for his own later efforts as archbishop of Canterbury to
draw closer the bonds between the church of England
and foreign Protestants. In reply to the chorus of con-
gratulation reaching him on his succession to the
primacy in 1716, he sought to initiate practical steps
towards this end. To Jean Le Clerc of Amsterdam he
expressed his fervent wish that the reformed churches
would restore episcopacy, affirmed—with a plain echo
of the words and sentiments of Andrewes—that he was
not so iron-breasted as to deny them a valid ministry
and sacraments, and urged agreement in polity as a
means to full union. To the Antistes of Zurich, Peter
Zeller, he went further; and together with the hope of
the reintroduction of episcopacy, he formally approved
and encouraged reciprocity of communion between
members of their church sojourning in England and
Anglicans visiting countries where the reformed religion
was the established church.[2] To Basle he wrote in similar
vein, acknowledging the agreement of their church with
his own in the fundamentals of faith, asserting that
differences in secondary matters should not be a barrier
to intercommunion, and appealing to the existing practice of reciprocal communion as evidence of his argument.

[1] Wake to Charlett, 21 April and 7 June 1707 (Ballard MSS., III, ff. 80, 83).

[2] 'Quotquot e nostris peregre ad vos proficiscuntur, ut juxta hanc sententiam
una vobiscum communicant, et permittimus et hortamur. Vestros hic agentes
libenter ad sacra nostra admittimus.'

With Dr J. F. Ostervald of Neuchâtel he went further still, exhorting him to complete the work which he had already begun through his introduction of a catechism and liturgy, by providing for the episcopal ordination of all future ministers, and hinting at the services of English bishops to this end. Furthermore, in a cordial and extensive correspondence with Jablonski, he accorded recognition to the Moravian Brethren as a true episcopal church and closest of all the Protestant churches to the English church.[1]

By giving thus formal authorisation and approval to reciprocity of communion between members of the church of England and those of foreign reformed churches sojourning respectively in each other's territories, Wake had taken a notable step forward in contemporary church relations. For whilst he had behind him an accepted tradition of welcoming Lutherans and Reformed to communicate with the Anglican church, there was no such unanimity of conviction or practice in respect of reciprocation of the custom on the part of English churchmen. On the one hand, for example, Cosin had advised Monsieur Testard

that both you and others that are with you, may (either in case of necessity when you cannot have the Sacrament among yourselves, or in regard of declaring your unity in professing the same religion, which you and they do), go otherwhiles to communicate reverently with them of the French Church.[2]

Similarly Ussher avowed that 'with the like affection I should receive the Blessed Sacrament at the hands of the Dutch ministers if I were in Holland as I should do at the hands of the French ministers if I were in Charenton'[3]; and even Sharp confessed that 'if he were abroad,

---

[1] N. Sykes, *William Wake*, vol. II, ch. I.
[2] Cosin, *Works*, vol. IV, p. 407.   [3] C. R. Elrington, *Life of Ussher*, p. 258.

he would willingly communicate with the Protestant churches where he should happen to be'.[1] Most remarkable of all, however, was the evidence of Dean Granville of Durham (afterwards a non-juror), whose advice about communicating with the French reformed was that

I conceive it your duty considering the circumstances we are and have been in, and like to be very much to edification. . . . [He was convinced that the foreign Protestants] were at their first Reformation and are still, in such circumstances that they could not then retain it [episcopacy], nor can have it now, if they would. . . . [Furthermore he thought it] a bad piece of service to Christendom and to the church of England itself, to unchurch therewith so great a part of Christendom as the reformed churches which want episcopal government, and to make our poor church of England a distinct thing from all other churches, and to stand by itself.[2]

On the other hand, many Anglican exiles during the interregnum had declined to communicate with the French reformed; included amongst whom were Bishops Bramhall and Sydserf and Dr George Morley and Richard Steward, whose grounds for refusal may perhaps be stated in the words of George Hickes, who also afterwards became a non-juror:

I freely own [he declared in 1707], that when I was in France thirty four years ago, I went to Charenton, and there received the Sacrament, and afterwards at Blois. But when I came to Montpellier, I declined the Sacrament, having by reading and conferring about the mission of the French Protestant ministers, altered my opinion.[3]

In recommending reciprocity of communion therefore Wake was advancing on his own former practice when resident in Paris and on that of many of his fellow-churchmen. But having recognised the validity of foreign

1 T. Sharp, *Life of John Sharp*, vol. 1, pp. 377–8.
2 R. Granville, *Life of Dennis Granville*, pp. 202–3.
3 A. J. Mason, *The Church of England and Episcopacy*, p. 322.

reformed ministries and sacraments, he took the logical step of approving and advising Anglicans sojourning abroad to communicate with the Protestant churches. Such an action, whenever performed, was warmly welcomed, as when in 1707 Ostervald commended cordially the reception of the communion at Geneva by the English envoy to the Swiss cantons: 'We regard this as an authentic sign of the sentiments which are felt in England towards our churches, and as a happy augury for that union so much desired.'[1] It was an especial misfortune, therefore, that all Wake's earnest endeavours towards this much-desired union failed of practical results. From the several churches of Switzerland to which he wrote, he received indeed many assurances of their respect for the English episcopacy and recognition of its services to the Protestant cause, but no readiness to adopt it in their own churches. The Antistes of Zurich replied that those who found the innocent term of bishop *invisum et exosum* should consider how great benefits bishops had procured for the Reformation and since in England and elsewhere; and should reflect that where agreement existed in doctrine, differences in regimen should not be grounds for contention. From Basle came the like assurance of unity in doctrine, and the affirmation that even in church government there would be no differences in principle if names and other externals (in which all agreed that the essence of religion did not consist) were laid aside. At Geneva the church, so far from condemning the Anglican episcopacy, reckoned it a peculiar felicity of the church of England, and accorded recognition to its ordinations. But beyond these formal compliments, nothing was even suggested towards the realisation of Wake's aspirations of a restoration of

[1] Ostervald to Werndly, 21 Oct. 1707 (Rawlinson MSS. 982, f. 14, Bodley).

the episcopal office and order in the foreign reformed churches. Except for his formal recognition of inter-communion, therefore, and the cultivation of friendly correspondence and understanding, his efforts produced little practical result.

The relationship of the church of England to the Lutheran churches received further important illus-tration and expression in the missionary enterprise supported by the Society for Promoting Christian Know-ledge in South India. The early history of the society's connection with missions in India, indeed, has been characterised in its official history as

curious, unique, anomalous, yet providential. By a chain of circumstances it became the patron and supporter of a Danish mission. By unexpected developments it had to employ Lutheran clergy. In default of English missionaries (to our shame be it spoken) it was driven to look to a German university for its agents.[1]

The beginnings of this work in 1705 were due to King Frederick IV of Denmark and Professor A. H. Francke of the University of Halle in Saxony, the former supply-ing the salaries and the latter the personnel of the first mission, namely, two Lutheran divines ordained by the Danish bishop of Zealand. Thanks to the circumstance that Queen Anne had married a Danish prince, in 1709 the interest and support of the Society for the Propa-gation of the Gospel were invited; but that society was prevented by the terms of its charter from undertaking work save in the English plantations and colonies, so that the request devolved upon the S.P.C.K. Accord-ingly this society warmly espoused the duty, and the Danish-German Lutheran mission at Tranquebar be-

1 W. O. B. Allen and F. McClure, *Two Hundred Years: The History of S.P.C.K. 1698–1898*, p. 258.

came one of its principal interests. In 1712 one of the two original missionaries, Henry Plutschau, visited London and addressed a special assembly of the society, a precedent which was followed in 1714 by his colleague Bartholomew Ziegenbalg. Already, however, the propriety of an Anglican society's sponsorship of missions conducted by Lutheran clergymen had been queried in 1713 by John Chamberlayne, a former secretary of the S.P.C.K. and then secretary to Queen Anne's Bounty. In a letter of 19 December, his successor in the secretaryship, Henry Newman, informed him that his communication had been laid before the Malabar committee:

and if you had heard the debate upon it, perhaps you would have thought the subject so nice that you would choose rather to have declared by word of mouth than in writing what you was pleased to communicate. For the Committee, being few in number, thought the matter of too much importance to be decided by them, and therefore ordered your letter to be laid before the Society, where it occasioned a long debate. . . . The major part seemed to wish the matter had never come in question before them for it was no secret to them that the missionaries are Lutherans or at least pass for such, in which it cannot be supposed they are countenanced and encouraged by the Society. . . . The members who have solicited for charities to this mission have thought it their prudence and charity to avoid as much as they could putting it into the heads of benefactors that the missionaries were Lutherans or ministers not episcopally ordained, because mankind are too apt to catch at objections to save their purses; and they considered that if it should please God to make these men instruments of propagating Christianity under some disqualifications, it would not misbecome good men, not only to rejoice at it, but to encourage such instruments, in hopes that their defects might by the good Providence of God be hereafter supplied. They considered that, though they unfeignedly wished to see the Gospel in its purity propagated without any bias to the sects or opinions that unhappily divide Christians, yet that it is rather to be connived at that the heathen should be Lutheran Christians rather than no Christians.[1]

Notwithstanding the hesitancy and reservations of some members, the society continued its employment and patronage of the Lutheran ministers; some of whom served as salaried chaplains to the East India Company, administering the word and sacraments according to the Book of Common Prayer to the English communities; and others under the direct auspices of the S.P.C.K. ministered to scattered congregations and groups of English settlers or Indians or half-castes, sometimes using Lutheran forms of service. Archbishop Wake as President of the S.P.C.K. not only wrote fulsome letters of praise and appreciation to the missionaries at Tranquebar, but also accepted the division of responsibility by which Francke at Halle provided the personnel and S.P.C.K. the financial support for the work. Twenty years later, the ordination to the ministry by the Lutheran missionaries in India of a native convert and catechist, Pastor Aaron, raised afresh the vexed question of non-episcopal orders; and the society called for a formal report from Professor Francke on the incident. On 6 June 1735, Newman wrote to thank Francke for his letter

in answer to the enquiry I was desired to make of the power vested in the missionaries at Tranquebar to confer Orders on such persons among the Malabarian converts to Christianity as shall be found fitly qualified for divine offices, particularly the administration of the Holy Sacraments. A translation of your letter was read at the last General Meeting of the Society, which happened to be a full one, and they unanimously expressed their entire satisfaction at the account you gave of that affair, and have ordered me to put them in mind of giving their directions at the next return of their ships to India, for preventing any difficulties or misunderstandings that may

1 S.P.C.K., Society's Letters, C.S. 2/3, f. 84.

hereafter grow in those parts upon a supposition of the Holy Orders conferred in India not being valid.[1]

By its unanimous approval of this Lutheran ordination the Society had nailed its colours to the mast; and Newman's unofficial interpretation of its action and attitude were equally revealing with the formal approbation. To Mr Wynch and Mr Howard, chaplains at Fort St George, he ventured the explanation, on 6 February following, that

when I asked for instructions to answer Mr Howard's letter of 2 September 1734, about the ordination of Pastor Aaron at Tranquebar, they declined giving me any, it being a tender point for the Society to engage themselves in, to make a comparison of the validity of episcopal with foreign ordinations; which could yield no service to the Mission but might do abundance of mischief. The sending over candidates for Orders to Europe would be attended with insuperable difficulties. You have seen the archbishop of Canterbury's [Wake] opinion in favour of Ordinations in India; and according to your desire I herewith send you copies of what the Society have received from Professor Francke in Germany to warrant the regularity of what the missionaries at Tranquebar have done and may further do as necessity may require on the like occasions. If the primitive Christians had been as scrupulous on this head, as some well-meaning persons now are, how much would it have obstructed the progress of Christianity; and some perhaps would have blamed the forwardness of the eunuch in being baptized by Philip before he was better informed of his commission; but though some lay more stress on the external than the internal call to divine offices, it is certainly right to retain a regard for both with all the decency which prudence, the custom of different countries, and the circumstances of different places will admit.[2]

The precedent thus set was copied in 1741 when another native catechist, Diogo, was ordained with the

[1] *Ibid.* Miscellaneous Letters, C.N. 2/1, f. 1.   [2] *Ibid.* C.N. 2/2, f. 11.

full acceptance of the society. Moreover European missionaries with Lutheran ordination continued to be sent out: in 1731 Sartorius being ordained in London by Mr Ruperti, one of George II's Lutheran chaplains, and Geister receiving similar ordination at Wernigerode in Germany; whilst Gericke was ordained likewise at Wernigerode in 1765, and Schwartz received ordination in 1749 at Copenhagen from a Danish bishop.

Equally interesting and illustrative of the standpoint of many churchmen of the period was Newman's further exposition of the rationale of the society's attitude in a letter to Dr Benjamin Coleman, minister at Boston, New England, on 24 September 1736:

In my little observation I have contracted all the disputes between churchmen and dissenters to the articles of Episcopacy and the use of Liturgy. The first concerns chiefly the clergy, and when they are agreed, I believe the laity will soon follow them; the last concerns both clergy and laity. . . . God forbid that any fence should stand that keeps out Christian unity and charity, the badge by which all men are to judge who are disciples of Christ; and this the Protestant cantons in Switzerland maintain, notwithstanding that variety of customs peculiar to each canton, while we are quarrelling about *words*; for if we consider every Bishop or Superintendent of the Christian Church as a *great Presbyter*, and every Presbyter with a cure of souls regularly ordained as a *little Bishop*, (though I am satisfied from my lord Chancellor King's 'Inquiry into the Constitution, Discipline, Unity, and Worship of the Primitive Church', many of them have now larger charges that some of the primitive bishops enjoyed), it might be a good way towards obviating the invidious distinctions that subsist among us. But where inveterate customs have established themselves, as episcopacy is, with the addition of temporalities, blended with the constitution in England, and presbyterianism in Scotland, it would be turning the world upside down to oblige people to alter an establishment that implies no idolatry nor deviation from the fundamentals of Christianity, and with which they may go to heaven, let them be on which side of the question they may please.[1]

Nevertheless, despite such impeccably latitudinarian sentiments, the ghost continued to haunt meetings of the society. In 1779 Lector Pasche of the German court chapel in London and a member of the East India Committee Mission of the S.P.C.K., reported the recrudescence of doubts concerning the propriety of an Anglican society's maintenance of a mission staffed by German Lutherans:

The matter of the ordination of the new missionaries must on such an occasion always be touched upon (because there are always fresh members present), and if it then turns out that it is not episcopal, one can notice in the case o í a considerable number of members that the same matter puts a check upon their feeling, that there is no longer agreement from the heart on the matter, and if they can, they rather evade it.[2]

Some years later the veteran missionary C. F. Schwartz, having asked Pasche in 1784 whether the society would agree to the ordination in India of John Caspar Kohlhoff, reported to the East India committee on 14 February 1787 that the candidate had been 'publicly ordained in the presence of the Danish governor and of the English and Danish missionaries at Tranquebar'; and on 5 February 1788 the society at a General Meeting 'agreed to concur with the Committee respecting Mr J. C. Kohlhoff, and the same Mr Kohlhoff is hereby admitted into the number of the Society's missionaries'.[3] In 1790 Schwartz also ordained a native catechist, Sattianaden, whose sermon preached on this occasion was translated into English and published by the society, in order to

1 S.P.C.K., New England Letters, C.N. 3/5, f. 8.
2 Hans Cnattingius, *Bishops and Societies*, p. 47.
3 S.P.C.K., East India Mission Committee Book, M.E. m./5, 19 December 1787 and 5 February 1788.

establish 'the capacity of the natives for undertaking the office of the ministry, and to shew that the efforts of the missionaries in India have not been in vain'.[1] It was indeed in explicit imitation of the practice of the S.P.C.K. that the Church Missionary Society at its foundation in 1799 followed the lead of 'the church society' by employing Lutheran (though in its case also Reformed) missionaries from the Basle Mission House.

In 1791, however, the annual report of the S.P.C.K. contained the statement that

we ought in time to give the natives a church of their own, independent of our support; we ought to have suffragan bishops in the country, who might ordain deacons and priests, and secure a regular succession of truly apostolical pastors, even if all communications with their parent church should be annihilated.[2]

There can be no doubt that this represented the long-term policy and ideal of the society, just as from the outset it would have preferred English clergymen as its agents in South India. But the realisation of these hopes must needs tarry until the revision of the charter of the East India Company made provision for the establishment of an Anglican bishopric at Calcutta, and the appointment in 1814 of Bishop Middleton to that see. Moreover the S.P.C.K. itself was passing under new influences; both at home, thanks to Bishop Howley of London, Joshua Watson, and its secretary from 1785 to 1823 George Gaskin, who was a close associate of such high-churchmen as Bishop Horne, William Stevens, and William Jones of Nayland; and abroad, thanks to successive bishops of Calcutta. A sign of impending changes was seen in the strong preference of Howley for missionaries ordained by the Danish bishop of Zealand; as, for

1 Allen and McClure, *op. cit.* p. 277.   2 H. Cnattingius, *op. cit.* p. 52.

example, when it was reported to the East India Committee on 8 May 1818 that

the Bishop of Zealand, having offered to the Society through the lord Bishop of London, the services of two young students in theology for the Society's Missions in India, whom he represented as entirely qualified for the Mission, the Committee agreed in opinion that, after receiving Holy Orders from the Bishop of Zealand, they be accepted by the Society as missionaries.[1]

But change could only come gradually; and so late as 18 November 1818 the committee received a letter of 6 April previous from Bishop Middleton, reporting that 'the Lutheran ordination had been conferred on three native catechists, which he considered to be necessary; a step however by no means superseding the necessity of missionaries from Europe'.[2]

Before this date the society had sent out its last German-Lutheran minister, in circumstances which merit detailed description alike for their intrinsic interest and for their importance as illustrating the traditional policy of the S.P.C.K. in regard to its East India Mission. At the meeting of the committee on 16 June 1818, with Bishop Howley in the chair, the secretary

reported that Dr Schwabe had introduced to him at the Society's House the Reverend John George Philip Sperschneider, who had just arrived in London with letters from the Reverend Dr Knapp, professor of Divinity at Halle, in consequence of application made to him by this Committee to furnish one or more missionaries to be engaged in the service of the Society's Mission in the East Indies.

With the letter from Schwabe there was enclosed a literal translation of Mr Sperschneider's Certificate of Ordination, in the following terms:

[1] S.P.C.K., East India Mission Committee, M.E. m./8, 8 May 1818.
[2] *Ibid.* 13 November 1818.

Whereas Mr John George Philip Sperschneider, intended Missionary of the Honourable Society for Promoting Christian Knowledge in London, had been duly examined, both orally and in writing by the Royal Commission for examinations in Halle, who were charged therewith by the Royal Consistory of the Province of Saxony, and whereas he had in this examination acquitted himself most honourably, and therefore his request of being ordained a Christian Minister had been consented to: Such Ordination was performed in the name and by the order of the said Royal Consistory of the Province of Saxony, by me, the undersigned Counsellor of the Consistory, and First Superintendent of the Circle of the Saale, Henry Balthazar Wagnitz, D.D. on the 6th day of May of the year 1818; and he, the said Mr John George Philip Sperschneider, received, with supplication to and in the Name of God, the Father, Son, and Holy Ghost, and after having solemnly promised that his most zealous endeavours shall be directed towards promoting to the utmost of his ability and under the influence of the Holy Spirit, the saving knowledge and worship of God and Jesus Christ, both by word and deed among the old and young, and extending the kingdom of truth and religion, both near and far, the Consecration to the office of a Christian Minister, the dignity of a Christian teacher, and the general privileges thereto attached, and particularly the right of administering the Holy Sacraments of the Evangelical Church. In testimony of which this Certificate has been given, with the wish that God may richly endow his newly consecrated servant with his strength for the beneficial performance of the duties entrusted to him, that he also in distant regions, may promote much good, and, according to the words of Jesus, bring forth fruit and his fruit may abide. Halle. May 8, 1818.

> Henry Balthazar Wagnitz, Dr and Professor of Divinity, Member of the Royal Prussian Consistory, and First Superintendent of the Circle of the Saale, and also Pastor Primarius at Halle.

It may occasion little surprise that the committee was

agreed in opinion that these testimonials in favour of Mr John George Philip Sperschneider are very satisfactory to the committee, and that he be desired to attend a meeting of this committee to be holden on Thursday the 23rd inst. at 10 o'clock.

When the young missionary duly appeared,

he was most suitably addressed by the chairman, and congratulated on his safe arrival in England, and on his religious disposition to be employed in the interesting work of propagating Christian knowledge in India.

After this interview the committee

agreed in opinion that the Reverend John George Philip Sperschneider be received by this Society to be employed as a Missionary in the East Indies, and to be engaged in the Society's Missions there, where his services may be deemed by the other missionaries there to be most wanted; provided the Bishop of Calcutta do not disapprove of this determination; in which case his Lordship's judgment is to be followed.

On 8 January 1820 the committee received a letter from the bishop of 20 March previously, stating that, after consultation with the Madras District committee, he had 'ultimately resolved upon his [Sperschneider's] going to join Mr Kohlhoff at Tanjore'.[1] Thus was recorded the ordination and reception of the last German-Lutheran minister to be sent out by the S.P.C.K. for service in its Indian missionary sphere.

It is impossible to interpret this policy of the society, maintained for almost a hundred years, otherwise than has been done by a recent Swedish historian:

The most natural interpretation seems to be that by using these Lutherans, the Society did recognise the validity of their Lutheran orders. It is difficult to contest this interpretation, since it turns out to be the conception of the time, as far as it is possible to find any references to it. The Lutheran missionaries had no doubt about it, though they were well aware that the Society preferred episcopal orders.[2]

[1] S.P.C.K., East India Mission Committee, M.E. m./8, 16 June, 23 June 1818, 8 January 1820.   [2] H. Cnattingius, *op. cit.* p. 43.

It is true that there was a recurrent and growing un-easiness as the century progressed on the part of some members of the society as to the propriety of its continuance of the custom; and that the maintenance of the tradition was only *faute de mieux*, namely in view of the virtual impossibility of inducing English clergymen, episcopally ordained, to volunteer for this difficult service. Moreover, the patronage and employment by the S.P.C.K. of the German-Lutheran ministers, though a recognition *de facto* of the validity (as distinct from the regularity) of their orders, did not imply an acceptance of them *de jure*. Nevertheless, it is difficult to explain the society's policy in sending out ministers ordained as Mr Sperschneider was testified to have been ordained, save on the basis of its recognition that Lutheran ordination was valid, though irregular. With the establishment of an Anglican bishopric at Calcutta, the anomaly was bound to cease, though gradually. A particularly decisive step was taken by the second bishop, Reginald Heber, when in November 1825 he reordained three Lutheran missionaries employed by the C.M.S. and thereby set forward the Anglicanisation of the existing personnel. In view of the importance of his action, it is particularly interesting and important to ascertain his own view of episcopacy, as expressed in his edition of Jeremy Taylor's works before he became bishop of Calcutta and in his pronouncements after going to India.

In commenting on Taylor's *Episcopacy Asserted*, Heber observed that 'in the few particulars where he has taken a different ground from that generally occupied by the assertors of episcopal government, I am not sure that he has been fortunate'. As a particular example, Heber remarked that Taylor sets out with asserting the absolute necessity that some form of church government should be found laid down in scripture; an assertion of precisely the same kind with that which was maintained by the puritans in the reign of Elizabeth, and which was so ably refuted by Hooker. . . . The reasons indeed on which Taylor rests his position are as unsound as the position itself is *prima facie* questionable.

The editor admitted that if Taylor had made good his contention

that our Lord while on earth appointed the two distinct offices of bishop and presbyter, no doubt could remain but that both of these would rest on the same foundation with that of those sacraments themselves, which all men allow to be immutable. But here too, the author, while attempting to prove too much, had assumed facts in which he is neither borne out by antiquity nor the tenor of the gospel history, when he finds in the apostles, during the abode of their Lord on earth, the first bishops, and in the seventy disciples whom Christ also selected from his followers, the first presbyters of his church. . . .

That the apostles thus left in charge of the faithful, thus commissioned by Christ, and thus guided by the Paraclete, delegated to three different orders of men distinct and different portions of the authority which they had themselves received; that they ordained in different parts of the world apostles or bishops like themselves, elders to act in subserviency to those bishops, and deacons to assist those elders—the author in what follows has indeed satisfactorily established. And it is plain that not only is the fact that episcopacy was instituted by the followers of Christ and the possessors of the holy Spirit sufficient to prove it neither an irrational nor unchristian form of polity, but that a very great and evident necessity must be shewn, before any human hand can be authorized to pull down or alter a fabric erected under such auspices. This and this only is the strong, and (if I may be allowed the expression) the impregnable ground of the episcopal scheme, and of Taylor's defence of it.

The conclusions of Heber himself were as follows:

Though I am far from confounding the relative value of institutions immediately authorized by Christ, immediately

tending to the salvation of souls, or of visible and universal
advantage to them, with those which chiefly respect ecclesiastical order, it can hardly I think be denied that those churches
are wisest who retain episcopacy; those sectaries least excusable
who dissent from it; and that the authority of apostolical
tradition cannot reasonably be rejected in this case, without
endangering many other observances of Christianity which are
almost universally accounted essentials.[1]

It is difficult to interpret these statements otherwise
than as indicating that Heber held episcopacy to be of
the *bene* or *melius esse* of the church rather than of the
esse; representing thereby the traditional pre-Tractarian
high-church position. This is confirmed by his observation regarding the desire of some rigid high-churchmen
to rebaptise persons baptised by non-episcopal ministers:

The German Lutheran clergy are as absolutely without episcopal ordination, and therefore in the view of an episcopal
church as merely laymen, as the dissenting teachers in our own
country. Yet . . . who has blamed the venerable Societies for
the Propagation of the Gospel and for Promoting Christian
Knowledge for recognising not only the baptism but the
ordination of Lutheran Superintendents and Elders, and employing as missionaries those who, if your correspondent were
correct, are not entitled to receive the Eucharist themselves?

Similarly, whilst avowing on the one hand that he was
'very far indeed from judging those who, from con-
scientious error, reject the form of episcopal government;
to [our] common Master they must stand or fall', on the
other hand he urged that only episcopally-ordained
clergy should be sent to India:

I . . . hope that the Society will supply us with episcopally-
ordained clergymen. English by nation as well as in church
discipline are on many weighty accounts to be preferred. But
if these are not forthcoming, I would earnestly recommend

[1] *Works of Jeremy Taylor*, edited by R. Heber, vol. I, pp. clix, clxi, clxii–clxiii
(rev. C. P. Eden, London, 1883).

recourse to the ancient and apostolical churches of Denmark and Sweden.[1]

Further, in defending against criticism his own action in reordaining Lutheran ministers in India, he remarked:

You suppose that I generally admit ordination by Presbyters without a Bishop to be valid. I do not admit this. All I said is that, when a Christian nation has, by unfortunate circumstances, lost its apostolical succession of Bishops, the continuance of Ministers being a thing absolutely needful and essential, those good men are not to be censured who perpetuate it by the best means in their power. And were I to return to Germany, I would again, as before, humbly and thankfully avail myself of the preaching and Sacramental ordinances of the Lutheran evangelical church, not doubting that they are a true Church of Christ, and that the Spirit of God is with them as, I trust, he is with us also.[2]

The action of Heber in reordaining Lutheran ministers, and the taking over by the S.P.G. from the S.P.C.K. of its missionary work in South India in 1825, combined to accelerate the process of elimination of non-episcopalian personnel from Anglican missions there.

The century dividing the Hanoverian accession from the passing of the first reform act saw indeed the widest diversity of opinion amongst English churchmen concerning ecclesiastical polity and the necessity of episcopacy. At the most extreme position the famous sermon on 'The Nature of the Kingdom or Church of Christ' of Benjamin Hoadly, bishop of Bangor, denied that Christ had delegated authority to any officers in the church: 'He himself is sole lawgiver to his subjects; and Himself the sole judge of their behaviour in the affairs of conscience and eternal salvation.' Indeed the precise *differentia* between the kingdoms of this world and the

---

[1] Cited in A. J. Mason, *The Church of England and Episcopacy*, pp. 433, 435–6.
[2] R. Heber, *Narrative of a Journey through the Upper Provinces*, vol. III, p. 411 (London, 1828).

kingdom or church of Christ lay in the circumstances that

He had in those points left behind him no visible human authority; no vicegerents who can be said properly to supply his place; no interpreters upon whom his subjects are abso-lutely to depend; no judges over the consciences or religion of his people.

From these premisses, it followed that in the church of Christ

all his subjects in what station soever they be, are equally sub-jects to him; and no one of them more than another hath authority, either to make new laws for Christ's subjects, or to impose a sense upon the old ones; or to judge, censure, or punish the servants of another master in matters relating purely to conscience or salvation.

Hoadly's conclusion, therefore, was that the church was simply 'the number of men, whether small or great, who truly and sincerely are subjects to Jesus Christ alone as their lawgiver and judge in matters relating to the favour of God and their eternal salvation'.[1]

Little discernment was needed to perceive that the bishop had subverted all claims to authority on behalf of the episcopate, all visible polity and order in the church, and that he had substituted an unrestrained individual-ism. William Law indeed summarised the effect of the sermon succinctly when he averred that it was designed 'to dissolve the church as a society'.

William Paley had no doubt of the practical necessity of the church as an organised society, but he applied the same mundane reasoning to its polity in his sermon 'A Distinction of Orders in the Church defended upon Principles of Public Utility'. Basing his argument upon

[1] B. Hoadly, 'The Nature of the Kingdom or Church of Christ' (*Works*, vol. II, pp. 404–6).

the difference between the immutable precepts of moral-
ity and the fundamental articles of faith on the one hand
and 'the laws which respect the discipline, instruction,
and government of the community on the other', he
held that the latter 'are delivered in terms so general and
indefinite as to admit of an application, adapted to the
mutable condition and varying exigencies of the Christian
church'. In his opinion 'the apostolic directions which
are preserved in the writings of the New Testament,
seem to exclude no ecclesiastical constitution which the
experience and more instructed judgment of future ages
might find it expedient to adopt'. Accordingly, the form
of church polity 'might be assimilated to the constitution
of each country'; and in England the threefold
ministry of bishops, priests and deacons was justified
by its correspondence with the orders of secular society:

The appointment of various orders in the church may be considered as the stationing of ministers of religion in the various
ranks of civil life. The distinctions of the clergy ought, in some
measure, to correspond with the distinctions of lay-society, in
order to supply each class of the people with a clergy of their
own level and description, with whom they may live and associate upon terms of equality.[1]

At the other end of the ecclesiastical firmament
William Law was drawn into literary combat against the
noxious doctrines of the Bangorian sermon, and in his
Three Letters to the Bishop of Bangor set forth a classic
defence of the high-church position. He had little difficulty in showing that the bishop had left Christians with
'neither priests, nor sacraments, nor church', but had
given them instead 'only sincerity; . . . that, which,
according to your lordship, will help us to the communion of saints hereafter, though we are in communion

[1] W. Paley, Sermon III (*Works*, ed. A. Chalmers, vol. v, pp. 35 *seq.*).

with anybody, or nobody, here'. Nor did his mordant satire spare the inconsistency of the preacher's personal position who had allowed himself to be consecrated to the office and work of a bishop and was prepared to lay hands upon candidates for confirmation and ordination, whilst believing that 'all human benedictions are useless niceties; and that to expect God's grace from any hands but His own, is to affront Him'. In particular, Law stated his own conviction of the necessity of apostolic succession:

This divine commission can only be had from such particular persons as God has appointed to give it, therefore it is necessary that there should be a continual succession of such persons, in order to keep up a commissioned order of the clergy. For if the commission itself be to descend through the ages and distinguish the clergy from the laity, it is certain the persons who alone can give this commission, must descend through the same ages; and consequently an uninterrupted succession is as necessary, as that the clergy have a divine commission.

In reply to the contention that such a succession is only of apostolic and not of dominical institution, he contended that

we do not say that episcopacy cannot be changed, merely because we have apostolical practice for it; but because such is the nature of the Christian priesthood, that it can only be continued in that method which God has appointed for its continuance. Thus, episcopacy is the only instituted method of continuing the priesthood; therefore episcopacy is unchangeable, not because it is an apostolical practice, but because the nature of the thing requires it.[1]

In dealing with the Reformation, Law confined himself to a defence of the Anglican breach with Rome, without considering the position of the Church of England in relation to the foreign reformed churches.

[1] W. Law, *Three Letters to the Bishop of Bangor* (ed. J. O. Nash and C. Gore, 1893), pp. 149, 159.

The evangelical revival, both in its Arminian-Methodist and Anglican-Calvinist forms, introduced a further complexity into the position. John Wesley moved from the traditional high-church standpoint to a belief and practice of presbyterian ordination. In a letter of 30 December 1745 he averred that

we believe it would not be right for us to administer either baptism or the Lord's supper unless we had a commission so to do from those bishops whom we apprehended to be in a succession from the apostles; [and he further added that] we believe there is, and always was, in every Christian church ... an outward priesthood, ordained by Jesus Christ, and an outward sacrifice offered therein, by men authorised to act as ambassadors of Christ and stewards of the mysteries of God; [and] we believe that the threefold order of ministers ... is not only authorised by its apostolical institution, but also by the written Word.[1]

Only three weeks later, an entry in his journal for 20 January 1746 recorded that on the way to Bristol

I read over Lord King's Account of the Primitive Church. In spite of the vehement prejudice of my education, I was ready to believe that this was a fair and impartial draught; but, if so, it would follow that bishops and presbyters are (essentially) of one order, and that originally every Christian congregation was a church independent on all others![2]

Together with Lord Chancellor King's book, Stillingfleet's *Irenicum* also influenced Wesley to adopt the position that 'I have as good a right to ordain as to administer the Lord's supper. But I see abundance of reasons why I should not use that right, unless I was turned out of the church.'[3] Four years after writing this letter, his 'scruples were at an end' against ordaining for

[1] *Letters of John Wesley* (ed. J. Telford), vol. II, pp. 55–6.
[2] *Journal of John Wesley* (ed. N. Curnock), vol. III, p. 232.
[3] *Letters of John Wesley* vol. VII, p. 21; cf. p. 238.

North America; and later for Scotland and finally for England.

An equal latitude of opinion prevailed amongst many of the Anglican evangelicals who were caught up by Whitfield's Calvinistic movement; of whom Thomas Haweis may be taken as representative. In his *Plea for Peace and Union among the Living Members of the Church of Christ*, he averred that

the diffusion of light hath begun to shame bigotry out of countenance; and I hope there are but few, really taught of God, in England and Scotland, who suppose the Church is confined to one side or other of the Tweed; that the good Francillion of Switzerland is not as really a Minister of Christ as the good Archbishop of Uppsala; or that a Lutheran Superintendent or a Huguenot pastor are not as truly ordained by Christ and his Church as the Archbishop of Canterbury or the Moderator of the General Assembly. Episcopalian as I am, were I in Scotland, though I should prefer my own mode, I should feel not the least objection to join in communion with all real Christians in the High Church, or in a meeting of faithful men among the Seceders, Burghers, or Antiburghers; if I were in Saxony my Lutheran brethren would meet me at their tables; at Nîmes I should sit down with St Etienne under the rock; at Berne break bread with that gracious Swiss correspondent as cordially as with the prelate of Uppsala if I were in Sweden. . . . I need not add that they would be equally welcome to the bread I break.[1]

In his *Impartial and Succinct History of the Rise, Declension, and Revival of the Church of Christ*, whilst affirming that episcopacy was 'most correspondent in my poor ideas, to the apostolic practice and the general usage of the Church in the first and generally esteemed purer ages', he qualified this by stating that

respecting the administration of this Church I am not convinced that the Lord of life and glory left any precise regulations.

[1] T. Haweis, *A Plea for Peace and Union*, 1796, pp. 29–30.

His kingdom could alike subsist under any species of government, and, having nothing to do with this world, was in
externals to be regulated by existing circumstances. Whether
episcopacy, a presbytery or the congregational order be
established as the dominant profession, it affects not the
Body of Christ.[1]

It was little surprising, therefore, that some Anglican
evangelicals should join with their dissenting Calvinistic brethren in the foundation of the London Missionary Society in 1796, of which it was declared

to be a fundamental principle . . . that our design is not to send
Presbyterianism, Independency, Episcopacy, or any other form
of Church Order and Government (about which there may be
differences of opinion among serious persons), but the glorious
Gospel of the blessed God to the heathen; and that it shall be
left (as it ought to be left) to the minds of the persons whom
God may call into the fellowship of his Son from among them
to assume for themselves such form of Church Government as
to them shall appear most agreeable to the Word of God.

Three years later the Anglican evangelicals formed their
own society, the Church Missionary Society, avowedly
on 'the church principle, not the high-church principle',
but standing firmly by the anglican tradition in respect
of episcopacy.

Against all aberrations from high-church principles in
regard to episcopacy the Clapton sect, with their sym-
pathisers in different parts of the country, stood firm and
set forth their *apologia* for that form of church polity.
Bishop George Horne of Norwich rebuked John Wesley
for ordaining superintendents for America, and in his
primary charge to his diocese laid down the principle
that the divine ordinances cannot be administered

to effect but by God's own appointment; at first by his immediate appointment, and afterwards by succession and de-
rivation from thence to the end of the world. Without this rule

[1] *Idem, An Impartial and Succinct History,* 1800, Introduction, p. x.

we are open to imposture, and can be sure of nothing; we cannot be sure that our ministry is effective, and that our sacraments are realities. We are very sensible the spirit of division will never admit this doctrine; yet the spirit of charity must never part with it. . . . [He allowed indeed that] the definition of the Church contained in our Articles was purposely less definitive than it might have been, to avoid giving further offence to those whom we rather wished to reconcile; [but he rejoiced that at the Reformation] the church of England . . . preserved its constitution and its doctrines, while many of the reformed fell off by degrees, some into disorder, some into dissolution.[1]

William Jones of Nayland likewise contended that

in the Christian Church throughout the world we find these three orders of ministers for fifteen hundred years without interruption. The fact therefore is undeniable that the church has been governed by bishops, priests, and deacons from the apostles downwards; and where we find these orders of ministers duly appointed, the word preached, and the sacraments administered, there we find the church of Christ with its form and authority.[2]

More rigid and extreme than the majority of his brethren, Archdeacon Charles Daubeny in his *Guide to the Church*, affirmed in its prefatory address to Wilberforce that

what form of government the apostles agreed to establish in the church, if not expressly communicated to them by Christ in person, must be considered established under the direction of the Holy Spirit. . . . What that form of government was, we shall be at no loss to determine, if we are disposed to enquire fairly into the subject. . . . [Moreover, he held that] the church of England in her canons exclusively appropriates the title of a *true and lawful Church* to that society of Christians in this country assembled under episcopal government; and determines all separatists from it to be schismatics.

Outside this country he championed the 'branch' theory of the catholic church, maintaining

[1] G. Horne, *Works*, vol. II, p. 570. [2] W. Jones, *Works*, vol. IV, p. 422.

174

every Christian society possessing the characteristic marks of the church of Christ . . . to be a separate branch of the catholic or universal visible church upon earth. The church of England, the church of Ireland, and the episcopal church of Scotland and America possess these marks. In the same light the churches of Denmark, Sweden, and Rome are to be considered; not to mention the great remains of the once famous Greek church, now to be found in the empire of Russia and the east.[1]

Similarly Bishop Van Mildert in his Bampton Lectures defined the church

as existing under that apostolical form of government, which from the date of its first institution, it has invariably exhibited in the far greater part of the Christian world. It is the church episcopally constituted, which forms our present subject of investigation; not any of those various modes of professing Christianity which may be found in communions of *other* kinds. For without entering into controversy with those who deny the divine origin of episcopacy, it can hardly be disputed that this form of ecclesiastical polity has so generally prevailed, that in every age from the time of the apostles until the separations which in some instances unhappily took place at the period of the protestant reformation, the catholic or universal church properly so-called, comprising many particular or national churches, was known and distinguished by its episcopal constitution.[2]

Between such various and contrasting schools of churchmanship it is not easy to discern the *via media* or to attain the highest common factor. But if the post-revolution epoch of Anglican church history saw a widening of the gulf dividing the several elements of its comprehensive tradition on the question of episcopacy, this divergence did not extinguish or invalidate the continuance of a typical Anglican norm. Perhaps the best expression of that norm may be found in the definition by a perceptive and discriminating high-churchman of

[1] C. Daubeny, *Guide to the Church*, pp. 10, 27; Appendix I, p. 130.
[2] W. van Mildert, *Theological Works*, vol. IV, p. 223.

the reign of Queen Anne, Jonathan Swift, in his *Sentiments of a Church of England Man with respect to Religion and Government*:

A Church of England man hath a true veneration for the scheme established among us of ecclesiastic government; and though he will not determine whether Episcopacy be of divine right, he is sure it is most agreeable to primitive institution, fittest of all others for preserving order and purity, and under its present regulations best calculated for our civil state.[1]

[1] Jonathan Swift, *Prose Works* (ed. Temple Scott), vol. III, p. 54.

'GIANT POPE'

In the *Oratio pro praesente Convocatione sive Synodo*, to be read daily during the session of convocation, there is a suffrage

that we, who according to the rule of our holy reformation, justly and earnestly repudiated the errors, corruptions and superstitions at that time surrounding us and also the tyranny of the pope, may all hold firmly and constantly the apostolic and truly catholic faith, and may serve Thee duly and intrepidly with a pure worship.[1]

In like phraseology Archbishop Sancroft, amid the gathering clouds of James II's reign, exhorted the bishops and clergy of his province to

have a very tender regard to our brethren, the protestant dissenters, . . . and . . . take all opportunities of assuring and convincing them that the bishops of this church are really and sincerely irreconcilable enemies to the errors, superstitions, idolatries and tyrannies of the church of Rome; [and he further bade them] to join with us in daily fervent prayers to the God of peace for an universal, blessed union of all reformed churches, both at home and abroad, against our common enemies.[2]

Yet again, the University of Oxford in its reply to the church of Geneva in 1706 referred to 'the war in which we are engaged against the tyranny of the pope', and to the unity of all Protestants in opposing 'the impious and

---

1 'Ut qui, ad amussim sanctae Reformationis nostrae, errores, corruptelas et superstitiones olim hic grassantes, Tyrannidemque Papalem, merito et serio repudiavimus, Fidem Apostolicam et vere Catholicam firmiter et constanter teneamus omnes, Tibique rite puro cultu intrepidi serviamus.'

2 E. Cardwell, *Documentary Annals of the Reformed Church of England*, vol. II, pp. 375–6.

most detestable innovations of the Romish church'. Such expressions were typical, not to say ubiquitous, in Anglican statements concerning Rome during the two centuries and a half dividing the papal excommunication of Elizabeth I from the passing of Roman Catholic emancipation. It is therefore against this background of hostility to 'Giant Pope' that the attitude of the church of England towards Lutheran and Reformed churches abroad must be seen and interpreted. Yet, notwithstanding their common bond of unity in opposition to the church of Rome, the church of England avowedly as a matter both of fact and sentiment was closer to the Roman church than any other of the churches which had renounced its obedience at the Reformation. It may be serviceable, therefore, to essay a brief survey of the relations between Canterbury and Rome, in order to appreciate better the points of difference and agreement between their two churches, and to understand that Janus-attitude of the church of England in discussions for restoring the shattered unity of Christendom, which then, as now, is difficult of interpretation to foreign churchmen.

In Jewel's *Apologia Ecclesiae Anglicanae*, the basis of his argument against the church of Rome was 'that God's holy gospel, the ancient bishops, and the primitive church do make on our side, and that we have not without just cause left these men, and rather have returned to the apostles and old catholic fathers'.[1] The breach with Rome he accepted, but denied it to be an act of schism:

it is true: we have departed from them; and for so doing we both give thanks to almighty God, and greatly rejoice on our own behalf. But yet for all this, from the primitive church, from the apostles, and from Christ we have not departed. . . . [Indeed,] we truly have renounced that church, wherein we could

1 Jewel, *Works*, vol. III, p. 56.

neither have the word of God sincerely taught, nor the sacraments rightly administered, nor the name of God duly called upon. . . . To conclude, we have forsaken the church as it is now, not as it was in old time ; . . . and we are come to that church, wherein they themselves cannot deny . . . but all things be governed purely and reverently, and, as much as we possibly could, very near to the order used in the old times.[1]

In setting forth the positive belief of the church of England, Jewel, whilst professing acceptance of the catholic and universal church, affirmed 'that there neither is nor can be any one man, which may have the whole superiority in this universal state'; and he cited the Council of Nicaea, 'that the bishop of Rome hath no more jurisdiction over the church of God, than the rest of the patriarchs, either of Alexandria or Antiochia have'.[2] Similarly in his famous sermon at Paul's Cross, first preached on 26 November 1559 and repeated on 31 March 1560, he challenged his adversaries:

If any learned man of all our adversaries, or if all the learned men that be alive, be able to bring any one sufficient sentence out of any old catholic doctor or father, or out of any old general council, or out of the holy scriptures of God, or any one example of the primitive church: whereby it may be clearly and plainly proved, that there was any private mass in the whole world at that time for the space of six hundred years after Christ; or that there was then any communion ministered to the people under one kind; Or that the people had their common prayers then in a strange tongue that they understood not; Or that the bishop of Rome was then called an universal bishop, or the head of the universal church; Or that the people was then taught to believe that Christ's body is really, substantially, corporally, carnally, or naturally, in the sacrament; Or that his body is, or may be, in a thousand places or more at one time; Or that the priest did then hold up the sacrament over his head; Or that the people did then fall down and worship it with godly honour; Or that the sacrament was then, or

1 *Ibid.* pp. 91, 92.   2 *Ibid.* pp. 59–60.

179

ought now to be, hanged up under a canopy; Or that in the sacrament after the words of consecration, there remaineth only the accidents and shews, without the substance of bread and wine; Or that the priest then divided the sacrament in three parts, and afterward received himself all alone; Or that whosoever had said the sacrament is a figure, a pledge, a token, or a remembrance of Christ's body, had therefore been judged for a heretic; Or that it was lawful then to have thirty, twenty, fifteen, ten, or five masses said in one church in one day; Or that images were then set up in the churches, to the intent the people might worship them; Or that the lay people was then forbidden to read the word of God in their own tongue—if any man alive were able to prove any of these articles by any one clear or plain clause or sentence, either of the scriptures, or of the old doctors, or of any old general council, or by an example of the primitive church; I promised then that I would give over and subscribe unto him.[1]

Notwithstanding this comprehensive catalogue, it was implicit in Jewel's challenge that the Roman church, stripped of such excrescences and corruptions, held the fundamentals of faith, and was therefore still a branch of Christ's universal church, albeit in present need of purgation and reform. What was implied by Jewel was made explicit by Hooker:

Touching those main parts of Christian truth wherein they constantly still persist [he wrote of its members], we gladly acknowledge them to be of the family of Jesus Christ, and our hearty prayer unto God almighty is, that they may at length (if it be His will) so yield to frame and reform themselves that no distraction remain in anything, but that we all may with one heart and one mouth glorify God, the Father of our Lord and Saviour, whose church we are.[2]

Similarly he refused to accept the Puritan contention that whatever had been used by the Roman church was forbidden to churches of the Reformation:

[1] Jewel, *Works*, vol. i, pp. 20–21.
[2] Hooker, *On the Laws of Ecclesiastical Polity*, iii, i, 10.

To say that in nothing they may be followed which are of the church of Rome were violent and extreme. Some things they do in that they are men, some things in that they are wise men and Christian men, some things in that they are men misled and blinded with error. As far as they follow reason and truth, we fear not to tread the selfsame steps wherein they have gone and to be their followers. Where Rome keepeth that which is ancienter and better, others whom we much more affect leaving it for newer and changing it for worse, we had rather follow the perfections of them whom we like not, than in defects resemble those whom we love.[1]

Throughout the reign of Elizabeth I a fierce and protracted literary controversy was conducted between Anglicans and Romanists on the points specified in Jewel's catalogue; to which the Romanists retorted by challenging the lay character of the Anglican settlement, the validity of the consecration of Archbishop Matthew Parker and consequently of all subsequent consecrations and ordinations, and the doctrine of the Book of Common Prayer and of the Articles of Religion concerning the real presence and the eucharistic sacrifice. But these were skirmishes conducted at long range; and perhaps the first encounter at close quarters may be seen in 1622–4, in Laud's controversy with Fisher, which is of particular interest as illustrating the standpoint of an unequivocally high-church theologian. At the outset Laud, whilst affirming that he 'never did grant of the Roman church, nor ever mean to do', that it was 'the only true church', nevertheless freely acknowledged that it was 'a true church'.

For so much very learned Protestants have acknowledged before me. . . . For that church which receives the Scriptures as a rule of faith, though but as a partial and imperfect rule, and both the sacraments as instrumental causes and seals of grace, though

---

[1] *Ibid.* v, xxviii, 1.

they add more and misuse these, yet cannot but be a true church in essence.[1]

Indeed, he held of Rome that

a particular church it is, and was, and in some times right, and in some times wrong; and then in some things right, and in some things wrong; but 'the right church' or 'the Holy Catholic Church', it never was nor ever can be.[2]

Accordingly the schism of the sixteenth century had been caused not by the Protestants, but by Rome itself:

The cause of the schism is yours; for you thrust us out from you, because we called for truth and redress of abuses. . . . [For] the Protestants did not get that name by protesting against the church of Rome, but by protesting (and that when nothing else would serve) against her errors and superstitions. Do you but remove them from the church of Rome and our Protestation is ended, and the separation too. . . . [Meanwhile, however, such separation was fully justified.] For another church may separate from Rome, if Rome will separate from Christ. And so far as it separates from Him and the faith, so far may another church sever from it. And this is all that the learned Protestants do or can say; and I am sure all that ever the church of England hath either said or done.[3]

Nor did Laud confine the abuses of Rome to moral and financial matters:

But that there are errors in doctrine, and some of them such as most manifestly endanger salvation, in the church of Rome, is evident to them that will not shut their eyes. . . . Now, had I leisure to descend into particulars, or will to make the rent in the church wider, it is no hard matter to prove that the church of Rome hath erred in the doctrine of faith, and dangerously too.[4]

Under pressure of discussion, he was driven to specify some of the doctrinal errors of Rome, in fashion not unlike Jewel:

---

[1] W. Laud, *Works* (L.A.C.T.), vol. II, pp. 143-4.
[2] *Ibid.* p. 147.   [3] *Ibid.* pp. 150, 152, 156.   [4] *Ibid.* p. 166.

For the pope teaches in and by the Council of Lateran, confirmed by Innocent III, Christ is present in the sacrament by way of transubstantiation; and in and by the Council of Constance, the administration of the sacrament to the laity in one kind, notwithstanding Christ's institution of it in both kinds for all; and in and by the Council of Trent, Invocation of Saints and Adoration of Images, to the great scandal of Christianity and as great hazard of the weak. Now that these particulars, among many, are errors in divinity, and about the faith, is manifest both by Scripture and the judgment of the primitive church.[1]

With regard to the papal supremacy, he was equally clear:

The Roman patriarch, by ecclesiastical constitutions, might perhaps have a primacy of order; but for principality of power, the patriarchs were as even, as equal, as the Apostles were before them. . . . [Consequently] A 'primacy of order' was never denied him by the Protestants; and an 'universal supremacy of power' was never granted him by the primitive Christians.[2]

Per contra, the relationship between the several parts of the universal church was not one of subordination but of equality:

The Roman church and the church of England are but two distinct members of that catholic church which is spread over the face of the earth. Therefore Rome is not the house where the church dwells; but Rome itself, as well as other particular churches, dwells in this great universal house.[3]

Laud's positive claim for his own church was that it held the catholic faith as expressed in the three creeds, acknowledged the authority of scripture and of the fathers, accepted the two dominical sacraments and the threefold order of ministry, and further believed in the real presence of Christ in the eucharist; and that in this sacrament

we offer up to God three sacrifices, one by the priest only, that

[1] *Ibid.* p. 306.   [2] *Ibid.* pp. 186, 208.   [3] *Ibid.* p. 346.

is the commemorative sacrifice of Christ's death, represented in bread broken and wine poured out; another by the priest and people jointly, and that is, the sacrifice of praise and thanksgiving for all the benefits and graces we receive by the precious death of Christ; the third, by every particular man for himself only, and that is, the sacrifice of every man's body and soul to serve Him in both all the rest of his life, for this blessing thus bestowed on him.[1]

In summary of his entire argument, he affirmed that

I have lived, and shall, God willing, die in the faith of Christ as it was professed in the ancient, primitive church, and as it is professed in the present church of England. And for the rule which governs me herein, if I cannot be confident for my soul upon the Scripture, and the primitive church expounding and declaring it, I will be confident upon no other.[2]

With the accession of Charles I to the throne, his wife's entourage became a natural centre of Roman Catholic proselytism; and for the first time since the excommunication of Elizabeth I the possibilities of reunion between Rome and Canterbury were canvassed. It is probable that the missions of Dom Leander a Sancto Martino and of Gregorio Panzani were exploratory in intent rather than accredited approaches towards formal negotiation; and it is certain that both envoys saw the Anglican position through rose-coloured spectacles and were unduly sanguine as to the prospects of corporate union. Certainly Laud as archbishop of Canterbury was impervious both privately and publicly to flattering advances; but the episode was important as producing the first (even unofficial) venture from the Roman side to reconcile the Thirty-nine Articles with the decrees of the Council of Trent. Laud indeed had affirmed of these Articles that

the church of England never declared that every one of her Articles are fundamental in the faith. For it is one thing to say, None of them is superstitious or erroneous; and quite another

<hr/>

[1] W. Laud, *Works* (L.A.C.T.), vol. II, pp. 340–1.   [2] *Ibid.* p. 373.

to say, Every one of them is fundamental, and that in every part of it, to all men's belief.[1]

The detailed examination of the Articles in the light of post-Tridentine Roman Catholicism was undertaken by a convert from Anglicanism, Christopher Davenport, whose name in religion was Franciscus a Sancta Clara, in his *Paraphrastica Expositio Articulorum Confessionis Anglicanae*.[2] In the first five Articles he found 'no matter for examination'; and he reserved the first paragraph of Article 6, 'Of the Sufficiency of the Holy Scriptures for Salvation', for later consideration in respect of the relationship of scripture to tradition and of the authority of the church and of general councils. Articles 7 and 8 ('Of the Old Testament', and 'Of the Three Creeds') he adjudged to be 'catholic throughout'; and he approved likewise of the former part of Article 9, 'Of Original or Birth-sin', whilst the latter part which declared 'that concupiscence and lust hath of itself the nature of sin', he wished to interpret thus: 'because it is not subject to the divine law, and no more; it has not therefore, formally the nature of sin, but only by way of disposition'. The following Article 10, 'Of Free-Will', was pronounced satisfactory; whereas Article 11, 'Of the Justification of Man', naturally raised more difficult questions.

Sancta Clara indeed believed the difference between the Anglican Article and the definition of the Council of Trent to be largely one of words; since both agreed 'concerning the efficient cause of justification', namely God; 'concerning the meritorious cause, which . . . is

[1] *Ibid.* p. 60.
[2] Franciscus a Sancta Clara, *Paraphrastica Expositio* (ed. F. G. Lee, London, 1865), Latin text with English translation, from which all the following extracts are taken. In his later *Enchiridion Fidei* Sancta Clara retreated from his earlier position.

Christ alone or His passion'; concerning 'the material cause', and 'the final cause'; so that the divergence related only to 'the formal cause'. In this matter, he understood the Article to mean 'that justification is acquired by faith, as applying or laying hold of the merits or righteousness of Christ', and held that 'this may bear a sound and catholic sense'. Indeed,

the difference really is as to what is to be understood by 'Faith'. They think that it means a leaning on, or act of confidence in, the promises of God; while we think this to be the same thing with that faith of Christ, preached to the nations everywhere, by which we believe all the promises of God; . . . here, then, we might very easily come to an agreement.

His conclusion therefore was that 'in reality no discrepancy can now be found between the Anglican confession and the Tridentine definition'.

Little difficulty was found in accepting Article 12, 'Of Good Works'; whilst in Article 13, 'Of Works before Justification', the statement that such works 'neither make men meet to receive grace, or (as the School-authors say) deserve grace of congruity', was accepted in the sense intended by St Augustine (Ep. 105). More delicate was the assertion that these works 'have the nature of sin'; which was interpreted to mean that 'the intention is to call the works in question *sins*, improperly; or according to the schools, negatively; . . . and this is the common doctrine of the schoolmen'. Even Article 14, 'Of Works of Supererogation', though appearing at first sight 'somewhat hard', was capable of a catholic interpretation, when it was remembered that 'the Article speaks of the Works of a man in a state of pure nature— that is, not prevented nor assisted by God's grace'. The following Article 15, 'Of Christ alone without Sin', was agreed so far as concerned Christ himself; and in respect of the statement that 'all we the rest . . . offend in many things', was interpreted in such wise that 'the Blessed Virgin is not included with the common dregs of sin', but that the authors 'plainly excluded her', thereby allowing belief in the Immaculate Conception. Of Articles 16, 'Of Sin after Baptism', 17, 'Of Predestination and Election', and 18, 'Of obtaining eternal Salvation only by the Name of Christ', it was allowed severally that they 'contain excellent doctrine' and were 'catholic'.

The three Articles relating to ecclesiastical authority, 19, 'Of the Church', 20, 'Of the Authority of the Church', and 21, 'Of the Authority of General Councils', came near to the root of differences between Canterbury and Rome; and therefore demanded and received fuller treatment. The actual definition of the visible church of Christ was accepted as being 'sound, having in it nothing to exclude the truth', although 'inadequate as a definition'. The further reference to the church of Rome (together with those of Jerusalem, Alexandria, and Antioch) as having 'erred . . . in matters of faith' was met by interpreting it as relating to Rome 'as distinct from other particular churches' and not as 'the church universal', just as the bishop of Rome may signify either 'simply the bishop of the city' or 'bishop of the world'. In the narrower interpretation of 'the church of Rome', Sancta Clara held that 'the statement is not contrary to the *faith*, though it be contrary to the *truth*'; whilst in the wider interpretation 'the Article does not assert her to have erred, which alone is of the faith'. The first clause of Article 20, affirming the authority of the church in matters of faith, rites, and ceremonies, was pronounced to be 'clear and in agreement with all antiquity'; and likewise the prohibition against ordaining anything contrary to God's Word written and the definition of the church as 'a witness and keeper of Holy Writ' were approved. The conclusion drawn in the Article from these premisses, that 'besides the same ought it not to enforce anything to be believed for necessity of salvation', required 'interpretation line by line'. Accordingly, 'by *besides* must be understood what is not either actually or virtually in them—that is, neither expressed in terms nor can be deduced as a consequence from them'. In the Article relating to General Councils, the requirement of the consent of princes was accepted as a statement of historical fact, but not 'of councils in themselves—that is, considering only the Divine Law'. The further affirmation that such General Councils have erred 'even in things pertaining unto God' was allowed, because councils 'may err in matters which do not concern the faith or morals, in things necessary to salvation', and 'provided only they be not matters necessary in respect of faith and morals, which is not asserted in the Article'. Even so, the final clause, requiring that 'things ordained by them as necessary to salvation' must 'be declared that they be taken out of Holy Scripture', needed to be so interpreted as to allow councils 'to extract the truth from the more abstruse parts of Holy Scripture and the sayings of the Apostles'; not 'for the purpose of making anything of faith which was not before of faith, but only for the purpose of declaring those things which directly or indirectly affect the faith'.

In anticipation of *Tract XC*, Article 22, 'Of Purgatory', was explained by observing that, though its words were 'without doubt at first sight most difficult', a distinction must be drawn between '*the Romish doctrine*', that is, 'what is supposed to be their doctrine', and 'the Roman doctrine'. Between the official Roman doctrine and the Anglican Article there was no contradiction; whilst Rome would concur in the repudiation of 'the Romish doctrine'. The next Article, 23, 'Of Ministering in the Congregation', was pronounced to be 'in agreement with Holy Scripture, the doctrine of the holy Fathers, and the practice of the Universal church'; whilst Article 24, 'Of speaking in the Congregation in such a Tongue as the people understandeth', was interpreted to exclude the Mass from its definition; and the author even contended that

on the strength of this Article it may be probably inferred, that the offices of the church and the Sacraments of Christ ought at the present time to be celebrated amongst us in Latin, because it is, speaking generally, ... the common language and commonly understood, and publicly taught in every place; and it is only asserted in the Article that public prayer should be in a language understood by the people, which ought undoubtedly to be explained of general understanding everywhere, not of accidental variations.

In considering Article 25, 'Of the Sacraments', the first two paragraphs, defining the nature of sacraments and specifying the dominical sacraments of baptism and the supper of the Lord, were accepted as 'catholic'. The third paragraph, concerning 'those five commonly called Sacraments', was held to 'require explanation'. Sancta Clara insisted that it was 'a most received truth, as well in the Eastern as in the Western church, that there are seven Sacraments'; that 'they are properly called Sacraments'; and therefore

it must be noticed that in this Article some nature of Sacraments is not denied to the other five specified, but only a difference is made in the necessity and greater dignity of Baptism and the Eucharist in respect of the rest, with which all antiquity agrees and the whole theology of the schools. But it is clear that this is the true sense of this Article, because there is added *have not the like nature*; it does not deny that they are Sacraments at all, which it had before called them, but says that they are so in a different degree, which we readily grant.

The last paragraph of the Article, concerning the gazing upon and carrying about of the sacraments, was reserved for later comment.

Both Articles 26, 'Of the Unworthiness of the Ministers, which hinders not the effect of the Sacrament', and 27, 'Of Baptism', were said to be 'the very doctrine of the church and of all the Fathers'. The first paragraph of Article 28, 'Of the Lord's Supper', 'with all its clauses stated, as there affirmatively only', was held to be 'catholic'. To deny transubstantiation, however, as the second paragraph did, was 'contrary to the truth of the faith, as it has been defined in the Lateran and Tridentine councils'. The clause must therefore 'be explained thus; that the authors only condemn the old error of the Capharnaïtes, namely, the carnal presence of Christ, that is, as though Christ was present in the Sacrament in a natural or carnal manner, and were chewed by the teeth'. This sense 'is wholly repugnant to Scripture and would destroy the nature of a Sacrament', for then 'Christ would be present under the species or consecrated elements in a carnal or sensible manner, not sacramentally'. It was this error, 'and no more', which the Article condemned. Sancta Clara cited Bishops Andrewes and Montagu as evidence that Anglicans confessed 'a *change*, an *alteration*, a *transmutation*, and that not only in form but in nature'; and also he appealed to Andrewes and Jewel in support of his contention that the adoration forbidden in the Article was 'only the worship of *latria*', and not that of *dulia*, whilst he emphasised that the decree of Trent 'does not say that the Sacrament, but that Christ in the Sacrament is to be adored with *latria*'. Finally the statement of the Article that the

Sacrament 'was not by Christ's ordinance reserved, carried about, lifted up, or worshipped', was explained to signify 'that those things are not formally commanded by Christ, which may nevertheless be rightly instituted by the church'. In Article 29, 'Of the Wicked which eat not the Body of Christ in the use of the Lord's Supper', it was 'not so much the conclusion as the reasons for the conclusion, which require consideration'. These reasons were based on a misunderstanding of St Augustine; so that the Article

must then be explained according to St Augustine's meaning, ... or we must say with respect to this Article, as Bellarmine does upon St Augustine, that the wicked receive not the Lord, that is, as the Lord (because they receive not the grace of the Lord), in partaking of this Sacrament; in other respects all receive our Lord there under a veil, according to St Augustine ... and the true faith.

Article 30, 'Of both kinds', was interpreted as not asserting 'that communion in both kinds was so commanded by God, as that it is necessary to salvation, or that it may not be understood as capable of accommodation to circumstances'.

In confronting Article 31, 'Of the one Oblation of Christ finished upon the Cross', Sancta Clara confessed indeed that 'the whole of this Article seems most difficult, but by looking into it more correctly, I should not consider it very dissonant from the truth'. Once more anticipating the argument of *Tract XC*, he pointed out that

nothing is said against the Sacrifice of the Mass in itself, but against the vulgar and commonly-received opinion about it, namely that priests in this Sacrifice offer Christ for the living and the dead, for remission of pain and guilt, so that by virtue of this Sacrifice offered for them, independently of the Sacrifice of the Cross, they gain remission for the people. This is the popular opinion which the Article here condemns.

191

In affirming that the mass is a true sacrifice, he stated that 'it is not primarily propitiatory, for this pertains to the Sacrifice of the Cross, though it may well be called so in itself, and, as it were, secondarily'. Again he appealed to the authority of Andrewes and Montagu as evidence that 'there will be no difficulty whatever on this point with the more learned Protestants', who accepted the doctrine of an unbloody sacrifice.

Article 32, 'Of the Marriage of Priests', was regarded as stating 'the common opinion of the schools', and Article 33, 'Of excommunicate Persons', was 'catholic and agreeable both to Holy Scripture and Antiquity'. Even Article 34, 'Of the Traditions of the Church', since 'the Traditions here treated of are not doctrinal', was held to be 'most true and agreeable to the practice of the church'. The following Article 35, 'Of the Homilies', evoked the comment that they contained 'many things worthy of all praise', together with some which

neither please us nor the more learned among them. Nor are Protestants, because of these words in the Article, bound to hold every word or sentence in the Homilies. . . . Those things therefore, which savour of sound doctrine, should prudently be read by the people, the rest should be neglected.

It was to be expected that the longest commentary thus far should be devoted to Article 36, 'Of Consecration of Bishops and Ministers', because it contained the *gravamen* of Roman objections against Anglican orders. Moreover Sancta Clara, being a convert, had the advantage of being well acquainted with the Edwardine Ordinal. In regard to the consecration of bishops, he observed that

the matter is the imposition of hands; let the more learned judge whether it be right to declare their consecration void on this account, especially since Vasquez and others think that the imposition of hands and those words (Take the Holy Ghost, etc.) are sufficient *jure divino*, for the essence of the ordination of a Bishop;

and he cited authorities to prove that neither the tradition of the instruments nor unction was essential for the admission of either bishops or priests to their respective orders. After quoting the Anglican formula at the imposition of hands in the ordering of priests and at the giving of the Bible, he observed that the commission to minister the holy sacraments implied the power to offer sacrifice, since 'Christ himself, by giving the power of consecrating, gave at the same time that of sacrificing'. In so arguing, he added: 'I merely explain the Article in a favourable sense, and the rather because I find that the more distinguished doctors of the Protestants... acknowledge priests and a sacrifice.' Although the Anglicans had erred in rejecting the Roman pontifical, the question at issue was whether their form was 'sufficient for conferring the priesthood? It seems (I do not assert it, still less do I hold to the opinion) that, according to some, it might be answered affirmatively from Innocent IV (*De Sacramentis non iterandis*: Cap. Presbyt).' Having cited his authority, Sancta Clara commented that

according to this opinion, therefore, Christ only appointed that ordination should be conferred with some form of words and symbols, and from this it follows *a fortiori*, that equivalent words are wholly sufficient, because words prescribed by the church can much more readily be changed than if they had been prescribed by Christ.

He concluded therefore that the Anglican form might be sufficient 'because it includes the power of sacrificing and absolving'. In the Office for the Making of Deacons

'to many it seems that nothing essential is here omitted';
and his general conclusion was thus stated:

I do not examine the other points respecting the succession of
Bishops or Ministers (which has been treated at length and
learnedly by others), but only the bare words of the Article,
whether, that is, in point of form and matter (if nothing else
hinder) a valid Ordination is performed.

Equally important and crucial was Article 37, 'Of
the Civil Magistrates', since it treated of the royal and
papal supremacies. Indeed, Sancta Clara held that it
afforded

by far the most weighty subject of examination: whether, that
is, laics are capable of exercising spiritual jurisdiction. First, it
must be observed, that by consent of all they are not capable
of exercising the power of the keys, for then they would be able
to confer absolution or remission of sins. Secondly, it must be
observed that spiritual jurisdiction, or the power of jurisdiction,
is not directly the power of the keys itself; indeed they are
separable, and are not always actually united, either by divine
or positive law. Thirdly, it must be supposed that the Sovereign
Pontiff in every matter, in virtue of his absolute power, can
confer such jurisdiction on laics, because it is not directly
against divine law; . . . and this not only in respect of men, but
also of women. . . . But to shew my own opinion in a matter of
such gravity, I think it should be said, that by no right, as has
been said before, are they capable of spiritual power or jurisdiction, . . . whereby spiritual grace is procured, that is to say,
the power of administering the Sacraments. And my opinion is
the same respecting the power which flows from the former,
such as the infliction of spiritual penalties, the exposition of
the Scriptures, the institution, confirmation, or examination of
the ministers of the church, and many things of that kind. For
everything of this kind is by divine law absolutely restricted to
spiritual men, or consecrated to God. . . . But as respects the
power or antecedent right, not of itself and necessarily annexed
to spiritual offices, this may occasionally rest with laics, such as
the presentation or collation of benefices, the temporal punish-

ment of clerks, and many other things of that kind, . . . principally by concession of the church, or sanctioned by long custom, the prelates of the church assenting to it. And I said with good reason, sanctioned by long custom, because not only concession but custom itself gives jurisdiction, even in spiritual matters . . . especially when the exercise of the custom is proved to have been from time immemorial.

Sancta Clara was sufficiently acquainted with English history to give many concrete examples of the power in ecclesiastical matters claimed and exercised by sovereigns during the middle ages, as well as to cite precedents from France; and he appealed to Anglican divines to show that the Article granted 'no spiritual jurisdiction whatever to our kings, but the civil and temporal government, indirectly and incidentally, for the peace of the state, extended over the abovementioned ecclesiastical persons and causes'.

More delicate was the statement in the Article that 'the Bishop of Rome hath no jurisdiction in this realm of England'; which required 'a wider explanation'. It might refer to the repudiation of King John's surrender of his kingdom to the Pope; or it might mean 'that every kind of subjection and communion with the Apostolic See is denied'; or, more narrowly,

a departure from the obedience not of the Apostolic See, or of the authority annexed to that See as respects the act primarily, but only as respects the act when exercised, . . . that is, as respects the exercise of that authority by such a person to whom for a time that See is entrusted.

The complete repudiation of all authority of Rome was, of course, to Sancta Clara 'plainly contrary to the opinion of both the Eastern and Western churches'; nor did he construe the Article as making this statement. There remained, however, the questions: 'whether at a certain point it is lawful for any kingdom to withdraw itself from the obedience of any Pontiff for a time'; and 'were there sufficient causes in this kingdom?' Even if these were answered affirmatively, which was impossible to any Romanist, it would still be a problem 'whether they have not gone too far, at least in their manner'. These matters therefore were commended by the author to 'especial consideration at the hands of Anglicans', with the pious hope 'that by public authority the matter, as its greatness deserves, . . . were weighed with a desire of reunion'. Since nothing in the last two Articles called for comment, Sancta Clara concluded his exposition by affirming his pious and peaceful intentions; and by an exhortation to his readers that though

you will esteem the bare words sometimes deserving of a severe censure, the hidden sense which I have drawn out, you will rightly esteem not very dissonant from the truth, except when men choose to twist it another way.

The verdict of a recent commentator that Sancta Clara 'navigue habilement entre Charybde et Scylla' in his essay towards reconciling the Anglican Articles with the decrees of Trent, yet at times his task 'a vraiment été laborieuse et peu naturelle en certain cas', would seem to be just and perceptive.[1] Moreover, though his efforts produced no tangible results, they had at least brought the two parties to the controversy within negotiating distance; and they were to be followed by later divines and centuries.

The latter half of the seventeenth century was fecund in projects of ecclesiastical reunion, eminent amongst which was the correspondence between Molanus and Bossuet; but the next important stage in England came with the correspondence between Archbishop Wake and

[1] Maurice Nédoncelle, *Trois Aspects du Problème Anglo-Catholique au XVIIième Siècle*, pp. 94–5.

two Gallican theologians of the Sorbonne, Dr L. E. Du Pin and Dr Piers Girardin. These divines represented the opposition of the Sorbonne to the anti-Jansenist policy of the papacy, especially as expressed in the bull *Unigenitus* of 1713, which condemned Père Quesnel's *Reflexions Morales sur le Nouveau Testament*. They had the support, albeit vague and vacillating, of the archbishop of Paris, Cardinal de Noailles; and in their irritation against the attitude of Pope Clement XI, they turned to the idea of a possible union of the Gallican and Anglican churches, in which connection they requested a correspondence with the English primate. The protracted and scholarly interchange of letters which ensued was accompanied also by a more personal and intimate correspondence between Wake and the English chaplain in Paris, William Beauvoir, in which the archbishop offered more revealing and forthright comments than were possible in the formal diplomacy of Latin treatises. Du Pin was supplied with French and Latin translations of the Book of Common Prayer, the Ordinal, and the Thirty-nine Articles; on the basis of which he compiled a *Commonitorium*, in which he set forth his own project for union. Wake insisted from the outset that unity must be based upon agreement in the fundamentals of faith with agreement to differ on other issues, both of faith and practice:

I make no doubt but that a plan might be framed to bring the Gallican church to such a state, that we might each hold a true catholic unity and communion with one another, and yet each continue in many things to differ, as we see the Protestant churches do; nay, as both among them and us many learned men do differ in several very considerable points from each other. To frame a common confession of faith, or liturgy, or discipline for both churches is a project never to be accomplished. But to settle each so that the other shall declare it to be a sound part of the catholic church and communicate with each other as such—this may easily be done without much difficulty by them abroad, and I make no doubt but the best and wisest of our church would be ready to give all due encouragement to it.[1]

The translation of general sentiments into particular projects is notoriously beset with pitfalls; but the archbishop accepted the challenge to define what he considered to be the fundamentals:

In the meantime so far are they right, to distinguish matters of doctrine from matters of order and discipline; in which last national churches may vary without breaking the unity of the catholic church. But then they should in points of doctrine too distinguish fundamentals in which all ought to agree from others of lesser moment in which error or difference may be tolerated. And I am much mistaken if they must not at last come to the creeds of the four first General Councils, if ever they mean to restore peace to the church.

Wake emphasised in a series of extensive theses the Anglican claim to have maintained an unbroken episcopal succession and a valid ministry and sacraments, as well as an orthodox belief; and his chief concern was to impress upon his correspondents the preservation of the apostolic succession at the reformation of the church of England. It was equally essential in his opinion that the Gallican church should follow the example of its English sister by renouncing the papal obedience and supremacy. Rome was the obstacle

from which if we could once divide the Gallican church, a reformation in other matters would follow of course. The scheme that seems to me most likely to prevail is, to agree to the independence, as to all matters of authority, of every national church on any others; of their right to determine all matters that arise within themselves; of an union with one another by

1 N. Sykes, *William Wake*, vol. i, ch. iv.

circular letters, whereby a person for example who is excommuni-
cated in one church shall not be received into communion by
any other; and for points of doctrine, to agree as far as possible
in all articles of any moment (as in effect we either already do
or easily may); and for other matters to allow a difference, till
God shall bring us to an union in those also. Only one thing
should be provided for; to purge out of the public offices of the
Church all such things as hinder a perfect communion in the
service of the Church, so that when any come from us to them,
or from them to us, we may all join together in prayers and in
the holy Sacraments with each other. In our Liturgy there is
nothing but what they allow of, save the single rubric relating
to the Eucharist; in theirs nothing but what they agree may be
laid aside, and yet the public Offices be none the worse or more
imperfect for want of it.

This was strong doctrine even for the digestion of
quasi-rebellious Gallican theologians; but Du Pin and
Girardin took a long step to meet Wake in their winnow-
ing-away of the papal prerogatives. Except for the right
of appeal to Rome allowed by Canons 3 and 7 of the
Council of Sardica in 343, Du Pin reduced the papal
authority to a mere primacy of honour: 'inter episcopos
primum locum tenere; sed primatus ille non ei dat
superiorem gradum inter episcopos; eorum tantum
coepiscopus est, licet inter episcopos primus'. On his
side the English archbishop would concede to Rome
only a primacy of honour, and that by ecclesiastical
tradition, not by dominical appointment:

As to the pope's authority, I take the difference to be only this;
that we may all agree, without troubling ourselves with the
reasons, to allow him a primacy of order in the episcopal
college. They would have it thought necessary to hold communion with him, and allow him a little canonical authority
over them, as long as he will allow them to prescribe the bounds
of it. We say fairly we know of no authority he has in our
realm. But for actual submission to him, they as little mind it
as we do.

The discussion was terminated by political events in France, and by the death of Du Pin. Nor could it in the nature of things have enjoyed the character of an official negotiation, but only of a courteous and friendly interchange of letters; for Wake was convinced throughout that no project of union could become practicable unless it were supported by the civil authority in both France and England. The summary of the matter was thus stated by the primate to Professor Turrettini of Geneva:

Some letters upon this subject, very friendly and Christian, but general, did pass between us. At last we came to consider the episcopal government and succession as it stood in our church; and so far they owned themselves to be perfectly satisfied with us. Then we came to doctrine; our Articles of Religion were proposed, and some advances made in shewing how far, for peace sake, they would come into them. Our Liturgy had been before communicated to them, and was not disliked by them.

From the Gallican side the most important contribution was the *Commonitorium* of Du Pin, which was thus described by its author:

M. Du Pin dressa ... un mémoire contenant les Articles dont on convenait; ceux qui étaient indifférents; et ceux sur lesquels il fallait entrer en conférence pour les éclaircir; articles qui se reduisent à peu.

It is a circumstance of the greatest misfortune that Du Pin's treatise has disappeared; so that its contents are known only from a summary printed as an appendix to Dr A. Maclaine's translation of Mosheim's *Ecclesiastical History*.[1] Unlike Sancta Clara's pioneer work, the arguments of Du Pin are known therefore only at second hand and in part; so that a comparison between their

[1] N. Sykes, *William Wake*, vol. i, ch. iv for description of the rediscovered *Commonitorium*.

conclusions must necessarily be imperfect.[1] Like Sancta Clara, the first Article which arrested Du Pin's attention was the 6th, where he would readily grant the Anglican position in respect of the sufficiency of the holy scriptures for salvation.

provided that you do not entirely exclude Tradition, which doth not exhibit new articles of faith, but confirms and illustrates those which are contained in the Sacred Writings; and fences them by new safeguards against those who are otherwise minded, so that nothing new is said, but only the old in a new way.

With regard to the books of the Apocrypha, he was of opinion that they 'ought to be deemed Canonical', but was prepared to compromise by considering them as deutero-canonical. The next Article which occasioned comment was the 10th, 'Of Free-Will', which he was prepared to accept, provided that its statement that 'we have no power to do good works' were understood in the scholastic sense of *potentia proxima*; since without a *remote* power of doing good works, sin could not be imputed. Again like Sancta Clara, he paused to examine carefully the next Article, 'Of the Justification of Man'; where from the Roman side he averred that 'we do not deny that it is by faith alone that we are justified, but we maintain that faith, charity, and good works are necessary to salvation; and this is acknowledged in the following Article' (i.e. the 12th, 'Of Good Works'). In considering the cognate Articles 13 and 14, 'Of Works before Justification' and 'Of Works of Supererogation', he allowed in respect of the former 'that there will be no dispute, since many divines of both communions embrace the doctrine contained in that article

[1] The citations from Du Pin's *Commonitorium* are taken from A. Maclaine's translation of J. L. Mosheim's *Ecclesiastical History* (5 vols., London, 1768), vol. v, pp. 129–33, appendix III.

(viz. that works done before the grace of Christ are not pleasing to God, and have the nature of sin)'; and though he held 'it very harsh to say, that all those actions are sinful which have not the grace of Christ for their source', yet he wished to relegate this point for theological discussion and not to make it a term of communion. In respect of Article 14, he stated that 'works of Supererogation mean only works conducive to salvation which are not matter of strict precept but of counsel only; and that the word, being new, may be rejected, provided it be owned that the faithful do some such works'.

The next series of Articles which called for comment were those relating to the church and its authority. Du Pin accepted the definition of the church in Article 19, desiring only that the words 'under lawful pastors' should be added; and remarking that though all particular churches, even that of Rome, may err, it is needless to say this in a confession of faith. He concurred with Article 20 that the church had no power 'to ordain anything that is contrary to God's Word written'; but observed that it must be taken for granted that the church will never do this in matters 'which overturn essential points of faith' ('quae fidei substantiam evertant'). The statement of Article 21 that General Councils 'may err and sometimes have erred, even in things pertaining unto God', he countered by observing that such councils as have been received by the universal church cannot err; and that though particular councils may, yet every private man has not a right to reject what he thinks in their decrees to be contrary to scripture. The strong statements of Article 22, 'Of Purgatory', Du Pin qualified by remarking that souls must be purged, that is, purified from defilement of sin, before they are

admitted to celestial bliss; that the church of Rome
does not affirm this to be done by fire; that indulgences
are only relaxations or remissions of temporal penalties
in this life; that Roman Catholics do not worship the
cross, nor relics, nor images, nor even saints before their
images, but only pay them an external respect, which is
not of a religious nature; and that even this external
demonstration of respect is a matter of indifference,
which may be laid aside or retained without harm. In
respect of Article 24, 'Of speaking in the Congregation
in such a Tongue as the people understandeth', he
allowed that divine service may be performed in the
vulgar tongue where that is customary, whilst defending
the Latin and Greek churches for preserving their
ancient languages, and observing that great care had
been taken that everything be understood by translations.

As with Sancta Clara, the Articles relating to the
sacraments were amongst the most difficult of reconciliation. In regard to Article 25, Du Pin insisted that
the five 'commonly called Sacraments' be acknowledged
as such, whether instituted immediately by Christ or not;
and in respect of Article 28, he was willing to omit the
term 'Transubstantiation', and to define its meaning as
teaching 'that the Bread and Wine are really changed
into the Body and Blood of Christ, which last are truly
and really received by all, though none but the faithful
partake of any benefit from them'. The administration
of the eucharist in both kinds he held to be an *adiaphoron*;
in which he advocated mutual toleration and the liberty
of each church to follow its own customs. The loss of the
text of Du Pin's *Commonitorium* is particularly unfortunate
in relation to Article 31, dealing with 'the sacrifice of
Masses'; upon which the editor of Mosheim only

comments that 'he is less inclined to concessions, and maintains that the Sacrifice of Christ is not only commemorated, but continued in the Eucharist, and that every communicant offers him along with the priest'. The marriage of priests, defended in Article 32, Du Pin would allow as a local custom of particular churches; and Anglican ordinations, referred to in Article 36, he 'would not have . . . pronounced null, though some of them perhaps are so; but thinks that, if an union be made, the English clergy ought to be continued in their offices and benefices, either by right or indulgence, *sive ex jure sive ex indulgentia Ecclesiae*'. The last Article to command detailed comment was Article 37, 'Of the Civil Magistrates', which he

admits so far as relates to the authority of the civil power; denies all temporal and all immediate spiritual jurisdiction of the pope; but alleges that by virtue of his primacy, which moderate church of England men don't deny, he is bound to see that the true faith be maintained, that the canons be observed everywhere, and when anything is done in violation of either, to provide the remedies prescribed for such disorders by the canon laws (*secundum leges canonicas, ut malum resarciatur, procurare*). As to the rest, he is of opinion that every church ought to enjoy its own liberties and privileges, which the pope has no right to infringe. He declares against going too far . . . in the punishment of heretics, against admitting the Inquisition into France, and against wars without a just cause.

Perhaps the most striking concessions were contained in Du Pin's final, general reflections; to the effect

that an union between the English and French bishops and clergy may be completed, or at least advanced, without consulting the Roman Pontiff, who may be informed of the union as soon as it is accomplished, and may be desired to consent to it; that, if he consents to it, the affair will then be finished; and that even without his consent, the union shall be valid; that, in case he attempts to terrify by his threats, it will then be expedient to appeal to a general council.

Even allowing for the irritation of the Sorbonne against the papacy as a consequence of *Unigenitus*, the conclusions of Du Pin seem remarkable. Naturally he was little disposed to contend for the prerogatives of Rome, to which he allowed only a primacy of honour. Notwithstanding, his *Commonitorium* did not placate his English correspondent. Wake wrote to Beauvoir:

I cannot well tell what to say to Dr Du Pin. If he thinks we are to take their direction what to retain and what to give up, he is utterly mistaken. I am a friend to peace, but more to truth; and they may depend upon it, I shall always account our church to stand upon an equal foot with theirs; and that we are no more to receive laws from them than we desire to impose any upon them. In short, the church of England is free, is orthodox; she has a plenary authority within herself. She has no need to recur to other churches to direct her what to believe or what to do; nor will we otherwise than in a brotherly way and with a full equality of right and power, ever consent to have any treaty with that of France. And therefore if they mean to deal with us, they must lay down this for the foundation, that we are to deal with one another upon equal terms. If, consistently with our own establishment, we can agree upon a closer union, well; if not, we are as much and upon as good ground, a free, independent church as they are. . . . With the Doctor's *Commonitorium*, I shall never comply. The matter must be put into another method; and whatever they think, they must alter some of their doctrines and practices too, or an union with them can never be effected. . . . If anything is to come of this matter, it will be the shortest method I can take of accomplishing it, to put them in the right way. If nothing (as I believe nothing will be done in it), 'tis good to leave them under a plain knowledge of what we think of ourselves and our church; and to let them see that we neither need nor seek the union proposed, but for their sake as well as our own or rather neither for theirs nor ours, but in order to the promotion of a catholic communion as far as is possible among all the true churches of Christ.

In forwarding the *Commonitorium* for Wake's perusal, Beauvoir had ventured the observation that 'Dr Du Pin's design is a noble one indeed, but it is not likely to succeed in this generation.' But it was not for this reason a vain endeavour. Rather, as the British ambassador wrote to the archbishop, it was 'perfectly right' for his grace to keep up 'a correspondence here, and thereby lay a foundation for an union which may meet with more encouragement hereafter, and which without such a preparatory would possibly never be brought about or attempted'. Furthermore, the sequel to the correspondence, namely an exhaustive examination of the problem of Anglican ordinations undertaken by Pierre François Le Courayer, exploded completely the Nag's Head fable and other unhistorical fictions surrounding the consecration of Archbishop Matthew Parker, and opened the debate concerning the sufficiency of the form and matter of the Anglican Ordinal in a more dispassionate atmosphere than had been possible before. Wake himself shared indeed the stiffness of Laud in asserting unequivocally the claims and character of the church of England, and in resisting any pretensions to supremacy on the part of Rome. Thus he insisted on emphasising 'the subject of the pope's authority as the first thing to be settled in order to an union'. But at least the foundations had been laid for an eirenical reconsideration by theologians of both churches of their several confessions and formularies: on the Gallican side by examining the relationship of the Thirty-nine Articles to the decrees of the Council of Trent and by weighing the evidence for the Anglican episcopal succession since the breach with Rome; and on the Anglican side by measuring the differences in faith and practice which divided the two churches, and by pondering the degree of primacy which might be accorded to the Roman pontiff. It was significant of the general temper and tradition of the times, however, that Wake was at pains to represent his tentative approaches to the Sorbonne in the most favourable light to his foreign Protestant correspondents; as in his ingenuous assurance to Professor Turrettini that

the doctors of the Sorbonne are truly, to all appearance, well disposed to a union with us, and though, in pursuance of their notions of episcopacy and succession of bishops (which from our public records they allow to have been proved beyond exception as to the church of England) they extend their opinions and desire of union no farther than to and with the episcopal church here; yet could we once bring them so far, and break them off from the court of Rome, and make them an independent church, we should soon see them insensibly go on to all we could farther desire of them.

The ecclesiastical milieu of the later eighteenth century indeed was not conducive to sympathetic overtures to Rome; and the Gordon riots illustrated the ease with which popular fanaticism could be aroused against Roman Catholics. The excesses of the French revolutionaries, however, and the asylum accorded in England to Gallican clerical *émigrés* contributed not inconsiderably to mutual understanding and to the assuagement of antipathies; as may be seen in the change of tone between Bishop Shute Barrington's charge of 1806 on 'The Grounds on which the Church of England separated from the Church of Rome', and that of 1810 on 'Grounds of Union between the Churches of England and Rome considered'. But it was to be the task of the Oxford Movement to create a new and more friendly atmosphere for the reconsideration of Anglo-Roman relations; in which Newman's *Tract XC* was to follow the path opened by Sancta Clara and Du Pin, and a later generation of Anglo-Catholics were to find themselves occupying much of the positions formerly set forward by Davenport and the divines of the Sorbonne; whilst their Roman Catholic counterparts, meanwhile, thanks to the definitions of the Immaculate Conception in 1854 and of the Papal Magisterium and Infallibility at the Vatican Council in 1870, had receded still further from the *Consensus Quinquesaecularis*, which had been the *beau idéal* of seventeenth-century English churchmen.

VIII

VIA MEDIA: A MODERATE IMPARITY

'IT is plain', wrote Newman in the first of the *Tracts for the Times*, of the function of the bishop in ordination,

that he but *transmits*; and that the Christian ministry is a *succession*. And if we trace back the power of ordination from hand to hand, of course we shall come to the Apostles at last. We know we do, as a plain historical fact; and therefore all we who have been ordained clergy, in the very form of our ordination acknowledged the doctrine of the Apostolical Succession. And for the same reason we must necessarily consider none to be *really* ordained who have not *thus* been ordained.[1]

These words, written, as R. W. Church said, 'like the short, rapid utterances of men in pain, and danger and pressing emergency', and marking the inauguration of the Tractarian movement, testified to the emergence of a new emphasis upon, if not a novel doctrine of, episcopacy in the church of England. Echoes of the earlier tradition indeed survived at first; as when Tract 4, on 'Adherence to the Apostolical Succession the safest Course', in reply to the question, 'Do you then unchurch all the Presbyterians, all Christians who have no bishops', affirmed that 'we are not judging others but deciding on our own conduct'; and allowed that '"necessary to Salvation" and "necessary to Church Communion" are not to be used as convertible terms'. More specifically, it was stated that 'neither do we desire to pass sentence on other persons of other countries'; and the caution was offered that 'it is one thing to slight and disparage this holy Succession where it may

---

[1] *Tracts for the Times*, no. 1, p. 3.

be had, and another thing to acquiesce in the want of it, where it is (*if it be anywhere*) really unattainable'. These were, however, but echoes of the past; for the present and future the new note struck was that episcopal ordination 'marks us, *exclusively*, for God's ambassadors'.[1] By this emphasis on the exclusive authority conferred by episcopal ordination, the Tractarians were seeking to remedy that defect in the Anglican tradition which Keble noted in his edition of Hooker; namely, that Hooker and his contemporaries did not assert the 'plea of exclusive apostolical prerogative', nor in defending episcopacy did they 'venture to urge its exclusive claim, or to connect the succession with the validity of our holy Sacraments'.

This latter deficiency was likewise now to be corrected; for it was fundamental to the Tractarian position that the validity of the sacraments should depend upon ordination by a bishop. At a meeting in Oxford in August 1833, Newman, Keble, Froude, and Palmer agreed to put forward as the first of a six-point programme:

The doctrine of Apostolic Succession as a rule of practice, that is:

(1) That the participation of the body and blood of Christ is essential to the maintenance of Christian life and hope in each individual.

(2) That it is conveyed to individual Christians *only* by the hands of the successors of the Apostles and their delegates.

(3) That the successors of the Apostles are those who are descended in a direct line of succession from them by imposition of hands, and that the delegates of these are the respective presbyters whom each has commissioned.[2]

Furthermore, Tract 74, 'Catena Patrum: No. 1, Testimony of Writers in the Later English Church to the

[1] *Tracts for the Times*, no. 4, pp. 1, 5–6.
[2] A. P. Perceval, *A Collection of Papers connected with the Theological Movement of 1833* (London, 1842), p. 12.

doctrine of Apostolical Succession', embraced a series
of extracts from forty-three writers ranging from Bilson
to Mant, and exhibiting the Anglican defence of episcopacy as having descended from the apostolic age. But,
whilst the catena established the positive Anglican adherence to episcopacy, it is doubtful whether it could be
pressed so far as to substantiate the exclusive claims now
being advanced by the Tractarians. For a not inconsiderable number of the most eminent divines there
cited, including Hooker, Andrewes, Hall, Bramhall,
Mason, Taylor, Stillingfleet, Sharp, and Wake, in addition to their staunch defence of episcopacy in the church
of England, had explicitly allowed the orders and sacraments of the foreign Protestants who lacked bishops.
Indeed, one of the most candid and learned of a later
generation of Anglo-Catholics, Dr Darwell Stone, confessed that

there always seems to me to have been something providential
in the notion of the Tractarians that they had support for their
position in a post-Reformation tradition, because without this
belief they very likely would not have had the heart to go on.
But I think that we have now to face the facts that, so far as the
Reformation and post-Reformation formularies and divines are
concerned, there are loopholes which we can use but not the
support for an exclusive position.[1]

His own conclusion was that 'any reference to the sixteenth and seventeenth centuries' English formularies
and divines is a broken reed for anything except the
practical requirement' of episcopal ordination for
ministry in the Church of England. This was based on
his opinion that Article 23 was not

necessarily to be interpreted in the light of the ordinal so as to
commit those who accept it to the necessity of episcopal

[1] F. L. Cross, *Darwell Stone*, p. 245.

ordination. I think it more probable that this Article was design-
edly left ambiguous . . . so that whilst care was taken that the
ministers of the church of England were episcopally ordained,
declaration of belief in the necessity of bishops as a speculative
opinion was not required from those who subscribed the
Article.

Accordingly he held that complete discomfiture must be
expected to be the lot of attempts 'to argue that the
present formularies and the post-Reformation English
divines are committed to the necessity of episcopal
ordination as distinct from the practical requirement in
the church of England'.[1]

Notwithstanding the novelty of the Tractarian emphasis on the *exclusive* validity of the orders and sacraments
of episcopal ministries, its influence was to be profound
and pervasive on the future relationship of the church
of England to the foreign Protestants. An early evidence
of this occurred in relation to the Jerusalem bishopric
scheme. This amiable proposal of the Chevalier Bunsen
and his sovereign Frederick William IV of Prussia, by
which the pastoral oversight of those Christians in the
Holy Land who were not otherwise ecclesiastically protected was to be undertaken by a Protestant bishop,
chosen alternately from the Anglican and Lutheran
Evangelical churches and consecrated according to the
English ordinal, divided churchmen in England pro-
foundly. Most probably Gladstone was right in seeing in
the cordial support accorded to it by Archbishop Howley
and Bishop Blomfield, 'an opinion on the part of the
ruling authorities of the English Church that some effort
should be made to counteract the supposed excesses of
the [Tractarian] party . . . by presenting to the public
mind a telling idea of catholicity under some other

1 *Op. cit.* pp. 232, 244; cf. pp. 235–6.

form'.[1] Certainly it was precisely this aspect of the matter which aroused the hostility of the Oxford high-churchmen. Newman made a vigorous protest and denunciation of Lutheranism and Calvinism as 'heresies repugnant to Scripture, springing up three centuries since, and anathematised by East as well as West'[2]; whilst Pusey, who at first had been not unfavourable to the venture, at least to the extent of trying 'to make the best of the experiment', later evinced determined hostility to the prospect of an union by this means of the church of England with the Lutheran churches in the Prussian dominions: 'What a misery it would be if the ultimate object of the Prussian government were obtained and they were to receive episcopacy from us, and we were to become the authors of a heretical succession.'[3] The contrast between such sentiments and the cordial welcome given by Archbishop Sharp and other high-church bishops and clergy in the reign of Anne to the project then ventilated for the introduction of episcopacy into the churches of the Prussian territories was eloquent of the new climate of ecclesiastical orthodoxy introduced by the Tractarians and of the gulf dividing them from their seventeenth-century predecessors.

The Caroline tradition, however, was not left without witness in this controversy; and it was from the pen of Frederick Denison Maurice that it found restatement and application to the Jerusalem bishopric proposal. Maurice had no doubt of the affinities of the church of England with other Protestants: 'we may cease to be Protestants, but at present we are Protestants, and have been so for the last three hundred years'; but at the

1 D. C. Lathbury, *Correspondence on Church and Religion of W. E. Gladstone*, vol. I, p. 229 (2 vols., 1910).
2 J. H. Newman, *Letters and Correspondence*, vol. II, p. 362.
3 F. W. Cornish, *A History of the English Church in the XIXth Century*, vol. I, p. 269.

same time he was equally sure that the English church must not surrender that episcopacy which it held in trust for the future reunion of Christendom:

Now Bishops, being as we believe the witnesses and representatives of Christ's universal kingdom, are the very instruments of our communion with other nations. If there be no such institution—no apostleship—in the Church now, then the Church has lost its universal character. . . . We cannot then recognise a Church without bishops. We cannot do it for our own sakes, because we believe that we have a solemn trust and responsibility to uphold this great universal institution of episcopacy; because we believe that it has been preserved to us in a wonderful manner for the last three centuries, when there was scarcely anything in our minds to make its meaning intelligible; because we believe that all the circumstances of this age are declaring to us its meaning and necessity. And we cannot do it for your sakes. We will not use the name of Charity, when we have rejected the thing. Now it is not charity to tell you that you have not lost the sense of being members of a Catholic body, for your wisest men know that you have. . . . It is, therefore, not charity to tell you that you can dispense with an institution, which, if received livingly and practically, in the way we believe that you have been prepared by God's discipline and grace to receive it, as the witness of Christ's presence, and not as the substitute for it, might, we believe, be the remedy for all these evils.

From these premises he deduced that 'it would be a sin to reject' the Prussian proposal, since it seemed to him 'the most satisfactory recognition of episcopacy as a permanent institution, and yet as one especially adapted to this day, which we could have received from any quarter'. He concluded therefore that

if we labour that our Protestant brethren may unite with us on Catholic principles and for Catholic objects, we shall find out better than all doctors can teach us, what Catholicity is, how necessary it is to the support of Protestantism, how impossible it is that it can thrive without Protestantism.[1]

[1] F. D. Maurice, *Three Letters to the Reverend W. Palmer*, II, pp. 19, 34–5, 36–7; iii, p. 73 (London, 1842 edition).

These were the authentic accents of traditional high-churchmanship; but amid the strife of tongues Maurice's plea for a cordial welcome to the Jerusalem bishopric was little heeded.

Reverberations of the storm continued to be heard in a number and variety of quarters. Archbishop Sumner came into conflict with the polemical Henry Phillpotts, bishop of Exeter, anent some expressions used by him of the status of ministers of the foreign Protestant churches. To a correspondent who had asked whether 'these foreign clergymen were not true pastors of the church, but were to be considered as mere laymen', the primate had replied that he hardly imagined 'there were two bishops on the bench, or one clergyman in fifty throughout our church, who would deny the validity of the orders of these clergy, solely on account of their wanting the imposition of episcopal hands'. Furthermore, he amplified his answer by explaining that, since he had understood the point raised by his correspondent to be 'equivalent to the question whether we held that no person, in any country or under any circumstances, could be entitled to minister in the church of Christ except through the imposition of episcopal hands', he had therefore stated:

I imagined this to be as far as possible from the general opinion of our bishops and clergy. I knew that neither our Articles nor our Formularies justified such an opinion. I knew that many of our divines had disclaimed such an opinion; and I knew that such an opinion would amount to declaring that no valid sacrament or other ministerial act had ever been performed, except under an episcopal form of government. And therefore I could not believe, and I still do not believe, that many of our clergy would venture seriously to maintain such an opinion.

Notwithstanding, two hundred and twenty clergymen of the diocese of Exeter forthwith desired earnestly to record their conviction, in agreement with the judgment of our Church, consentient with that of the Catholic Church, that they only can be deemed validly ordained who have received the laying-on of hands by those to whom the apostolic succession has descended.

In this opinion they were supported by an eighty-page pamphlet from the pen of their redoubtable diocesan, who concluded with the avowal

that while faithfulness to our own principles bids us refuse to acknowledge Christ's Commission in them who receive it not as He hath been pleased to appoint, yet far from us is the presumptuous dogma, that the ministry of such men is never blessed because we see not any promise of a blessing to it.[1]

A more intimate and domestic strife arose from the invitation by the dean of Westminster, A. P. Stanley, to the members of the committee appointed to revise the Authorised Version of the New Testament, to partake together of the holy communion in Henry VII's chapel within the abbey before entering on their work on 22 June 1870. One of the members, Dr F. J. A. Hort, described the occasion as

one of those few great services which seem to mark points in one's life. There was nothing to disturb its perfect quietness and solemnity; everything was kept out except the place, the occasion, the communicants, and the service itself; and these combined together into a marvellous whole.[2]

Nevertheless, furious controversy ensued, centring chiefly in the person of Dr Vance Smith, a Unitarian minister, but embracing also the propriety of the admission to the holy communion of presbyters of the church of Scotland and of English Nonconformist ministers. In the various memorials which poured into Lambeth Palace,

---

[1] *A Letter to the Archdeacon of Totnes by Henry, Lord Bishop of Exeter*, pp. 7, 9–10, 12, 87 (London, 1852, 2nd edition).
[2] A. F. Hort, *Life and Letters of F. J. A. Hort*, vol. II, p. 136 (2 vols., London, 1896).

the general question of occasional communion was raised in terms too profane and painful to permit of mention, save as examples of the new bitterness introduced into the controversy. Archbishop Tait made a formal reply to the effect that

Some of the memorialists are indignant at the admission of any Dissenters, however orthodox, to the Holy Communion in our Church. I confess that I have no sympathy with such objections. I consider the interpretation which these memorialists put upon the rubric to which they appeal, at the end of the Communion Service, is quite untenable.

As at present advised, I believe this rubric to apply solely to our own people, and not to those members of foreign or dissenting bodies who occasionally conform. All who have studied the history of our Church, and especially of the reign of Queen Anne, when this question was earnestly debated, must know how it has been contended that the Church of England places no bar against occasional conformity.

While I hail any approaches that are made to us by the ancient Churches of the East and by the great Lutheran and Reformed Churches of the continent of Europe, and while I lament that Roman Catholics, by the fault of their leaders, are becoming further removed from us at a time when all the rest of Christendom is drawing closer together, I rejoice very heartily that so many of our countrymen at home, usually separated from us, have been able devoutly to join with us in this holy rite, as the inauguration of the solemn work they have in hand. I hope that we may see in this Holy Communion an omen of a time not far distant when our unhappy divisions may disappear, and, as we serve one Saviour and profess to believe one Gospel, we may all unite more closely in the discharge of the great duties which our Lord has laid on us of preparing the world for His second coming.[1]

On the historical issue of the attitude of the church of England to occasional conformity and the inapplicability to such a custom of the rubric requiring episcopal

[1] R. T. Davidson and W. Benham, *Life of A. C. Tait*, vol. II, pp. 71–2 (2 vols., London, 1891).

confirmation or the intention for it, as a condition of receiving the holy communion, Tait was to be supported later by the two historian-bishops, William Stubbs and Mandell Creighton. The former in reply to a question about the admission of a communicant member of the Free Church of Scotland to occasional communion with the church of England in 1897, observed that he had not 'any conviction that the rubric in the Prayer Book applies to persons' in such a position; and continued: 'I do not think that the Presbyterian was in the eye of the Church when the rubric was inserted.' On another occasion, in 1900, in relation to the admission of a schoolboy, without intention of being confirmed, to holy communion in the church of England, he wrote: 'If, after your pupil has been admitted as fully qualified to receive the Sacrament in the Scottish Kirk, he presents himself for Communion . . . I should not raise any objections to his receiving it. I really do not see that the point need be argued.'[1] Similarly Creighton contended

for an *historical* interpretation of the rubric, on the ground that it was framed for normal cases and did not contemplate the case of nonconformists. They were baptized outside the Church of England, but their baptism is valid. They went through instruction for the completion of their baptism and that completion of their spiritual maturity was recognised by the officers of their own body; but here rises the vital question—can that recognition be regarded as valid, i.e. as taking the place of Confirmation. The statement of the position which you lay before me leads up to the answer, Yes.[2]

With the assembly of the first Lambeth Conference in 1867, the question of the relationships of the church of England with other churches assumed a different aspect, for these conferences represented the entire Anglican

[1] W. H. Hutton, *Letters of William Stubbs*, pp. 331–2.
[2] L. Creighton, *Life of Mandell Creighton*, vol. II, pp. 63–4.

communion. This first conference solemnly recorded its conviction

that unity will be most effectually promoted by maintaining the Faith in its purity and integrity, as taught in the Holy Scriptures, held by the Primitive Church, summed up in the Creeds, and affirmed by the undisputed General Councils, and by drawing each of us closer to our common Lord, by giving ourselves to much prayer and intercession, by the cultivation of a spirit of charity, and a love of the Lord's appearing.[1]

The translation of these general aspirations into concrete proposals was the work of the third Lambeth Conference in 1888, amongst the formal resolutions of which was the following:

That, in the opinion of this Conference, the following Articles supply a basis on which approach may be by God's blessing made towards Home Reunion:—

(a) The Holy Scriptures of the Old and New Testaments as 'containing all things necessary to salvation', and as being the rule and ultimate standard of faith.

(b) The Apostles' Creed as the Baptismal Symbol; and the Nicene Creed as the sufficient statement of the Christian faith.

(c) The two Sacraments ordained by Christ himself—Baptism and the Supper of the Lord—ministered with the unfailing use of Christ's words of Institution, and of the elements ordained by Him.

(d) The Historic Episcopate, locally adapted in the methods of its administration to the varying needs of the nations and peoples called of God into the unity of His Church.[2]

Thus the now familiar Lambeth Quadrilateral made its appearance on the stage of ecclesiastical reunion. Moreover, from the outset the Lambeth Conferences were concerned with relations with the Scandinavian churches, the Old Catholic churches, the Eastern Orthodox

[1] Lord Davidson of Lambeth, *The Six Lambeth Conferences: 1867–1920*, pp. 53–4.
[2] *Ibid.* Conference of 1888, pp. 122 *seq.*

churches, and the *Unitas Fratrum*; all of which found a place, together with the non-episcopal churches, in the Encyclical Letter and Resolutions of the 1888 Conference. In particular the conference desired that

earnest efforts should be made to establish more friendly relations between the Scandinavian and Anglican churches; and that approaches on the part of the Swedish church, with a view to the mutual explanation of differences, be most gladly welcomed, in order to the ultimate establishment, if possible, of intercommunion on sound principles of ecclesiastical polity.

Similarly 'more frequent brotherly intercourse' was sought with the Old Catholics of Holland and elsewhere on the European continent, a committee was recommended to confer with representatives of the Moravian Brethren, and it was hoped that 'the barriers to fuller communion' with the Eastern Orthodox churches might be progressively removed 'by further intercourse and extended enlightenment'.[1]

The next Conference of 1897 contented itself with reaffirming 'this position as expressing all that we can formulate as a basis for conference'; but the report of its Committee on Church Unity contained some important and interesting observations. Thus in regard to the presbyterian churches it noted that

in America many of our Presbyterian brethren appear to have been not unwilling to remember that in England in 1660 their forefathers would have been prepared to accept episcopacy with such recognition of the laity as now exists in the United States and in the Irish and many of the Colonial Churches. We naturally turn to the Established Church of Scotland, which approached us at the beginning of the present Conference with a greeting so gracious and so tender. That body has amongst its sons not a few who are deeply studying the question of the three Orders in their due and proper relation.[2]

1 Davidson, *op. cit.* pp. 123–4.   2 *Ibid.* Conference of 1897, pp. 247, 249.

At the next Conference of 1908 further steps forward were registered by the resolution that 'any official request of the *Unitas Fratrum* for the participation of Anglican Bishops in the consecration of Bishops of the *Unitas* should be accepted', provided that certain conditions were fulfilled, including doctrinal agreement in all essentials between the two churches and the adoption by the *Unitas* of 'a rule as to the administration of Confirmation more akin to' the Anglican tradition; by the visit of the bishop of Kalmar on behalf of the archbishop of Uppsala and the consequent recommendation of the appointment of an Anglican commission to correspond further with the Swedish church; and by the formal opinion expressed in a resolution of the Conference that

in the welcome event of any project of reunion between any church of the Anglican Communion and any Presbyterian or other non-episcopal church, which, while preserving the Faith in its integrity and purity, has also exhibited care as to the form and intention of ordination to the ministry, reaching the stage of an official negotiation, it might be possible to make an approach to reunion on the basis of consecrations to the episcopate on lines suggested by such precedents as those of 1610. Further, in the opinion of the Conference, it might be possible to authorise arrangements (for the period of transition towards full union on the basis of episcopal ordination) which would respect the convictions of those who had not received episcopal orders, without involving any surrender on our part of the principle of church order laid down in the Preface to the Ordinal attached to the Book of Common Prayer.

The Report of the Committee on Reunion and Intercommunion, on which these resolutions were based, bore the evident impress of its chairman, Bishop John Wordsworth of Salisbury. It declared its belief

that the most pressing need of the present day is advance in the direction of what is usually in England called Home Reunion. ... Next to this they believe that development of friendly relations already existing with the orthodox and separate churches of the East, with the Old Catholics, with the churches of Scandinavia especially that of Sweden, and with the *Unitas Fratrum* will be most fruitful of results.

In regard to the Scandinavian churches, it recommended conferences between Anglican and Swedish divines concerning 'the spiritual validity of the Holy Orders of the Church of Sweden' and 'certain lesser points', particularly 'the form in which the Diaconate is retained, and the rite and minister of Confirmation'. The Committee devoted 'special attention to the relations between the Presbyterian Churches and the Churches of the Anglican Communion'. It recognised the presbyterian churches as already possessing the first three qualifications of the Lambeth Quadrilateral; and in respect of the fourth,

though they have not retained 'the historic episcopate', it belongs to their principles to insist upon definite ordination as necessary for admission into their ministry. Their standards provide that 'the work of ordination' should be 'performed with due care, wisdom, gravity and solemnity', [and] 'by imposition of hands and prayer, with fasting' by the presbytery; they regard and treat ordination as conferred by those who have themselves been ordained and authorised to ordain others. Many leading Presbyterian divines maintain the transmission of orders by a regular succession through the presbyterate. Facts such as these seemed to point to the Presbyterian churches as those amongst the non-episcopal bodies with whom it would be most natural and hopeful at the present time for our own Church to enter into closer relations.[1]

These points were emphasised further in an 'Appendix of Extracts on the Presbyterian Doctrine of Ordination', taken from official standards and formularies.

Before the next Lambeth Conference of 1920 there intervened two episodes of unequal importance, the

[1] Davidson, *op. cit.* Conference of 1908, pp. 334–6, 422, 430, 431–2, 434–9.

Kikuyu controversy of 1913–14 and the first world war of 1914–18. The former arose from a meeting of all the Protestant missions in British East Africa in 1913 under the chairmanship of Bishop Willis of Uganda to consider a scheme of federation; and particularly from the united communion service at its conclusion, conducted in the Scottish church by Bishop Peel of Mombasa according to the Anglican rite. This provoked a characteristic protest from Bishop Weston of Zanzibar, the reverberations of which were speedily muffled by the outbreak of war. But the incident produced a typically judicious and balanced statement of the traditional Anglican position from Archbishop Davidson; in which he examined

the question whether the Church of England, in addition to the emphasis she deliberately sets upon our episcopal system, has laid down a rule which marks all non-episcopalians as *extra ecclesiam*. The threefold ministry comes down to us from apostolic times, and we reverently maintain it as an essential element in our own historic system, and a part of our Church's witness to 'the laws of ecclesiastical polity'. We believe it to be the right method of church government, a method which no new generation in the Church of England would be at liberty to get rid of, or treat as indifferent. We believe further that the proper method of ordination is by duly consecrated bishops, as those who, in the words of the Article, 'have public authority given to them in the Congregation to call and send ministers into the Lord's vineyard'. But to maintain that witness with all steadfastness is not the same thing as to place of necessity *extra ecclesiam* every system and every body of men who follow a different use, however careful, strict, and orderly their plan. The words and acts of many leading high-churchmen in Caroline days, as well as the carefully-chosen sentences, and, it may perhaps be added, the significant silences of some of our formularies, throw a grave *onus probandi* upon those who contend for the rigid and uncompromising maintenance of the absolutely exclusive rule.[1]

[1] G. K. A. Bell, *Randall Davidson*, pp. 705–6.

If the exigences of war prevented the immediate discharge of this *onus probandi* on the part of the rigorists, the lapse of a further generation since the end of that war has not seen its successful realisation. But the immediate consequences of the cataclysm led to a new searching of heart at the Lambeth Conference of 1920 and to the issue of the *Appeal to all Christian People*; which rephrased the fourth requirement of the Quadrilateral in the words, 'a ministry acknowledged by every part of the Church as possessing not only the inward call of the Spirit, but also the commission of Christ and the authority of the whole body'; and followed this by the interrogative interpretation, 'May we not reasonably claim that the Episcopate is the one means of providing such a ministry?'[1] In the hope of a ready response to its appeal the Conference approved a limited interchange of pulpits subject to episcopal regulation, and the admission to communion of baptised but unconfirmed communicants of non-episcopal congregations 'in the few years between the initiation and the completion of a definite scheme of union' between their respective churches and the church of England. Furthermore it accorded 'general approval' to the suggestions of its Committee on Reunion that during the interim period in which ministers of a uniting church not episcopally ordained would continue, they should enjoy 'equal status in all Synods and Councils of the United Church'; but not 'the right to administer the Holy Communion to those congregations which already possess an episcopal ministry'; although they should have 'the right to conduct other services and to preach in such churches', subject to episcopal licence. At the same time the Conference rejected 'general schemes of intercommunion

[1] Davidson, *op. cit.* Conference of 1920, p. 28.

and exchange of pulpits'; and set forth 'the general rule' that Anglicans should receive the Holy Communion only at the hands of ministers of their own church or of churches in communion with it. With regard to particular churches, the Conference welcomed the appointment of an Eastern Churches Committee on a permanent basis as a means of forwarding reunion with the Orthodox Church, and expressed its hope for closer relations with the Separated Churches of the East. It welcomed the Report of the Commission set up after the Conference of 1908 concerning 'The Church of England and the Church of Sweden'; and recommended that communicants of the Swedish Church should be admitted to communion in the Church of England, that Swedish ecclesiastics should be invited to give addresses in Anglican churches, and that if an invitation were received for Anglican bishops to take part in the consecration of a Swedish bishop, it should be accepted. *Per contra*, negotiations with the *Unitas Fratrum* had reached a deadlock owing to the practice of that church to allow the celebration of the Holy Communion by deacons.[1]

From the Appeal and Resolutions of the Lambeth Conference of 1920 contemporary relationships between the Church of England and other churches received a new direction and impetus. In respect of the Church of Scotland, a mutual interchange of compliments followed; but, as the Church of Scotland and the United Free Church of Scotland were then preoccupied with their own negotiations for reunion, no practical steps were taken to confer with the Church of England until 1932. At a series of subsequent conferences between representatives of the two churches, agreement was reached on the first three points of the

---

[1] *Ibid.* pp. 30–4.

Quadrilateral; and in regard to the fourth, agreement was also recorded

that the Ministry is the gift of the Lord Jesus Christ to the Church; that in accordance with His purpose it is a ministry not of any section of the Church but of the Church Universal; that He calls to this sacred service whom He wills; and that admission to it is through prayer and the laying-on of hands by persons commissioned thereto.[1]

Amongst 'things that might be undertaken in common', it was recommended that there should be a regulated interchange of pulpits, and a provision 'by which communicant members of either Communion at home or abroad, when out of reach of their own accustomed ordinances, are welcome in the other, as members of the Catholic Church of Christ to the Table of the Lord'.[2] In May 1934 the General Assembly instructed its Committee to inform the representatives of the Church of England

that any agreement with regard to the Orders and Sacraments of the conferring Churches can only be based on the recognition and equal validity of the Orders and Sacraments of both Churches, and of the equal standing of the accepted communicants and ordained ministers in each.[3]

Therewith the conferences ended; only to be resumed after the present archbishop of Canterbury's university sermon at Cambridge on 3 November 1946, published under the hopeful title of 'A Step Forward in Church Relations'. In 1947 a Report of the Inter-Church Relations Committee to the General Assembly of the Church of Scotland recommended the implementing of the two practical proposals relating to interchange of pulpits and occasional communion, put forward in 1934 but having meanwhile 'remained inoperative'; and the Assembly, welcoming this, authorised its representatives

[1] G. K. A. Bell, *Documents on Christian Unity*, 3rd series, p. 128.
[2] *Ibid.* pp. 129–30.   [3] *Ibid.* p. 122.

to enter into conference with representatives of the Church of England. A new series of conferences has begun in accordance with this resolution.

An important consequence of the universal character of the Lambeth Appeal of 1920 was that discussions carrying the official approval of the archbishop of Canterbury and of the Pope were initiated between groups of Anglican and Roman Catholic scholars under the presidency of Cardinal Mercier at Malines. Hitherto approaches of Anglican and Roman Catholic churchmen had been unofficial and at long distance. The Oxford Movement indeed had given a new impetus to the question of Anglo-Roman relations, not only by the secessions of Newman, Manning, and others of its leaders, but also by the ideals and aspirations of its pro-tagonists, particularly Dr Pusey, who remained faithful to their own church. Newman also before his departure had carried forward from the Anglican side in *Tract XC* the endeavour towards the reconciliation of the Thirty-nine Articles with the decrees of the Council of Trent, which Sancta Clara and Du Pin had essayed earlier from the Roman standpoint. Pusey likewise, in republishing this tract, avowed that 'the general principle, that the Articles were directed not against the Council of Trent, but against the popular system, had long been familiar to his mind'.[1] Furthermore, in his *Eirenicon*, whilst castigating severely, with especial relation to popular Mariolatry, Purgatory, and Indulgences, 'that vast practical system which lies beyond the letter of the Council of Trent', he maintained his position

that there is nothing in the Council of Trent which could not be explained satisfactorily to us, if it were explained authorita-tively, . . . [and] nothing in our Articles which cannot be

[1] *Tract XC; with a historical preface by E. B. Pusey*, Preface, p. xxxii (London, 1870).

explained rightly, as not contradicting anything held to be *de fide* in the Roman Church. The great body of the faith is held alike by both.[1]

The definition by Pius IX in 1854, however, of the Immaculate Conception of the Virgin Mary as a dogma *de fide*, and by the Vatican Council in 1870 of the Papal Magisterium and Infallibility, added new obstacles to existing doctrinal differences between Rome and Canterbury. Accordingly the first Lambeth Conference of 1867 warned Anglicans against 'the pretension to universal sovereignty over God's heritage asserted for the see of Rome', and 'the practical exaltation of the Blessed Virgin Mary as mediator in the place of her Divine Son'; whilst that of 1878 declared

that the act done by the Bishop of Rome in the Vatican Council in the year 1870—whereby he asserted a supremacy over all men in matters both of faith and morals, on the ground of an assumed infallibility—was an invasion of the attributes of the Lord Jesus Christ.

The Conference of 1888 rejoiced that between the Anglican communion and the Eastern churches

there exist no bars such as are presented to communion with the Latins by the formulated sanction of the Infallibility of the Church residing in the person of the supreme pontiff, by the doctrine of the Immaculate Conception, and other dogmas imposed by the decrees of papal councils;

and its Committee on Reunion affirmed that 'under present conditions, it was useless to consider the question of Reunion with our brethren of the Roman Church'.[2]

Before the next Conference in 1897 there had occurred the ill-starred episode of the condemnation of Anglican orders by Leo XIII in 1896. Arising out of a chance

[1] H. R. T. Brandreth, *The Oecumenical Ideals of the Oxford Movement*, p. 41.
[2] Davidson, *The Six Lambeth Conferences*, (i) p. 50, (ii) p. 94, (iii) pp. 115–16, 159.

meeting, which ripened into a cordial friendship, between Lord Halifax and Abbé Portal, the idea was conceived of an impartial examination by a joint-commission of Anglican and Roman Catholic scholars of the historical and theological issues underlying the controverted question of the validity of Anglican orders. Instead Leo XIII appointed an exclusively Roman Catholic commission, which reported unfavourably; and in his Bull *Apostolicae Curae*, the Pope pronounced Anglican orders to be null and void, both on historical grounds of the reordination during the reign of Mary Tudor and subsequently of Anglican clergymen by Rome, and on theological grounds of the insufficiency of the English Ordinal in respect of an intention to ordain a sacrificing priesthood and of the lack of a doctrine of eucharistic sacrifice in the Order of Holy Communion in the Book of Common Prayer. The papal decision produced a formal reply from the archbishops of Canterbury and York, rebutting the grounds of its argument and setting forth the Anglican doctrine of priesthood and sacrifice.

With the issue of the *Appeal to all Christian People* by the Lambeth Conference of 1920, the veteran Lord Halifax approached Cardinal Mercier of Malines with the request that he would preside over conversations between Anglican and Roman Catholic scholars on the wider question of the reunion of their respective churches. The earliest conversations were unofficial; but for their continuance the authorisation of Archbishops Davidson of Canterbury and Lang of York on the one side and of Pope Pius XI on the other was sought. On 10 January 1923 (the initial conversations having been held in December 1921) Mercier informed Davidson that 'His Eminence the Cardinal Secretary of State has been authorised to inform me that the Holy See approves and encourages such conversations, and prays God with all its heart to bless them.'[1] On 2 February Davidson expressed his satisfaction

that the position of the members of the Church of England who take part as your guests in the discussions to which your Eminence invites them, corresponds to the position accorded to the Roman Catholic members of the group, and that the responsibilities, such as they are, which attach to such conversations, are thus shared in equal degrees by all who take part in them.

Perhaps the most surprising feature of the conversations was that on two occasions the participants discussed practical means of integrating the Anglican and Roman Catholic communions, with especial reference to the position of the see of Canterbury, if agreement had been previously reached on dogmatic issues. In a memorandum prepared by the Anglicans for the conferences in March 1923 such possibilities as the grant of a pallium to the archbishop of Canterbury and other metropolitans, recognition of 'the papal see as the centre and head on earth of the Catholic Church', the use of a vernacular liturgy, communion in both kinds, and marriage of the clergy were adumbrated; and at the meetings in May 1925 Mercier himself read a paper on *L'Église Anglicane unie non absorbée*. If to many observers this seemed to be putting the cart before the horse, it should be remembered that doctrinal issues relating to the authority of the papacy in regard to the episcopate and the relationship of scripture and tradition were also discussed. The conversations came to an end with the death of Mercier in 1926 and as a result of a change of policy at Rome, where in January 1928 Pius XI by his encyclical

---

[1] G. K. A. Bell, *Randall Davidson*, pp. 1258 *seq.* It should be noted that on 22 November 1922 Cardinal Gasparri wrote: 'Il [the Pope] autorise votre Éminence à dire aux anglicans que le Saint Siège approuve et encourage vos conversations', i.e. not merely Pius XI in his personal capacity.

Mortalium Animos virtually closed the door to further conferences sanctioned by authority. Nevertheless, it was a matter of surprise, not to say consternation, in informed circles to learn that Mgr Pierre Batiffol, one of the Roman Catholic members, had informed the papal nuncio in Paris in 1926: 'Quel est donc le bénéfice de ces Conversations? De préparer une union en corps des deux Églises? Non'; and that in the following April he had assured the Pope himself that

Les Conversations de Malines n'ont jamais traité de la réunion de l'Église anglicane au catholicisme romain, ce qui est un chimère, mais avec le Cardinal Mercier, nous y avons toujours parlé du rapprochement des anglicans croyants et de nous. La grande pensée du Cardinal Mercier était d'encourager ces anglicans croyants à se romaniser de doctrine et d'esprit, comme ils y ont tendance, et je crois que les Conversations de Malines, avec la grâce de Dieu, ont eu cet effet.[1]

This was indeed the lie direct to the evidence of the conversations. Accordingly the Lambeth Conference of 1930 expressed regret

that by the action of the pope all such meetings have been forbidden, and Roman Catholics have been prohibited for the future from taking part in conferences on reunion.... They regret also that in the encyclical the method of 'complete absorption' has been proposed to the exclusion of that suggested in the Conversations, as for example in the paper read at Malines *L'Église Anglicane unie non absorbée*.[2]

With the Old Catholics who had separated from Rome after the Vatican Council of 1870, on the other hand, intercommunion was achieved in 1932 on the basis of three articles:

[1] *The Times Literary Supplement*, 3 February 1950: 'The Malines Conversations'. Bell, *Documents*, 3rd series, no. 149, 'The Church of England United not Absorbed'; and no. 150, Letter from Mercier to the author of this memorandum, pp. 21–33.
[2] *The Lambeth Conferences 1867–1948*, p. 230 (S.P.C.K., 1948).

I. Each Communion recognises the catholicity and independence of the other and maintains its own.

II. Each Communion agrees to admit members of the other Communion to participate in the Sacraments.

III. Intercommunion does not require from either Communion the acceptance of all doctrinal opinion, sacramental devotion, or liturgical practice characteristic of the other, but implies that each believes the other to hold all the essentials of the Christian Faith.[1]

This agreement had been preceded by the recognition of the validity of Anglican orders by the Old Catholic Church of Utrecht in 1925, followed by the conference of Old Catholic bishops at Berne in the same year.

The Lambeth Conference Appeal of 1920 resulted also in further approaches to the Eastern Orthodox Church and a revival of the traditional, though avowedly intermittent, interest of the Church of England in the Eastern Orthodox Church which had continued since the seventeenth century. A special delegation from the Oecumenical Patriarchate of Constantinople had visited England for consultation with the Anglican bishops assembled in 1920; and in 1930 the Patriarch of Alexandria led a further delegation to the Lambeth Conference of that year. A theological committee in the following year discussed such topics as the Christian Revelation, Scripture and Tradition, the Creed of the Church, the Doctrine of the Holy Spirit, the variety of usages and customs in the church, and the Sacraments. Accordingly the Patriarchates of Constantinople, Jerusalem, and Alexandria, and the Church of Cyprus and the Holy Synod of the Rumanian Orthodox Church at various dates testified their formal recognition of the validity of Anglican orders; but the political obstacles to the summons of a Pan-Orthodox Synod have prevented further

[1] Bell, *Documents*, 3rd series, nos. 167–9, pp. 60–2.

concerted action in the closer development of Anglican-Orthodox relations.

With the Scandinavian churches outside Sweden discussions were also initiated, though with less complete results. The Lambeth Conference of 1930 recommended the appointment of a committee to consider relations with the Church of Finland, which reported in 1934 in favour of a permissive interchange of bishops between the Churches of England and Finland to officiate at each others' consecrations; of the admission of communicants of the Church of Finland to communion in the Church of England; and an interchange of bishops at episcopal conferences of the two churches. Similar recommendations in respect of the Churches of Latvia and Estonia were made in 1938; but in neither case was the recommendation concerning the reception of communicants reciprocal, though the Churches of Finland and of Latvia and Estonia from their standpoint were willing to welcome Anglicans to communicate with them. The changed political conditions resulting from the war of 1939–44, however, prevented the implementing of closer relations with these churches. In 1947 discussions with representatives of the Churches of Denmark and Iceland were initiated; and these were continued in 1951, when a delegation from the Church of Norway was officially commissioned to participate. The report of the 1951 conferences recommended that communicants in good standing in these churches should be made welcome to receive holy communion in the Church of England.

On the home front, which to the Lambeth Conference Committee of 1908 had seemed 'the most pressing need of the present day', little progress resulted from the renewed impetus at first sight accorded by the Appeal of

233

1920. During the intervening time, indeed, a considerable number of conferences were held, and a not inconsiderable number of schemes and projects, some of which contained elements of promise, were set forth; none of which succeeded, however, in breaking the impasse which divided the participants on the vexed question of episcopacy.[1] Meanwhile a novel experiment was being prepared in South India, where a practical programme was taking shape for an organic union on an episcopal basis of the non-episcopal South India United Church, the South India Provinces of the Wesleyan Methodist Church, and the four southern dioceses of the Anglican Church of India, Burma, and Ceylon. The future polity of the united church was to be episcopal, and its ministry episcopally ordained; whilst during an interim period of thirty years there would be a mixed ministry, embracing episcopally and non-episcopally ordained ministers. The Lambeth Conference of 1930, whilst 'not ready to express approval of every detail of the scheme', was 'desirous that the venture should be made and the union inaugurated'. It approved the entry of Anglican churchmen, clerical and lay, into the united church; and recommended that communicant members and ordained ministers of the united church should be received to communion in dioceses of the Anglican communion 'wherever this can be done consistently with the regulations of each province'; and that episcopally ordained ministers of the united church 'should be qualified, at the discretion of the bishop, to officiate subject to the regulations of the diocese for its own ministers'. It was recognised that these provisions represented 'certain restrictions upon full communion,

[1] Bell, *Documents*, 1st series, nos. 30–47; 2nd series, nos. 118–31; 3rd series, nos. 175–7.

that is to say, upon complete interchangeability of ministers and complete mutual admissibility to communion'; and the hope was expressed that 'when the unification within the united church . . . is complete, full communion in that sense will be secured between the united church and the churches of the Anglican communion'. In a series of comments on detailed points in the projected scheme of union, it was agreed that acceptance *de facto* of the historic episcopate should not involve 'any one particular interpretation of it'; and that 'acceptance of confirmation should not be insisted on as a prerequisite term of union'. Furthermore, recognition was given to the 'anomalous situation' in which the Anglican communion would 'at least to the extent already described, be in communion with the united church, which will itself be in communion with bodies not in communion with the Anglican communion'; and it was agreed that 'such a situation may be covered by the principle of "economy"'. Likewise consecration *per saltum* to the episcopate was allowed to be justifiable 'in the special circumstances of the inauguration of the united church'.[1]

Accordingly in September 1947 the Church of South India came into existence; and the Lambeth Conference of 1948 was called upon to implement the hopes and promises made in 1930. Much to its regret, it found itself unable 'to recommend with complete unanimity that every part of the Anglican communion should immediately enter into full communion with the Church of South India'. It was unfortunate that one of the bases of this inability rested upon a historical inaccuracy; for the statement that 'we have never yet entered into full communion with any church which does not possess a

1 *The Lambeth Conferences 1867-1948*, pp. 224-8.

fully unified ministry, episcopally ordained' ignored the historical precedent of the relationship of the Churches of England and Scotland between 1610 and 1638. It was agreed that members of the Church of South India who had not been episcopally confirmed 'would be admissible to Holy Communion or other church privileges in any church, province, or diocese of the Anglican communion in which their admission would be in accordance with the regulations of the church, province, or diocese concerned'. But it was with respect to the bishops consecrated in the Church of South India, and to the presbyters and deacons therein ordained, that acute division of opinion occurred. All these consecrations and ordinations indeed had been regular and valid in form and matter. Accordingly a majority of the Lambeth bishops were

able and felt bound . . . to accept the church of South India as a living part of the one, holy, catholic and apostolic church of Christ, to recognise bishops and presbyters consecrated or ordained in the church of South India as true bishops and presbyters in the church of Christ, and to recommend that they be accepted as such in every part of the Anglican communion.

A substantial minority, however, were 'unable to associate themselves with any such recommendations', because they held 'that it is not at present possible to make any definitive judgment on the church of South India and its ministry'. The Conference therefore was 'unable to make one recommendation agreed to by all' on this issue, and had to content itself and its readers with the somewhat cold comfort that 'no member of the Conference desires to condemn outright or to declare invalid the episcopally consecrated and ordained ministry of the church of South India'. Recognising, moreover, that the South India scheme would probably become a fruitful parent of further projects of reunion (an expectation which has proved justified), the Conference further recommended that 'the theological issues, especially those concerning the church and the ministry, should be faced at the outset'; that 'the unification of the ministry in a form satisfactory to all the bodies concerned, either at the inauguration of the union or as soon as possible thereafter, is likely to be a prerequisite to success in all future proposals for the reunion of the churches'; that 'the integral connexion between the church and the ministry should be safeguarded in all proposals for the achievement of intercommunion through the creation of a mutually recognised ministry'; that the goal of local schemes of reunion 'should always be a church with which the Anglican church could eventually be in full communion'; and that any part of the Anglican communion participating in a scheme which would involve its withdrawal from that communion 'should consult the Lambeth conference or the provinces and member churches of this family of churches before final commitment to such a course'.[1]

From the survey of these several approaches to reunion during the present century and especially of the varying results flowing from the Lambeth Appeal of 1920, it is evident that episcopacy constitutes still the chief barrier to agreement. Moreover the challenge of the single successful experiment in reunion from the Church of South India and the contrast between its unequivocal taking of episcopacy into its system and the equivocal response of Lambeth 1948 have raised the query whether from the Anglican side episcopacy has not assumed the elusive characteristic of the ghost of

---

1 *The Lambeth Conferences 1867–1948*, pp. 38–9, 41–8; and cf. pp. 51–66 for comments on other reunion projects.

Hamlet's father '*Hic et ubique:* then we'll shift our ground'. The differences between Lambeth in 1930 and in 1948 have evoked the suspicion that in fact a particular interpretation of the historic episcopate (and not the adoption of that institution alone) is being asked of non-episcopal churches as a condition of full union or inter-communion; and further, that this interpretation is not the traditional Anglican doctrine of episcopacy but the exclusive theory of Tractarian *provenance* and champion-ship. It is proper, therefore, to ask which interpretation is more consonant with the Anglican principle to require nothing to be believed of necessity 'but that which is agreeable to the doctrine of the Old or New Testament and that which the catholic fathers and ancient bishops have gathered out of that doctrine'.[1]

So far as the scriptural evidence is concerned, there is general agreement that the testimony of the New Testa-ment is indecisive and indeterminate. In the apostolic age there may be discerned apostles, presbyter-bishops, and deacons; and also apostolic delegates such as Timothy and Titus, and in the *Epistle of Clement* the 'other approved men' (*ellogimoi andres*). But the gulf dividing this incipient church order from the localised monarchical episcopate is still unspanned. Substantially, though with modifications in detail, the position of Lightfoot's excursus on 'The Christian Ministry', written eighty years ago, still holds its ground as the most satisfactory interpretation of the evidence. This essay argued that the most comprehensive explanation was that the episcopate was created out of the presbyterate by elevation, by a process of gradual development, the

[1] Canons of 1571: *Concionatores*: 'Ne quid unquam doceant pro concione, quod a populo religiose teneri et credi velint, nisi quod consentaneum sit doctrinae Veteris aut Novi Testamenti, quodque ex illa ipsa doctrina catholici patres et veteres episcopi collegerint.'

progress of which varied in different churches and regions. Generally speaking, the verdict of Armitage Robinson in 1918 still stands:

It has been said of Lightfoot in another connexion that 'he chose his ground so well' that it was not easy to dislodge him. That is eminently true in the present instance. Subsequent research or discovery has left his position as strong as ever. He would not claim more than to have given a reasonable interpretation of the available facts. New theories have since been offered to us; we can hardly say that new facts have come to light which require that his interpretation should be modified.[1]

The Lambeth Conference of 1930 Committee on the Unity of the Church therefore judged wisely when remarking that

when we speak of the Historic Episcopate, we mean the episcopate as it emerged in the clear light of history from the time when definite evidence begins to be available. . . . If the episcopate, as we find it established universally by the end of the second century, was the result of a like process of adaptation and growth in the organism of the church [with the canon of scripture and creeds], that would be no evidence that it lacked divine authority, but rather that the life of the Spirit within the church had found it to be the most appropriate organ for the functions which it discharged. . . .

As an institution, it was, and is, characterised by succession in two forms: the succession in office, and the succession in consecration. And it had generally recognised functions: the general superintendence of the church and more especially of the clergy; the maintenance of unity in the one eucharist; the ordination of men to the ministry; the safeguarding of the faith; and the administration of discipline.[2]

In respect of the conception of episcopal succession at the end of the second century, it must be observed that it was succession in office, and not yet succession by

---

[1] H. B. Swete (editor), *Essays on the Early History of the Church and Ministry*: J. A. Robinson, 'The Christian Ministry in the Apostolic and Subapostolic Periods', p. 90.

[2] Bell, *Documents*, 3rd series, pp. 7–10.

consecration, which was emphasised as the cardinal feature. In Irenaeus and in the episcopal succession lists of Hegesippus,

the succession consists of a continuous series of legitimate holders of the episcopal office, from the bishops appointed by the Apostles to the present leaders of the church. In the second century there is no trace of the idea of a continuous series of ordinations.[1]

The emphasis on a sacramental succession conveyed by the imposition of hands in consecration became explicit first in Hippolytus and Cyprian towards the middle of the third century. Moreover, in regard to the consecration of Irenaeus himself to the episcopate, 'the probable solution is that Irenaeus was consecrated by his fellow-presbyters at Lugdunum without the assistance of any Eastern bishops'.[2] Recent investigation furthermore has verified the tradition of a similar procedure in the church of Alexandria, where the early bishops received the episcopal office at the hands of their fellow-presbyters.[3] Duchesne was of opinion that the same was true at an early stage in Antioch and Rome also: 'Il ne serait pas étonnant que la même situation eût porté les mêmes conséquences à Antioche, à Rome, à Lyon, partout où les églises locales avaient un ressort extrêmement étendu.'[4] What has become, then, of the confident assertion in No. 15 of the *Tracts for the Times* that

we know that the succession of bishops, and ordination from them, was the invariable doctrine and rule of the early Christians. Is it not utterly inconceivable that this rule should have

[1] Einar Molland, 'Irenaeus of Lugdunum and the Apostolic Succession', *Journal of Ecclesiastical History*, vol. I, i, April 1950, p. 24.
[2] *Ibid.* p. 28.
[3] W. Telfer, 'Episcopal Succession in Egypt', *Journal of Ecclesiastical History*, vol III, i, April 1952.
[4] L. Duchesne, *Histoire ancienne de l'Église*, vol. I, p. 94.

prevailed from the first age, everywhere and without exception, had it not been given them by the Apostles?

The melancholy answer must be that 'in view of such a history the Tractarian emphasis upon the continuous imposition of episcopal hands will not endure the test of the Vincentian Canon'.[1]

During the third century the consecration of a newly elected bishop by fellow-bishops established itself as the rule, and the 4th Canon of the Council of Nicaea made the presence of three bishops the norm. The church of England at the Reformation claimed to have preserved three elements in its episcopal polity, the *successio localis, doctrinalis et personalis*. The first and last were maintained by the unbroken succession of bishops in its sees and by the rule requiring three bishops for the consecration of a bishop; and in regard to the second, the Anglican reformers laid great stress upon the reform of the church in order to ensure purity and soundness of doctrine, 'the most precious jewel of the Gospel' as Downham described it, 'which is to be redeemed (if need be) with the loss of all outward things'. Accordingly, whilst rejoicing in their own felicity in retaining pure doctrine together with episcopacy, they recognised the difficult circumstances of some of their foreign brethren who had to choose between the *successio doctrinalis* and *personalis*. If, by ineluctable historical necessity (which the Anglican divines admitted), the foreign reformed churches had to sacrifice either sound doctrine or episcopal consecration, they determined rightly in relinquishing the latter. This

---

1 Telfer, *op. cit.* p. 12. Notwithstanding, the assertion persists; cf. E. R. Fairweather: 'The most striking fact of all, however, as far as the question of sacramental succession is concerned, is the complete absence from the first fifteen centuries of Christian history of positive evidence for the ordination of bishops or presbyters by anyone except an apostle or apostolic bishop' (E. R. Fairweather and R. F. Hettlinger, *Episcopacy and Reunion*, p. 18: Mowbrays, 1953).

traditional ascription of superior importance to right faith over right order on the part of Anglicans was expressed by the Lambeth Conference of 1920 in welcoming the Report of the Commission of 1911 on relations with the Church of Sweden; and accepting *inter alia* 'the conclusions there maintained on the succession of the bishops of the Church of Sweden and the conception of the priesthood set forth in its standards'. These conclusions, as set forth by the Swedish churchmen and regarded as satisfactory by the Anglican bishops, were that

no particular organisation of the church and of its ministry is instituted *jure divino*, not even the order and discipline and state of things recorded in the New Testament; [and that] the object of any organisation and of the whole ministry being included in the preaching of the Gospel and the administration of the sacraments . . ., our church cannot recognise any essential difference *jure divino* of aim and authority between the two or three Orders into which the ministry of grace may have been divided *jure humano* for the benefit and convenience of the church;

from which it followed that the episcopal succession in the Church of Sweden was regarded 'with the reverence due to a venerable legacy from the past', and as 'a blessing from the God of history accorded to us'.[1]

Between the Lambeth Conferences of 1920 and 1948 there may seem, therefore, to be a great gulf fixed in respect of the requirements relating to the historic episcopate, which challenges explanation. In part the change is due to the little weight attached in some contemporary ecclesiastical circles to the 'blessings from the God of history accorded to us', and in part to the prevalence of a theological temper antipathetic to history. 'The theologian', wrote Gibbon in the opening of his

[1] Bell, *Documents*, 1st series, pp. 10, 187–8.

famous fifteenth chapter, 'may indulge the pleasing task of describing Religion as she descended from Heaven, arrayed in her native purity. A more melancholy duty is imposed on the historian. He must discover the inevitable mixture of error and corruption which she contracted in a long residence upon earth, among a weak and degenerate race of beings.'[1] The dominant tendency in some contemporary schools of Anglican theology is reluctant to admit the testimony of history to the reality of the corruptions and errors from which the church was cleansed at the Reformation; and consequently to allow the plea of necessity to those churches which, faced with the harsh choice between reform of doctrine and continuity of polity, chose the former at the cost of sacrificing the latter. The anti-historical temper, however, has penetrated more deeply, and is offended by the intrinsic limitations attaching to historical evidence, where 'probability is the very guide of life'. In face of the avowed complexity of the evidence for the early history and evolution of the Christian ministry, it seeks to dispel historical incertitude by dogmatic presupposition and assertion. When Lightfoot wrote his essay on 'The Christian Ministry', it seemed to him clear that

in this clamour of antagonistic opinions history is obviously the sole upright, impartial referee; and the historical mode of treatment will therefore be strictly adhered to in the following investigation. The doctrine in this instance at all events is involved in the history.[2]

At the present time this approach seems in danger of being abandoned in favour of Manning's axiom in respect of papal infallibility that 'the dogma must conquer history'. Thus the unproven premise of 'the primitive wholeness' of Catholicism is put forward at the outset as the maxim

[1] E. Gibbon, *The Decline and Fall of the Roman Empire* (ed. Bury), vol. II, p. 2.
[2] J. B. Lightfoot, *Philippians*, p. 187.

by which to fill the gaps in the historical evidence and to read back into the apostolic and subapostolic ages the settled rules of later epochs; or again, it is asserted that 'not only *a* ministry, but *the* ministry is so much a part of the church's God-given life, that its destruction would mean the disappearance of the church as God founded it through Christ and his Apostles'.[1]

From such an approach the Anglican tradition has been delivered by its tenacious hold upon the historical method. When Creighton ventured the bold affirmation that 'the formula which most explains the position of the church of England is that it rests on an appeal to sound learning', he added the rider that 'sound learning must always wear the appearance of a compromise between ignorance and plausible hypothesis. . . . It is the function of learning to assert what is known and to leave perverse ingenuity steadily alone.'[2] Accordingly the church of England has never set forth any theological or doctrinal theory of episcopacy, but in its Articles, the Preface to the Ordinal, and the writings of its representative divines has contented itself with a historical statement of its intention to continue the threefold ministry, on the ground of its tradition in the church since the apostolic age. As Lightfoot observed in the conclusion of his essay,

if the preceding investigation be substantially correct, the threefold ministry can be traced to Apostolic direction; and short of an express statement we can possess no better assurance of a Divine appointment or at least a Divine sanction. If the facts do not allow us to unchurch other Christian communities differently organised, they may at least justify our jealous adhesion to a polity derived from this source.[3]

---

[1] *Catholicity*, p. 17, (Dacre Press, 1947); Fairweather and Hettlinger, *op. cit.* pp. 30–1.
[2] M. Creighton, *The Church and the Nation*, pp. 251, 259–60.
[3] J. B. Lightfoot, *op. cit.* p. 267.

Moreover the temerarious procedure of going beyond the historical evidence and imposing dogmatic premisses upon insecure foundations may lead as easily and logically to the papal claims as to those of an episcopal apostolic succession; as was ruefully avowed in a recent puzzled enquiry into *Spiritual Authority in the Church of England*, which concluded that Anglicans could not

on historical grounds alone *insist upon* the episcopal succession as of the church's *esse*. For that matter, no finality could possibly be reached as between the place and function of bishops in general and the papal claims in particular. . . . Looked at from a strictly objective standpoint both the doctrine of apostolic succession and the doctrinal claims of the apostolic see are in the same category; they can only be justified and insisted upon in accordance with presuppositions concerning the nature of the church and her ministry.[1]

The traditional Anglican position in regard to episcopacy therefore commends it on the strength of its long historical continuance since the apostolic age, as being of the *bene* or *plene esse* of the church; and consequently a condition of union of other churches with itself. The Lambeth Quadrilateral required acceptance of this historic episcopate; and Stubbs in 1890 offered a gloss on the phrase to the effect that

the historic episcopate, not merely as a method of church government—in which sense it could scarcely be called historic —but as a distinct, substantive, and historical transmission of the commission of the apostles, in and by which our Lord formed his disciples through all generations into a distinctly organised body or church—the historic episcopate is of the very essence of the Church of England.[2]

Similarly the Lambeth Conference Committee on the Unity of the Church in 1930 urged that

[1] E. C. Rich, *op. cit.* p. 194.
[2] W. Stubbs, *Visitation Charges* (ed. E. E. Holmes), p. 130 (London, 1904).

what we uphold is the episcopate, maintained in successive generations by continuity of succession and consecration, as it has been throughout the history of the church from the earliest times, and discharging those functions which from the earliest times it has discharged.[1]

What, then, may be required of the Anglican church and of non-episcopal churches desiring to effect a union by mutual acceptance of 'the historic episcopate'? As defined at Lambeth in 1930 the characteristic functions of the bishop are

the general superintendence of the church and more especially of the clergy; the maintenance of unity in the one eucharist; the ordination of men to the ministry; the safeguarding of the faith, and the administration of the discipline of the church.

The episcopate therefore may be considered under two aspects, as exercising a *potestas jurisdictionis* and a *potestas ordinis*. In the former sphere no insuperable difficulties may be anticipated in a fusion of episcopal and presbyterian church orders. A considerable number of Anglican divines, as has been already illustrated, recognised a close kinship, amounting to virtual identity, of function between the superintendent and bishop in respect of pastoral oversight and administration of discipline. Even Laud allowed this of the Lutheran churches and Andrewes of the reformed, testifying that they had the *res* without the *nomen* of episcopacy in these respects; whilst of the superintendents of the church of Scotland, Hall wrote that

their power, by your own allowance and enacting, is the same with your Bishops; their Dioceses accordingly divided; their residence fixed; ... also the particularities of the function and power of these Superintendents; amongst the rest, these: that they have power to plant and erect churches; to set, order, and appoint ministers in their countries; that after they have

1 Bell, *Documents*, 3rd series, p. 10.

remained in their chief towns three or four months, they shall enter into their Visitation; in which they shall not only preach, but examine the life, diligence, and behaviour of the ministers; as also they shall try the estate of their churches and manners of the people; they must consider how the poor are provided and the youth instructed; they must admonish, where admonitions need; and redress such things as they are able to appease; they must note such crimes as are heinous, that by the censures of the church, the same may be corrected. And now, what main difference, I beseech you, can you find betwixt the office of these Superintendents and the present Bishops?[1]

The acceptance of episcopacy by the presbyterian and other non-episcopal churches would involve indeed the abandonment of the principle of parity of ministers; but the existence of moderators both in the Church of Scotland and even in such champions of independency as the Congregational Union implies a tacit acceptance of imparity. And the taking of episcopacy into their systems would be the allowance of a moderate imparity. For it is evident that the episcopate so adopted must needs also be adapted to a constitutional framework and organisation. But for the unfortunate political association in the seventeenth century, both in England and Scotland, of prelacy with monarchy, the ideal of a constitutional episcopacy advocated in England by Ussher and practised in Scotland by Leighton might have laid the foundation for the reconciliation of episcopacy and presbytery, and set forward the union of the two churches, according to the 'true, ancient, primitive episcopacy or presidency as it is balanced or managed by a due commixture of presbytery therewith'. Assuredly the bishop would be a perpetual moderator, not a temporary officer; but after the pattern set by Leighton, he would

[1] Joseph Hall, *Episcopacy by Divine Right: Conclusion*, section I (*Works*, vol. x, pp. 267–8).

247

be bound to co-operation with a council of presbyters and also with representatives of the laity. In both these respects the church of Scotland has much to teach its southern neighbour; and the Lambeth Conference committee of 1930 recognised that 'in this respect we have much to learn and to gain from the traditions and customs of the non-episcopal churches'.[1] In aspiration indeed the church of England upholds the ideal of a constitutional episcopacy; as the requirement of the association of presbyters with the bishop at the imposition of hands in the ordering of priests on the one side and the ancient provincial convocations and the modern church assembly on the other sufficiently testify. But the actual needs to be approximated more closely to the ideal, as the history of the convocations shows, and the practice of most other provinces of the Anglican communion illustrates. For in the Protestant Episcopal Church in the United States each diocesan bishop has a 'council of advice', composed usually of four presbyters and four laymen, whose recommendation is necessary, for example, before a bishop can accept a candidate for the ministry or ordain him after training. The principle of constitutional episcopacy is writ large in each convention and synod of the American church, so that the bishop's 'constitutional power is distinctly limited; he is still, what the fathers of the American church intended him to be, a constitutional executive'. Nearer home the powers of the laity in the church of Ireland also are such as to make that church 'unique among Anglican churches'.[2]

In the church of England there is urgent need for closer association of presbyters with bishops in adminis-

[1] Bell, *Documents*, 3rd series, p. 9.
[2] *Episcopacy Ancient and Modern* (ed. C. Jenkins and K. D. Mackenzie), ch. IV, sections IV and V.

trative and judicial matters; and for the association of the laity with the episcopate and clergy in safeguarding the faith. By its present constitution the church assembly is expressly disabled from deciding questions of doctrine, because of the presence of its house of laity; a curious anomaly in a church distinguished historically by the prominent part played in its reformation by the laity. For when the convocation of Canterbury in February 1559 explicitly affirmed that 'the authority to treat of and define matters concerning the faith, sacraments, and discipline of the church hitherto has belonged, and ought to belong, to the pastors of the church alone, and not to laymen', the first parliament of Elizabeth I retorted by passing the Acts of Supremacy and Uniformity, with all the bishops present in the House of Lords voting against both bills. Moreover the researches of Professor Neale, already mentioned, have emphasised the importance of the part played in this episode by the Puritan members of the House of Commons and their success in frustrating the intentions of the queen. Nor did Figgis tire of iterating that

it is the lay power which is ultimately supreme in the Reformation theory . . . . Now this fact must be faced, for it affords the only serviceable theory of continuity. . . . The laity are an active, not a passive part of the church. To Hooker, all power flows from the people to the prince. If this be not admitted, I do not believe that it is ultimately possible to argue for our continuity.[1]

In this respect particularly the church of England has much to learn from the non-episcopal churches. For in contemporary times, with the higher level of general education, it is no longer possible to contend for the exclusive competence of the episcopate to determine matters of doctrine. Furthermore, it might well prove to

[1] J. N. Figgis, 'National Churches' in *Our Place in Christendom*, pp. 129, 133.

249

be the case that reunion between the churches of England and Scotland would lead to a considerable multiplication of the number of dioceses and bishops in England, in order to enable episcopacy to function constitutionally with greater ease and smoothness at local levels. Such a development would provide a solution for the present anomaly of suffragan bishops, who are not members of the upper houses of convocation but must jostle for membership of the lower houses with representatives of the inferior clergy; yet who nevertheless, along with assistant bishops, are full members of the Lambeth Conferences, although they cannot be said to testify to the tradition of any church. Finally a constitutional episcopacy, functioning in each diocese as Ussher or Leighton designed, would provide a useful local check to the authority of Lambeth Conferences, by reviving the Cyprianic doctrine of episcopacy, once the favoured tradition of the church of England.

But if the church of England would have to make the greater concessions as regards the episcopal *potestas iurisdictionis* in a reunion with presbyterian churches, in respect of the *potestas ordinis* the non-episcopal churches would be required to modify considerably their traditions and practice. It is here that the chief difficulty is likely to arise, and particularly in any project of organic union between episcopal and non-episcopal churches, whose respective ministries need to be integrated during the period between the inauguration of union and the realisation of a fully-episcopal ministry. The precedent set by Anglo-Scottish church relations between 1610 and 1638, by which presbyters of the church of Scotland were consecrated *per saltum* to the episcopate whilst the parochial presbyters were not required to submit to episcopal ordination but retained their presbyterian orders, suggested itself to the Lambeth Conference of 1908 as a means of reuniting the two churches in the present century. Moreover the Lambeth Conference of 1930 approved consecration *per saltum* in relation to the proposed union in South India as an emergency measure to meet an extraordinary situation. Bishop John Wordsworth also was convinced that

as regards the promotion to the episcopate of certain ministers in non-episcopal churches, without raising the question of the validity of their existing ministerial character, under the special circumstances contemplated by recent resolutions of the Lambeth Conference of 1908 . . . it would be the right course to pursue, if the conditions were otherwise satisfactory.[1]

His brother, Bishop Charles Wordsworth of St Andrews, likewise commented that

in 1662 this was the course formally adopted by the Scottish episcopate. The presbyterian ministers were left in possession of their parishes without reordination; and if doing this once has not unchurched us, doing it twice would not.[2]

This pattern has been followed by the church of South India, in which ministers in presbyteral orders have been consecrated *per saltum* to the episcopate, and, whilst providing that all future ordinations to the ministry shall be episcopal, the existing non-episcopal ministries are to be retained during the interim between the inauguration of union and the attainment of a universally episcopal ministry. The Scottish precedent also would allow of reciprocal intercommunion of the communicant members of each of the churches, since the action of the English bishops in 1610 implied, according to Bancroft, a recognition of the validity of presbyterian orders; and following the Lambeth Appeal of 1920 a

---

[1] J. Wordsworth, *Ordination Problems*, p. 112.
[2] *Idem, The Episcopate of Charles Wordsworth*, p. 284.

series of joint conferences between Anglicans and Free-
churchmen produced a statement from the Anglican
bishops that non-episcopal ministries

which imply a sincere intention to preach Christ's word and
administer the sacraments as Christ has ordained, and to which
authority so to do has been solemnly given by the church concerned, are real ministries of Christ's word and sacraments in
the Universal Church;

though the rider was added that such ministries 'may be
in varying degrees irregular or defective'.[1] Thus the
church of England would recognise the newly consecrated bishops of the church of South India and its
episcopally-ordained presbyters as the equivalent of its
own bishops and priests; and would allow its own members freedom in accordance with their individual judgment to receive the holy communion at the hands of
non-episcopal ministers of that church. But, in obedience
to that clause of the Act of Uniformity of 1662 which
forbade any person not episcopally ordained 'to consecrate and administer the holy Sacrament of the Lord's
Supper' in the church of England, these non-episcopal
ministers, though allowed to preach in Anglican pulpits,
could not celebrate the holy communion in Anglican
churches. It is this barrier to full intercommunion and
complete interchangeability of ministries which has led
to the search for other means of unification.

First among such alternatives may be placed the proposal for the conditional reordination by bishops of non-
episcopal ministers, according to the form used by
Bramhall in Ireland after the Restoration and included
in the projected comprehension scheme in England at
the revolution, or some similar formulae such as were
canvassed at conferences between presbyterian and

---

1 Bell, *Documents*, 1st series, no. 46, p. 159.

Anglican divines during the period between the Restoration and the revolution. The essential obstacle to the success of such projects, however, was stated by Stubbs in a passage of his visitation charge of 1890, immediately following his affirmation that the Lambeth Quadrilateral was 'the very minimum of what the church of England could advance without a practical renunciation of her own vital position'. Asking whether this involved the episcopal reordination of presbyterian ministers, he remarked that

to make this demand seems to me somewhat unreasonable; the very essence of presbyterianism is presbytery; and the essence of historic presbyterianism is the negation of historic episcopacy. To expect reunion on a basis which means with one of the two parties a renunciation of its essential principle seems, I say, unreasonable and unpractical. In saying this, I must not be understood to mean more than I say. There are Presbyterian churches with a historical succession of great authority and completeness. In affirming our historic episcopate I am throwing no doubt on their constitutional consistency or on their spiritual work. God has many ways of doing his work; and because I maintain that we have one of his ways in our church, I am not to be said to maintain that that which is in use in Scotland, we will say, is not of his way; or that other ministrations than ours are dead and useless. If I wanted to say so, or thought so, I should not be deterred from saying it by mere consideration of convenience.[1]

Conditional episcopal ordination is essentially unilateral; and this has ruled it out of practical consideration as a means of effecting the desired union between an episcopalian and a presbyterian church.

Accordingly proposals have been suggested to provide by mutual commissioning for a complete integration of the ministries of episcopalian and presbyteral churches from the inauguration of an union, notably in the

[1] W. Stubbs, *op. cit.* p. 131.

'Proposed Scheme of Church Union in Ceylon' of 1947 and the 'Plan of Church Union in North India and Pakistan' of 1951, revised in 1954. In the former scheme the objective is stated to be the acceptance 'of the historic episcopate in a constitutional form', and 'as it was known in the undivided church'; and the Preface to its Ordinal affirms the 'intention of this church to continue and reverently to use and esteem the threefold ministry of Bishop, Presbyter, and Deacon which existed in the undivided church'. At the inauguration of union, therefore, all the bishops-elect of the united church who have not already received episcopal consecration are to be consecrated by three bishops from outside Ceylon, representing different church traditions and acceptable to all the uniting churches; and after consecration, they are to be commissioned by prayer and imposition of hands 'from ministers of all the united churches duly appointed for the purpose' for the wider *episkopē* in the united church. The formula prescribed for use on this occasion declares that

Forasmuch as you have been consecrated to the office and order of Bishop in the church of God, and have been elected to be Bishop in the United church of Ceylon, we acknowledge you on behalf of the uniting churches, and commission you for the wider exercise of your ministry in the church of God. The grace of the Holy Spirit be with you, enlightening, strengthening and endowing you with wisdom all the days of your life, in the name of the Father and of the Son, and of the Holy Spirit. Amen.

Thereafter the bishops are to ordain by prayer and imposition of hands to the presbyterate of the united church all the clergy of the uniting churches desiring to become presbyters in the united church, according to the formula:

Forasmuch as you were called and ordained to the ministry of the church of God within the . . . church, and are now called to the ministry of the church of God as presbyter within this united church; receive from God at my hands the power and grace of the Holy Spirit to exercise the wider ministry of this office, and to nourish by Word and Sacraments all the members of Christ's flock within this united church, in the name of the Father and of the Son and of the Holy Spirit. Amen.

Take authority to preach and teach the Word, to fulfil the ministry of reconciliation and to minister Christ's Sacraments in the congregation whereunto you shall be duly appointed. Amen.[1]

An order of service for this commissioning makes clear in all its parts the above-mentioned intention of the united church.

The 'Plan of Church Union in North India and Pakistan' as revised in 1954 likewise declares its purpose that 'the ordained ministry in the united church shall consist of Bishops, Presbyters, and Deacons'; and that the uniting churches 'accept the Presbyteral, Congregational, and Episcopal elements in church order as necessary parts of the basis of union', and agree 'that the episcopate shall be both constitutional and historic'. Further, 'it is agreed that at the outset the ministry shall be unified and complete freedom of communion throughout the united church shall be realised', so that 'from the beginning of the union every bishop and every presbyter of the united church shall be recognised as competent to celebrate the holy communion in any congregation of the church'. Accordingly, 'at the inauguration of union, the existing bishops and presbyters of each of the uniting churches shall accept through the laying-on of hands of the duly authorized persons of the other churches uniting with them, the additional authority

1 'Proposed Scheme of Church Union in Ceylon', section on Faith and Order (1947), pp. 12–17.

that they lack in separation'; and careful emphasis is laid on the fact that the service of commissioning 'is not re-ordination, nor is it presumed to bestow again the grace, gifts, character or authority that have already been bestowed upon them'.

In the preface to the service for the unification of the episcopate the intention to accept the historic episcopate is further affirmed, together with that of 'securing a ministry fully accredited'; in the prayer before the imposition of hands God is asked to

pour out thy Holy Spirit to enrich each according to his need with grace and authority for the exercise of the office of a bishop in the united church within the church universal;

and at the laying-on of hands the formula to be used states that

Forasmuch as thou wast called and duly appointed within the ... church to the office of a bishop in the church of God, and art now called to the office of a bishop in the church of God within the united church, mayest thou receive from God the grace of the Holy Spirit for the fuller exercise of God's ministry in the office of a bishop, in the name of the Father and of the Son and of the Holy Ghost.

In the service for the inauguration of the union, the prayer at the mutual imposition of hands on bishops and presbyters of the united church in similar form declares that

Forasmuch as thou wast called and ordained within the ... church to the ministry of the church of God, and art now called to the ministry of the church of God within the united church, mayest thou receive from God the power and grace of the Holy Spirit for the wider exercise of the ministry as a presbyter (or bishop) within the united church, and for a more effectual service take thou authority to preach the Word of

God, to fulfil the ministry of reconciliation and to minister Christ's Sacraments in the united church; and see that thou do all these things in brotherly partnership with God's fellow-workers whom in this union of churches He has made thine.[1]

The Lambeth Conference of 1948 regarded the Ceylon scheme as being 'of singular interest and promise'; and it is clear that both it and the North India project, by providing for the unification of the various grades of the ministry from the inauguration of union, may be judged to have overcome both the difficulties of the South India union and those of proposals for unilateral re-ordination *sub conditione* of non-episcopal ministers. Thus a new way out of the impasse appears to be in sight. It should be observed, however, that in North and South India as well as in Ceylon the uniting churches reserve explicitly their right to be in full communion with other non-episcopal churches; as was stated in the Ceylon scheme, 'the fact that other churches do not follow the rule of episcopal ordination will not preclude it [the united church] from holding relations of communion and fellowship with them'. On the other hand, the Lambeth Conference of 1930 accepted this position in regard to the South India project, holding that, though anomalous, it 'may be covered by the principle of *economy*'.

Meantime a different kind of approach was being worked out by a joint conference of Anglicans and Free-churchmen at home in response to the present archbishop of Canterbury's sermon before the University of Cambridge in 1946. Their objective was not the organic union of the several participating churches, but the taking of episcopacy into their own ecclesiastical polity by the non-episcopal churches and the creation thereby

[1] 'Plan of Church Union in North India and Pakistan' (1954), pp. 10–16.

257

of a series of overlapping episcopal churches and ministries in England, as a means of realising full intercommunion between these non-episcopal churches now adopting episcopacy and the Church of England. The recommendations of these conferences were published in 1950 in a report under the title of *Church Relations in England*. It would seem indeed that comparatively little attention has been directed to the similarities between this report and a memorandum by Bishop Frere and Dr A. E. Garvie, approved generally by an earlier joint conference in 1925; which also had suggested the creation of a Free Church episcopacy with the resultant 'several co-existing jurisdictions', and recognised that those ministers of the Free Churches who did not accept a form of episcopal ordination from their own newly consecrated bishops 'would not have the right to administer the holy communion to Anglican congregations'.[1] The recommendations of the 1950 Report were confronted, however, by the same difficulties as those of the South India scheme, namely the failure to secure a complete interchangeability of ministries and full intercommunion. Accordingly the Lambeth Conference of 1948 did not regard with enthusiasm the further development of this method, believing that

as compared with constitutional schemes, they do not sufficiently provide for a real growing together such as would lead to an organic union; [and that] it is unlikely that non-episcopal churches will be attracted by this proposal if nothing more at the moment than partial intercommunion is offered.

Its own conclusions, therefore, were that

in spite of these disadvantages we are not prepared to discourage further explorations along this line of approach, if there are linked with it provisions for the growing together of

1 Bell, *Documents*, 2nd series, no. 122, pp. 87–93.

the churches concerned and likewise the definite acceptance of organic union as the final goal.[1]

In fact, the somewhat lukewarm reception accorded to the 1950 Report would appear to have seconded the caution of Lambeth in 1948. Meanwhile also in another direction and in a much wider context, the establishment of the World Council of Churches has brought the Anglican communion into close relations with other reformed churches as well as with the Eastern Orthodox Church; and, by revealing that even amongst the reformed churches it is far from being one of the largest communions, has given a further impetus to self-examination and to ask what is the particular contribution which the Anglican communion has to offer in respect of ecclesiastical polity to the fullness of Christ in the Oecumenical Movement. After four centuries of history how stands it with the *via media*?

'It hath been the wisdom of the Church of England', claimed the Preface to the Book of Common Prayer in 1662 in relation to its public Liturgy, 'to keep the mean between the two extremes of too much stiffness in refusing and of too much easiness in admitting any variation from it.' It has been the argument of these lectures that the same principle has been true in respect of polity; and that the Anglican tradition has espoused a *via media* in regard to episcopacy, constructed by its defenders against the two extremes of Rome and Geneva. In accordance with this tenacious adherence to the mean, the Church of England has nowhere formulated any theoretical or theological doctrine of episcopacy; but has contented itself with the assertion of the historical ground of the continuance of the threefold ministry in the church since the apostolic age. Certainly no exclusive claim can

1 *The Lambeth Conferences 1867–1948*, p. 54.

be substantiated from the statements in the Preface to the Ordinal, Articles 19 and 36, and Canon VIII of the Canons of 1604. During the several centuries of its history since the Reformation, its representative divines have so interpreted these formularies as to require episcopacy where it may be had without sacrificing purity of doctrine, and not to unchurch those churches deprived of it by ineluctable historical necessity. The *via media* indeed has not been trodden unswervingly by all its apologists, some of whom have deviated to one or other of the extremes of too much stiffness in refusing or too much easiness in admitting any variation from it. But the existence of such extremes does not disprove the prevalence of a norm. As Figgis observed

Extremes at either end of any society do not prove that there is no normal, no general type. Rather are they evidence of its existence. . . . So with the Church of England. It may have a mind, a general view, a common way of life; but that does not prevent there being many people on the fringe. . . . Short of coercion, such exceptions cannot be prevented, but there may be a very general type for all that, and it may be conformed to a very real authority.[1]

The evidence adduced in these lectures of a great and continuing cloud of witnesses to the Anglican *via media* in respect of episcopacy assuredly cannot be dismissed as that of 'laxist Anglicans', or as a 'widespread Anglican opportunism', or as 'certain anomalies in the past', nor by the assertion that 'the pragmatism that can speak of this or that element as being of the *bene esse* has no place' in the authentic Anglican tradition.[2] The apologetic position of a church thus placed in the strait of seeking to repudiate nearly four centuries of its history as 'the

[1] J. N. Figgis, *Hopes for English Religion*, pp. 84–5 (1919).
[2] E. R. Fairweather and R. F. Hettlinger, *Episcopacy and Reunion*, pp. 46, 49, 50. *Catholicity*, p. 17. (Dacre Press, London, 1947.)

times of ignorance which God winked at' would be hardly reassuring or sound.

Per contra, the *via media* affirms the maintenance of episcopacy by the Church of England as part of a continuity with the early and medieval church, its acceptance on the ground of historic continuance since the apostolic age, its requirement for ministering within its own communion, and its restoration to those churches which have lost it, as a condition of reunion, without asserting their non-episcopal ministries and sacraments to be invalid because of its loss. Perhaps the best statement of this Anglican *via media* may be found in a combination of the sentiments of Dean Swift and of Dr Samuel Johnson. To the former, 'a Church of England man hath a true veneration for the scheme established among us of ecclesiastic government; and though he will not determine whether episcopacy be of divine right, he is sure it is most agreeable to primitive institution, [and] fittest of all others for preserving order and purity'. The latter, in conversation with Boswell, remarked: 'Why, Sir, the Presbyterians have no church, no apostolic ordination'; and when asked: 'And do you think that absolutely essential, Sir?' replied in modified and mollifying tone, *more Anglicano*: 'Why, Sir, as it was an apostolical institution, I think it is dangerous to be without it.'

INDEX